Postpolitics and the Aesthetic Imagination

Postpolitics and the Aesthetic Imagination

Juan Meneses, Editor

UNIVERSITY OF MINNESOTA PRESS
MINNEAPOLIS • LONDON

Published by the University of Minnesota Press
111 Third Avenue South, Suite 290
Minneapolis, MN 55401-2520
http://www.upress.umn.edu

ISBN 978-1-5179-1917-7 (hc)
ISBN 978-1-5179-1918-4 (pb)

A Cataloging-in-Publication record for this book is available from the Library of Congress.

Printed in the United States of America on acid-free paper

UMP BmB 2025

Contents

Acknowledgments

This book was written in the midst of a number of crises and is aimed to underscore the fact that not only is a different world possible where life is better for all, but it is our duty to imagine it too. I want to thank the contributors to this volume for working so hard to produce brilliant chapters under such circumstances. Thank you, too, to all the friends of this project who have been inspiring and encouraging in equal measure, especially Emily Apter, Greg Forter, Kasia Marciniak, and Alan Rauch.

Thanks to Leah Pennywark for expressing initial interest in the project and for shepherding it so graciously and attentively as we worked to bring it to its present book form. Also, my gratitude to Doug Armato (a constant source of support and intellectual curiosity), Anne Carter, Shelby Connelly, David Drummond (for designing such a fantastic cover), Karen Hellekson (for great copyedits), Jeffery Moen, Heather Skinner, Mike Stoffel, Carla Valadez, and everybody else at the Press for their dedication to such a crucial endeavor as book publishing is for societies to flourish. Thank you for the often invisible labor you put into making this and so many other books exist.

INTRODUCTION

Sensing the Postpolitical

JUAN MENESES

To say that today's world is in turmoil is to say very little, or perhaps nothing at all. Anywhere one looks, instances abound of the debilitation of democratic institutions, the egregious violation of legal and ethical principles, the persistence of (neo)colonial forms of hegemony, the reaffirmation of white supremacy, the sense of living in a constant state of crisis, a deteriorated press, the creeping advance of exclusionary policies and sentiments, generalized anti-immigrant hostility, the entrenchment of a two-tier economic system of winners and losers, a reinforced patriarchy, a digital world dominated by the exploitative activities of a few companies, and the persecution of individual rights and the free expression of one's identity—all in the context of a dying planet. Of course, the severity of these circumstances varies significantly depending on who and where one is; yet this is becoming a generalized state of affairs. It is hard to put a name to it: Are we living in the era of disruption? Is this just a blip, or are these "the End Times"? Demarcating its historical contours is not always easy either: How long have things been this bad? Accompanying this searching anxiety, furthermore, is a preoccupation with the future ramifications of these events. Will things get better or much harder? Taken together, all of these symptoms, whose proliferation we witness with dismay as well as horror, are not the only problem.

Crucially, our troubled times are also defined by the strain put on our ability to act politically—and, more generally, how and whether politics can be practiced at all. The sense remains that things are not just bad, but that the ways to make them better are vanishing rapidly too. The widespread criminalization of dissent, the peddling of a fallacious "anything-goes" relativism, the certainty that much of what looks like activist engagement is defanged even before it occurs, the appearance of novel forms of propaganda, the primacy of beliefs and opinions over arguments and facts, claims that this situation is in fact business as usual, or the assertion that there is simply no alternative, among others, compound the precarity of the current political landscape. To be sure, this is not due to a simple curtailment of our rights, but the outcome of an agenda aimed at the gradual normalization of the circumstances. Antonio Gramsci called this phenomenon "consensus," that is, the "'spontaneous' consent given by the great masses of the population to the general direction imposed on social life by the dominant fundamental group."[1] Disguised as "common sense" (i.e., the idea that things are the way they are for rational, natural, and logical reasons), consensus determines that alternatives to the status quo are simply impossible, preposterous, dangerous, risible, or even prosecutable. Controlling the consensus, then, amounts to dictating the terms of what can and cannot be done politically.

One can be certain that this is, nonetheless, not a recent phenomenon or something that has appeared out of the blue. Neither have its roots, dynamics, and consequences passed unnoticed. Theorists such as Jacques Rancière, Chantal Mouffe, and Slavoj Žižek have exposed the processes by which political action has been eroded and sites for its practice are increasingly disappearing. These operations have given rise to a general critical discourse encapsulated by the term postpolitics. Drawing from those and other theorists, Japhy Wilson and Erik Swyngedouw defined postpolitics in their essential volume *The Post-political and Its Discontents: Spaces of Depoliticisation, Spectres of Radical Politics* as "a situation in which the political—understood as a space of contestation and agonistic engagement—is increasingly colonised by politics—understood as technocratic mechanisms and consensual procedures that operate within an unquestioned framework of representative democracy, free market economics, and cosmopolitan liberalism."[2] In response to this postpolitical order, much work has concentrated on illuminating the evacuation of the political by politics[3] as well as the need to formulate alternative ways to generate meaningful change. Appearing over a decade after they published their volume, this book updates Wilson and Swyngedouw's diagnosis of the postpolitical to focus on elements that have since become more prominent in both the constitution of political life and the factors occluding it. In the interim, things have changed dramatically for the worse, as I have already posited, but they have also varied in nature. The depoliticizing operations of postpolitics have become more blatant and more insidious. The volume, then, responds to contemporary developments such as the worrying normalization of far-right agendas across the world, the continued managerialization of politics to the point of the near-collapse of institutions of governance, and the heavily mediating role played by technology, which are often connected to one another in a variety of triangulations. At the same time, in seeking to expand the theoretical understanding of postpolitics, the chapters contribute to this effort by suggesting that avenues to identify the concrete dynamics of this phenomenon as well as strategies to counter it can be found on the aesthetic plane.

Given the general state of things, this might seem a trivial endeavor. In opposition to discourses of functionalism and instrumentality, aesthetics is often dismissed as the realm of mere appearances, romantic musing, and impermanence. Such a sentiment, however, is one symptom of the postpolitical with which this book strongly contends. There is indeed important political value in engaging in sustained contemplation and activities that do not pursue "productive" goals, yet the chapters below do not simply propose inward-looking critiques of beauty, advocate escapism as a solution to the current political impasse, or perform surface-level analyses. Their starting point is that politics and the political are primarily shaped by a range of imaginative operations anchored in creativity. These operations constitute what Ernesto Laclau called "a horizon," that is, "not one among other objects but an absolute limit which structures a field of intelligibility and is thus the condition of possibility for the emergence of any object."[4] The task, then, is to find ways to discern, by way of the power of the imagination, what our political possibilities may look like. As Swyngedouw has put it, postpolitization "relies on both including all in a consensual pluralist order and excluding radically those who posit themselves outside the consensus."[5] Thus, in the face of the consensual regulation of our political options—often in plain sight—by a number of hegemonic forces, *Postpolitics and the Aesthetic Imagination* meets the challenge by showing that there are still sites for resistance, work to be done, and new horizons to fight in the name of emancipation, justice, and solidarity.

In providing an initial response to that challenge, it is necessary to consider first the idea of postpolitics more concretely and how aesthetic inquiry is an appropriate method to confront it. In doing so, we will be able to name the theoretical space in which the chapters below think through an array of themes concerning public and private life at a time when, as the commonplace expression goes, it appears that "everything is political."[6] How can we, then, employ the vocabularies of political critique without diluting them or sacrificing their analytical vigor so as to attend to the dimensions of the postpolitical? An effective strategy will involve showing how aesthetic theory and criticism render visible and disaggregate the occluded horizon of politics while naming specific ways to reactivate the emancipatory work of the political. Interrogating the meaning of the "post" in "postpolitics" is a good entry point.

A Name for Our Times, or On the "Post" in "Postpolitics"

The use of the prefix "post" has been a habitual gesture since at least the advent of a movement itself containing the modifier (i.e., postmodernism), and it offers a great array of semantic possibilities. The result of applying it to different terms, however, is varied, as not all "posts" mean the same.[7] The "post" in "postfeminism" and "postracial," for example, is often meant to indicate the alleged obsolescence of the words it precedes in an effort to "move on" from the critical discourse that originally emerged around them. Proponents of these terms imply that we live—or at the very least that we must strive to live—in a society in which we no longer need to think critically about gender or race. This is undoubtedly *not* the "post" in postpolitics; scholars working on this subject—including the authors in this volume—do not advocate for moving on from politics (moving on to what?) but express instead their concerns for the possibilities of political struggles to succeed when "political struggle" itself has been co-opted and neutralized. Furthermore, to claim that battling against gender- or race-based injustice is no longer necessary is to refuse to acknowledge ongoing violence perpetrated explicitly as well as surreptitiously against an extremely large portion of the population. Along the same lines, theorizing the postpolitical is not to take part in another kind of "post" project, namely the hermeneutical approach known as postcritique. In favor of this critical approach, the editors of one of the most prominent books on the matter have argued that "the intellectual or political payoff of interrogating, demystifying, and defamiliarizing is no longer quite so self-evident."[8] It is hard to overstate that the current state of affairs makes it impossible for some of us to take this position (which I would in fact label postpolitical) and simply discount the political as a suitable frame for examination—aesthetic or otherwise.

Other uses of the modifier, such as in "postcolonial," on the other hand, are closer in substance and spirit to the "post" in "postpolitics." It is true that debates in the heyday of the discipline of postcolonial studies grappled precisely with the implication that deploying that term might erase the realities of colonialism and imperialism.[9] However, a largely settled definition of postcolonial (one to which a great deal of scholars in the area subscribe) is not predicated on the official end of colonialism but, instead, names both a history of violent colonial control over global South territories and the structures of power and depoliticization rooted in it that remain in the period following formal decolonization.[10] Far from resolving the question of colonialism, this "post" emphasizes its nature as a catastrophic event that prevails beyond its original scope. Postpolitics functions in a related way in that, as a deconstructive gesture that signals a departure from a past in which it is nonetheless anchored, it ushers in a new stage where politics, far from being accepted as an unalloyed good, is identified as the grounds for much existing inequality and disenfranchisement. And while postpolitics has been criticized precisely on the basis that it assumes an a priori foreclosure of the political,[11] that is indeed not how this book or the work it builds on mobilize the term. To describe the current moment as postpolitical is not to declare, in a self-defeating fashion, the impossibility of any and all political options; it is to indicate that politics is a failing category given the increasing occlusion, on all fronts, of truly emancipatory practices aimed at making our lives substantially better.[12]

Absorbed by the postpolitical order, politics is, to borrow Jacques Derrida's phrasing, rendered *sous rature,* or "under erasure."[13] This typographic move allows us to grasp how politics becomes neutralized without disappearing; necessary but insufficient, it remains present as ~~politics~~. This is a crucial step because successful strategies of depoliticization carried out under the auspices of postpolitics never qualify as direct or literal oppression; otherwise, many of them would be deemed intolerable and would give rise to a different kind of order. Instead, they must retain the form of the political while divesting the latter of its ability to change the status quo. In this sense, the meaning of the "post" in postpolitics is akin to that in certain uses of the term posthumanism. In those instances, the aim is not to dismiss the concept of the human but to show the inadequacy of established humanist discourses that have historically excluded key elements from their characterization of human existence.[14] The "post" in postpolitics similarly accentuates the need to historicize, complicate, and reveal the limitations of our idea of politics.

Recently, the prefix has also been used in ways that are closely connected to the erosion of the political with which this book is concerned. A case in point is "post-truth," which was named word of the year in 2016 by the publisher of the *Oxford English Dictionary.* The rationale for this choice was "a spike in frequency this year in the context of the EU referendum in the United Kingdom and the presidential election in the United States. It has also become associated with a particular noun, in the phrase *post-truth politics.*"[15] The widespread use of such terminology is symptomatic. Not least, it reflects the degradation of many of the fundamentals on which politics in principle rests. More concretely, it marks the realization of the Orwellian nightmare perhaps best illustrated by the famous "2 + 2 = 5" untruth that Winston Smith, the protagonist of *Nineteen Eighty-Four,* is beaten, gaslighted, and psychologically tortured into accepting as a logical and entirely valid formula.[16] This phenomenon has given way, among others, to the rogue discourses of "alternative facts" and "fake news" aimed to further the "de-democratization of democracy" (as Wendy Brown has put it in another context)[17] and is in fact one of the many dimensions of the postpolitical.

My reference to Orwell's novel is not simply a literary illustration of the question of the depoliticization of politics; nor is it exclusively an attempt to point to what the most egregious instances of institutional propaganda might look like. With great proleptic insight, for decades, the book has been instrumental in conceptualizing how controlling consensus means controlling the possibilities of the political, as I contended earlier. *Nineteen Eighty-Four,* in other words, has made an invaluable contribution to the ways in which we think politically precisely because, as a work of fiction, it exists in the peripheries of the sphere of politics (in the traditional sense of the word) and yet it can be taken politically seriously—the most salient proof is the ubiquity of terms coined in the novel such as "newspeak" and "doublethink" to describe concrete, historical phenomena occurring in the world. This should encourage the refutation of the claim that aesthetics is a mere accessory to more "pivotal" or "real" political thinking. That is where *Postpolitics and the Aesthetic Imagination* finds its footing. While already prominent in some scholarly circles in the social sciences (among others, political science, human geography, and urbanism) as well as in political philosophy, postpolitics is not as commonly explored in cultural and aesthetic criticism, although it is not entirely absent.[18] Thus, the chapters below raise a number of important questions. For instance, how can aesthetics define the contours of the postpolitical? If postpolitics does not spell out the end of politics, what does it allow us to imagine? And if it heralds the birth of something else, what creative and sensory operations are involved in the process? What is the role of the beautiful and the ugly, the strange and the familiar, and the interesting and the banal in our engagements with what, one may argue, increasingly looks like a political wasteland? Finally, and as counterpoint, how is the aesthetic enlisted to fulfill a postpolitical agenda? As with the political, the scope of the postpolitical is vast, and it affects virtually all aspects of public and private life. The critical work of the aesthetic imagination, itself an endeavor undergoing a manufactured postpolitical crisis of its own,[19] can thus be of crucial help in naming what "politics" has ceased to name, decoding postpolitics no matter how insidious or elusive its processes and the actors behind them are, and formulating a variety of responses that can counter its operations.

In order to offer a general picture, I want to draw attention now to an array of dimensions of the postpolitical, which will also include descriptions of the chapters so as to show their specific interventions. Before I do so, however, I want to establish that the book's goal to recuperate the political substance of politics is not exclusively anchored in the possibilities afforded by electoral representation. It is not solely commended to the public, state-sanctioned, and heavily coded work of party affiliation and identification either; nor do the chapters employ "politics" or "political" to designate mere partisan rivalry. Those are not chief concerns of ours—although it is true that party dynamics, policy making, and electoral representation have been subsumed by postpolitics too, and therefore will not disappear entirely from our scope of analysis.[20] I provide this caveat because, while a world whose protagonists are the politician, the voter, and their intermediaries is indeed central to the administration of life in common, restricting "politics" to that realm is extremely detrimental. It reduces the avenues, planes, and tensions that make the pursuance of better conditions for collective life possible; it contributes to forms of foreclosure that are contiguous with the ones this book attends to. The deep ideological structures that define party lines and approaches to governance are also not the only purview of our explorations. Politicking and grand gestures, hidden agendas, the calculated dissociation between electoral promises and enacted policies, party mythology, politicians-turned-celebrities and celebrities-turned-politicians, epic narratives of victory and loss, and so on, are indeed highly aestheticized elements that we must be vigilant about given their role in the advance of postpolitics.[21] Yet the scope must be much wider. In Jacques Rancière's formulation, politics here is that which

> exists when the natural order of domination is interrupted by the institution of a part of those who have no part. This institution is the whole of politics as a specific form of connection. It defines the common of the community as a political community, in other words, as divided, as based

> on a wrong that escapes the arithmetic of exchange and reparation. Beyond this set-up there is no politics. There is only the order of domination or the disorder of revolt.[22]

While the theoretical discourse of the postpolitical is multifaceted and contains many strains, as Wilson and Swyngedouw showed, the aim of this book is to recuperate such an understanding of politics by describing and combatting the order of domination underpinned by postpolitics. Generally following this Rancièrian conceptualization, it seeks to put into relief how aesthetic critique cuts through the consensual order of the given and, in doing so, weakens its power to eliminate any alternatives to its dictate. We can turn to a description of postpolitics and the labor of the chapters in formulating this aesthetic kind of resistance.

Postpolitics as Assemblage of Operations

The erosion of the political by postpolitics is rooted in specific and contingent junctures where productive antagonism cannot materialize. Therefore, it is necessary to consider postpolitics as a phenomenon comprised of many different dimensions. Identifying as many of these dimensions as possible will shed light onto the ways it precipitates, to use Rancière's terminology, the increasing inability for political struggle to detach itself from the order of domination (or "the police," as he calls it),[23] name a wrong, and create a new horizon of possibility that allows for the redressing of that wrong. Covering a range of forms of expression (literary fiction and nonfiction, digital media, music, and documentary filmmaking), the chapters below offer an overview that, though by no means exhaustive, will, I hope, provide a clear enough portrait of the crisis of the political that concerns us. The chapters are, furthermore, ordered in a kaleidoscopic manner so as to reflect the multiple, refracted, and simultaneous operations of postpolitics while underscoring the numerous possible connections among them.

The advent of neoliberalism has been at the forefront of most accounts of the postpolitical.[24] Described succinctly by David Harvey as the "financialization of everything,"[25] neoliberalism is an ideological position cemented in the rule of profit at all costs. In the 1970s, Margaret Thatcher in the United Kindom, Ronald Reagan in the United States, and Augusto Pinochet in Chile adopted it as a blueprint for a new form of government characterized by the abandonment of the operations of the state to the cannibalizing forces of the market, which now run rampant across the world.[26] Three of the chapters address this topic in their own distinct ways. Christopher Breu's "The Infrastructural Aesthetic: Materialist Politics in Karen Tei Yamashita's *I Hotel*" tackles the crisis of the political in the early days of the hypercapitalistic world we live in today. The chapter turns back to San Francisco's post-1968 turbulent anticapitalist struggles as dramatized in Yamashita's experimental novel to theorize how material infrastructure can be a vehicle to overcome the impasse between factionalism and collectivity. In doing so, Breu finds the necessary vigor to surpass such an impasse in a politics of structural organization or "material politics." Such a politics, he maintains, is capable of catalyzing cooperative solidarity and agency via physical, communicative, and social infrastructures, diffusing neoliberalism's individualist impulses while, at the same time, reifying the power of the common.

Beyond neoliberalism's takeover of the administration of public affairs, and moving closer to the present time, the profit-making ethos at the core of neoliberal ideology rears its ugly postpolitical head in other spheres as well. In her chapter "Irrational Exuberance: The Politics of Start-up Futurism," Sherryl Vint discusses the fantasies peddled by the gurus of Silicon Valley in their attempt to co-opt the revolutionary energies of utopianism. Focusing on a series of cultural texts such as Jed Rothstein's documentary *WeWork, or The Making and Breaking of a $47 Billion Unicorn; Wired* magazine; and the countercultural *Whole Earth Catalog*, Vint traces start-up capitalism's appropriation of a futurism first conjured up by science fiction writers now deployed in order to misrepresent its own capitalistic activities. This corrupt futurist rhetoric, Vint concludes, is currently being turned into a fundamentalist neoliberal cudgel with which to batter the emancipatory substance out of certain forms of collectivism.

In a related vein, my chapter at the end of the book, titled "A Haunted Present: Postpolitics, Nuclear Waste, and the Colonization of the Future," also addresses technocapitalism by foregrounding its goal to own the future and counterposing it to the sobering realities of our nuclear legacy. First, it argues how longtermism, an ideology ardently cultivated by certain tech circles, disguises the iniquity of its own operations behind the veil of a purportedly altruistic agenda aimed to do good for the deep future. The chapter then turns this historical relationship around and explores how Michael Madsen's documentary *Into Eternity: A Film for the Future* employs a "haunting aesthetics" to challenge the presentist politics of nuclear energy by defamiliarizing it. The film, I conclude, thematizes the fact that our disposal of radioactive waste forecloses the possibilities of political action in the ultra-far future.

Investigations of the postpolitical nature of neoliberalism have also shown its installation as a totalizing system. The success of this enterprise has hinged on the proclamation that, as Margaret Thatcher imperiously put it, "there is no alternative"[27] to the financialization of everything. To illustrate the fallacy of this doctrine, critics often turn to Francis Fukuyama's infamous formulation of "the end of history," which hailed the supposedly natural dissolution of global ideological antagonisms following the fall of the communist bloc and the victorious rise of Western capitalism as the new global order.[28] Such an account has been widely refuted with arguments explaining that this is not the organic disappearance of antagonism but its postpolitical subsumption by consensus. As Žižek has maintained, while "emphasiz[ing] the need to leave old ideological divisions behind," postpolitics "no longer merely 'represses' the political . . . but much more effectively 'forecloses' it."[29] In other words, disguised as nonideological, it stipulates the demise of antagonism as the motor for politics without having to fight dissenting positions against it. Mark Fisher would call this "capitalist realism," as it precludes the emergence of other ways to practice politics on the premise that the laws of the market simply do not allow for them.[30]

Yet this postpolitical "realism" is not exclusive of neoliberal hegemony and can be identified in other realms outside of the politicoeconomic. Robert Marzec's chapter "Thinking Jacques Rancière with Ursula K. Le Guin: Aesthetics and Politics in a Postpolitical Age" examines the imposition of growth as the unchallengeable linchpin of an apparatus of power that curtails the emergence of alternative political visions. Following an account of Rancière's work on the perceptual scope of the political, the chapter zeroes in on the critique against the promise of technological progress at the center of Le Guin's short story "Direction of the Road." While focusing on its employment of an oak as the focal point and narrative voice, Marzec elucidates how the violent intrusion of the automobile in the relationship between humans and their immediate natural environment inaugurates a new order that renders politics as a mere "mechanical tool of representation." This postpolitical foreclosure of alternatives intended to dictate the terms of what counts and what does not count as politically legible is also a central analytical target in Vint's chapter and my own, which tease out the exclusivist claims to modernity by start-up capitalists and the extractivist nuclear industry.

Apart from preempting the emergence of alternatives to the hegemonic order of consensus by regulating the narrative of what counts as political, postpolitics also eliminates dissent by other means. Notably, a great deal of what looks like political activity is absorbed in processes designed precisely to neutralize its capacity to challenge the status quo.[31] This is why, despite its great emancipatory potential, the antagonistic politics epitomized by Bartlebian refusal—the power of no—can easily become a self-defeating tactic.[32] Eric Lemmon's chapter, "Dissensus, Refusal, Participatory Music: Negation and Rupture in *Crowd in C*," explores the ripple effects of this dilemma. Focusing on Sang Won Lee's computer-based composition *Crowd in C*, the chapter begins by inspecting the assumed decentering power of audiences in their performance of participatory musical pieces via the use of digital devices. It then moves to describe the self-disciplinary dynamics of this involvement, as audiences' agency is limited to the creative and technical decisions made by the composer. Despite this tension, Lemmon argues that the open-endedness found in this kind of musical event contains possibilities for the subversion of the composer's instructions in the form of disruption—both planned and spontaneous. As a result, individuals' poietic power productively unsettles the consensual order (whether in the performative space or in the "real world"), opening up new avenues for the political to materialize.

The tension between participation and refusal is particularly charged for minority identities, who are significantly vulnerable given the potential costs (including violence and death) of taking either option. A few chapters consider this. While Breu's focuses in part on the risks of adopting a minority (Asian American) identitarian approach to activism, this is fully explored in Matthew Scully's chapter, "Wayward Possibilities: Errant Black Women and the Intimacies of Freedom." In it, Scully studies Saidiya Hartman's *Wayward Lives, Beautiful Experiments* for the inventiveness of both the Black women in Hartman's account and the author's own stylistic choices. Scully argues that Hartman's rebellious subjects exploit an embodied politics rooted in a creative errancy that escapes the grip of the consensual order forged by patriarchy and white supremacy. At the same time, he shows Hartman's creative dexterity in the establishment of an intimate bond between those women and the reader via the use of free indirect style, which reveals, in the words of Frédéric Gros, how the inspiring "common vibration of several 'non-delegable' selves" can make us "understand that obedience is nothing more than an indefinite series of inner negations."[33] Strategic disengagement may be one possible successful response by the most vulnerable minorities and disempowered collectives to their postpolitical disenfranchisement. So is a direct confrontation that redraws the terms of engagement.

Jacquelyn Arcy and Allison Page's "*Un violador en tu camino:* Reimagining the Political through Mediated Feminist Street Performance" discusses the power of staged antagonism to generate positions of resistance. The chapter examines how the pervasiveness of social media can be harnessed for that purpose as it considers the viral video of Chilean collective LASTESIS's performance of *Un violador en tu camino* (A rapist in your path) in the streets of Santiago. Discussing the performative elements of the recording and its transmission on social media, Arcy and Page unveil the affective strategies of LASTESIS's public intervention as one that mobilizes bodies against sexual and gender-based violence. Crucially, they demonstrate that the latter must be seen not only as patriarchal but as state violence too given its acceptance as an unexceptional element of society's normal operation—that is, the general consensus—by institutions and a large portion of the public. Yet Arcy and Page's chapter, like Vint's and Lemmon's, does not put forth an uncritical celebration of digital politics. Rather, it considers the perils of phenomena such as Las

Tesis's performance being caught up in what Jonathan Crary calls the "trap of social media . . . where activism will continue to occur innocuously, without attaining any radical or foundational changes."[34] Far from offering a utopian environment ruled by horizontal, universal, and equal participation, the omnipresence of digital technologies has instead facilitated the acceleration of the postpoliticization of our public and private lives by "too big to fail" tech companies, which continue to operate without proper check. This digital postpoliticization has many fronts, from the production and collection of personal data and the hijacking of our attention to the establishment of opaque policing systems and the promotion of toxic behavior on social media, and from the disruption of traditional accountability processes by blockchain technology (including cryptocurrencies) and the rise of AI to the destruction of jobs by automation, the emergence of the misleadingly called "sharing economy," and the racist "default discrimination" written into the code of the digital tools we use.[35]

Thus, while technology is not always politically detrimental,[36] there is overwhelming evidence that we must remain vigilant about the widespread installation of techno-corporate "innovations" (to use the lingo) as chief mediators of our social and political activities or their adoption as a path toward emancipation.[37] And while digital technologies have an immediate negative impact, this phenomenon can also occur in both the medium and long terms, which are explored in two aforementioned chapters that consider other technological realms. Marzec's chapter focuses on the relatively quick entrance of car culture in our immediate environment over a span of about three generations while mine reflects on the ways nuclear technology is already predetermining the kind of politics humans will be able to practice thousands of years from now (if they find the right conditions to survive on this planet). Additionally, Stephen Charbonneau's chapter is concerned with technologies of audiovisual capture in judicial and democratic processes, which play roles with potential historical consequences too. I will describe Charbonneau's chapter in more detail momentarily.

A final dimension of the postpolitical pertains to the rise of new antidemocratic political spectacles. Appearing in this introduction for a second time and much harder to consolidate around one term, this phenomenon can perhaps simply be called the post-truth order, and it is the latest frontier in the war against political agency. Assaults aimed toward weakening the political by epistemic means are currently carried out through more or less sophisticated methods such as covert propaganda (aimed, often with the help of social media platforms, to sow division) and other forms of manipulative digital media such as deep fakes, or they can adopt more familiar methods as is the case of both conspiracy theories passed as independent critical thinking and hypernationalist, crony capitalism refashioned as populist discourses of liberation.[38] A symptom that the fabric of democracy—and, with it, the possibilities of political action—is dangerously being undone is that, apparently, anyone can now dispute the trueness of world-shattering events (from pandemics to climate change) without concrete evidence and in direct defiance of verifiability processes and established facts. Sophia Rosenfeld posits: "truth, like democracy, isn't something that simply exists in the world. It is, rather, something that we must always consciously and collectively forge."[39] This renewed effort to bombard our capacities to discern what is certain and what is not—what is verifiable and what is fake—is particularly destructive because it removes indispensable elements for the formation of social relations, and is currently deployed by a range of actors to turn the tenets of democracy upside down in broad daylight.[40]

At one level, Arcy and Page's as well as Scully's chapters grapple with two representative orders (patriarchy and white supremacy) that often resort to gaslighting the collectives they seek to dominate in order to declare unchallengeable the consensual status quo they control. Stephen Charbonneau's chapter, however, addresses this environment more frontally in a different context. In "False Specters of the Political: Revisitation, Digital Documentary Vernacular, and the Postpolitical after January 6," Charbonneau interrogates the composition and public presentation of aestheticized documentary evidence employed at Donald Trump's second impeachment proceedings intended to establish the facts of what happened at the January 6, 2021, attack on the U.S. Capitol. Specifically, his chapter shows how the play-by-play video narrative of the events at the center of the proceedings exhibits qualities of what he calls a "digital documentary vernacular" that conflates fact and affect and, thus, drags the creation of digital documentary content away from its original purpose as a medium for knowledge production. The ritualized and theatrical exhibition of the video, Charbonneau concludes, dooms this effort to reaffirm the postpolitical order it intends to counter and, ultimately, reveals the limits of political restoration.

I hope it is clear by now that the aesthetic imagination can contribute something important in response to the many faces of postpolitics. In a final reflection on this question and the work done by the chapters, Erik Swyngedouw brings the volume to a close with a deconstructive meditation on the idea of "the end." His afterword, titled "Between Two Endings, or Prolegomena for Another End," offers a postmortem diagnosis of the political under the postpolitical hegemonic order and, moving past it, illuminates ways toward an urgent repoliticization of things given the calamitous times we are currently living in. Addressing certain imaginative elements of our engagement with the crises assailing us (fantasies of the end, dystopic visions, and more), the afterword explores the paradoxical nature of the end as the trope that announces the (foretold) death of politics and, simultaneously, the continuation of business as usual in an endless loop of depoliticization—that is, the extension ad infinitum of the end of politics at a time during which we are condemned to live "at the end." As a result, our world is plagued by a variety of real, connected crises while a phantasmic sense of an ending looms over the postpolitical horizon that never quite arrives. After taking stock of this "never-ending end," finally, Swyngedouw identifies the aesthetic register as a "pivotal" vehicle to galvanize our political imaginaries and reenergize the radicality of life in common in order to face the catastrophes besetting our times.

Aesthetics and the Political, Again and Again

The aesthetic exploration of postpolitics offered in this collection follows a rich intellectual history. It is not necessary to construct a full genealogy (that would be a gargantuan project) to easily recall that many political thinkers have identified aesthetic elements at the center of their critiques. Classic examples abound, from Karl Marx and Friedrich Engels's call for a "world literature" to carry the message of the international workers' movement to Antonio Gramsci's preoccupation with popular culture's role in the perpetuation of hegemonic consensus.[41] Additionally, the work of other thinkers has been concerned with the political nature of the aesthetic such as, among many others, Walter Benjamin's warnings about the aesthetics of authoritarianism, Theodor Adorno's examination of art in relation to modern capitalistic society, Roland Barthes's critique of bourgeois mass culture, Hélène Cixous's theorization of *écriture féminine,* Paul Virilio's exploration of the links between cinematic visuality and military technology, Gloria Anzaldúa's account of the gender, racial, ethnic, and national qualities of border cultures, Toni Morrison's critique of Africanism in the (white and male) American literary canon, and Edward Said's appraisal of the entanglement between culture and imperialism.[42] Finally, many of the thinkers associated with the theorization of the contemporary crisis of the political, from Alain Badiou to Giorgio Agamben (the latter's injudicious Covid-19 commentary notwithstanding), have turned to aesthetics as a way to either illustrate their points or find a terrain for their reflections.[43]

Building off such efforts, *Postpolitics and the Aesthetic Imagination* explores new avenues in which we, practitioners of aesthetic criticism, can contribute to the larger question of what it is to live in a postpolitical world. It remains to be seen whether pursuing a purely antagonistic method or, in line with Chantal Mouffe's work, engaging with it agonistically is the best approach for this task.[44] Either way, the relationship between aesthetics and postpolitics must be understood as one of mutual influence—and that goes, I would argue, for the work of political and cultural theorists too. That is this volume's exploratory epicenter, around which the analyses offered in the following pages revolve, providing a critical platform that reveals aesthetics not just as a mere site to typify elements of the postpolitical, but also as another language to name them, a conceptual landscape to reveal their rooting, and the antidote to combat the depoliticization they occasion.

Ultimately, the semantic richness of the verb "to sense" lends itself as conceptual framework for this book and underpins the theoretical efforts of the chapters below. In the first instance, and attending to the etymology of aesthetics, we seek to valorize that which we perceive via the senses. The work of Jacques Rancière is invaluable to uncover the operations of consensus, as I have already pointed out, but so is his theorization of the antonym "dissensus," which he defines as "a division inserted in 'common sense': a dispute over what is given and about the frame within which we see something as given" that produces a "conflict between a sensory presentation and a way of making sense of it, or between several sensory regimes and/or 'bodies.'"[45] Furthermore, while the aesthetic can indeed be enlisted for depoliticizing purposes, as some of the chapters here show, for Rancière certain works of art have a dissensual potency that can provoke a renovation of politics in the face of postpolitics, especially given that the latter aims primarily to occlude possible ways to register, expose, and resist the very disenfranchisement it engenders. In other words, imagining dissensually allows us to make another sense of the postpolitical order than the prescribed one.

At a time when the agents of postpolitics justify their positions and actions as reasonable, and when the work of postpolitics is predicated on the imposition of a (putatively) unchallengeable narrative of why things are the way they are, the liberatory work of aesthetics begins in the act of sensorily dismantling the obstinate and unshakable hegemony of consensus. It is then that we can speak of an "aesthetic democracy," or the radical process that emerges from our engagement with artistic objects as an experience of "the possible or the ambiguous."[46] Art can counter the anesthesia generated by postpolitics by way of an illuminating reactivation of the senses. In the best of cases, postpolitics will be visible to those who look in the right direction, or from the right angle; however, postpolitics enacts very often such an assault on the senses that we may only be capable of intuiting its presence due to either its sheer invisibility or the incremental erosion of the political at imperceptible speeds. That is where the aesthetic, in facilitating the development of an "egalitarian imaginary,"[47] can help in the recuperation of the ground that postpolitics has colonized. When asked in one of his last interviews how he dealt "with a future that feels so bleak," activist and intellectual Mike Davis responded: "I've always been influenced by the poems Brecht wrote in the late 30s, during the second world war, after everything had been incinerated, all the dreams and values of an entire generation destroyed, and Brecht said, well, it's a new dark ages . . . how do people resist in the dark ages?"[48] These may be radically different times from the war years. The chapters below, nevertheless, are motivated by a similar urge—to shine a light onto our own dark ages.

Notes

1. Antonio Gramsci, *Selections from the Prison Notebooks of Antonio Gramsci,* trans. Quintin Hoare and Geoffrey Nowell Smith (New York: International, 1971), 12.

2. Japhy Wilson and Erik Swyngedouw, "Seeds of Dystopia: Post-politics and the Return of the Political," in *The Post-political and Its Discontents: Spaces of Depoliticisation, Spectres of Radical Politics,* ed. Japhy Wilson and Erik Swyngedouw (Edinburgh: Edinburgh University Press, 2014), 6. See also Ali Rıza Taşkale, *Post-politics in Context* (London: Routledge, 2016).

3. The distinction between these two terms, however, has been the subject of debate. Badiou has argued that it is politics and not the political that a theory of emancipation should focus on, qualifying the political as "a fiction" in which "we have lost the fact that the real, of which *politics* comes to pass as the process, never occurs except in the figure without essence of the event," while describing politics as "the infinite assumption of being that gives a lasting latency to the existence of the Two." Alain Badiou, *Can Politics Be Thought?,* trans. Bruno Bosteels (Durham, N.C.: Duke University Press, 2018), 31, 107; emphasis in the original. In another context, Badiou calls for the need to escape the intellectual abstractions with which political philosophy concerns itself and proposes metapolitics as an alternative designation to speak of politics as an "evental," transformative process. Alain Badiou, *Metapolitics,* trans. Jason Baker (London: Verso, 2005).

4. Ernesto Laclau, *New Reflections on the Revolution of Our Time* (London: Verso, 1990), 64.

5. Erik Swyngedouw, *Promises of the Political: Insurgent Cities in a Post-political Environment* (Cambridge, Mass.: MIT Press, 2018), 36.

6. Dean rightly calls this a "cliché," making the case that perpetuating it is in itself a "depoliticizing" act, because if everything is political, then "there's no need to bother with organizing, consciousness-raising, or critique." Jodi Dean, "Political Theory and Cultural Studies," in *The Oxford Handbook of Political Theory,* ed. John S. Dryzek, Bonnie Honig, and Anne Phillips (Oxford: Oxford University Press, 2006), 762.

7. For a foundational text on this matter, see Kwame Anthony Appiah, "Is the Post- in Postmodernism the Post- in Postcolonial?," *Critical Inquiry* 17, no. 2 (1991): 336–57.

8. Elizabeth S. Anker and Rita Felski, eds., introduction to *Critique and Postcritique* (Durham, N.C.: Duke University Press, 2017), 1.

9. See, for example, Ella Shohat, "Notes on the 'Post-colonial,'" *Social Text,* no. 31/32 (1992): 99–113; Anne McClintock, "The Angel of Progress: Pitfalls of the Term 'Post-colonialism,'" *Social Text,* no. 31/32 (1994): 84–98; and Arif Dirlik, "The Postcolonial Aura: Third World Criticism in the Age of Global Capitalism," *Critical Inquiry* 20, no. 2 (1994): 328–56.

10. As Stuart Hall contends, "*postcolonial* is not the end of colonisation. It *is* after a certain *kind* of colonialism, after a certain moment of high imperialism and colonial occupation—in the wake of it, in the shadow of it, inflected by it—it is what it is because something else has happened before, but it is also something new." "Cultural Composition: Stuart Hall on Ethnicity and the Discursive Turn," interview conducted by Julie Drew, *JAC* 18, no. 2 (1998): 189; emphasis in the original.

11. Dean, for example, has maintained that it "overlooks the reality of politics on the ground" while giving up "in advance key terrains of activism and struggle." Jodi Dean, *Democracy and Other Neoliberal Fantasies: Communicative Capitalism and Left Politics* (Durham, N.C.: Duke University Press, 2009), 12.

12. Taylor has treated this paradoxical question in democratic terms. See Astra Taylor, *Democracy May Not Exist, but We'll Miss It When It's Gone* (New York: Metropolitan, 2019).

13. Jacques Derrida, *Of Grammatology,* trans. Gayatri Chakravorty Spivak (Baltimore: Johns Hopkins University Press, 1998), 15.

14. See, for instance, Rosi Braidotti, *Posthuman Knowledge* (Cambridge: Polity, 2019).

15. "Word of the Year 2016," *Oxford Languages,* languages.oup.com/word-of-the-year/2016; emphasis in the original.

16. George Orwell, *Nineteen Eighty-Four* (New York: Signet, 1963), 290. Tellingly, Radiohead would repurpose this motif to thematize a palpable unease with the postpolitical status quo in the early days of the twenty-first century in the opening track of their 2003 album *Hail to the Thief,* "2 + 2 = 5 (The Lukewarm)."

17. Wendy Brown, "American Nightmare: Neoliberalism, Neoconservatism, and De-democratization," *Political Theory* 34, no. 6 (2006): 690–714.

18. For some attempts to illuminate this question through a variety of lenses, see Marc James Léger, *Brave New Avant Garde: Essays on Contemporary Art and Politics* (Winchester, Eng.: Zero/Collective Ink, 2012); Matt Tierney, *What Lies Between: Void Aesthetics and Postwar Post-politics* (Lanham, Md.: Rowman & Littlefield, 2015); Robert P. Marzec, *Militarizing the Environment: Climate Change and the Security State* (Minneapolis: University of Minnesota Press, 2015); and Juan Meneses, *Resisting Dialogue: Modern Fiction and the Future of Dissent* (Minneapolis: University of Minnesota Press, 2019).

19. We can see this clearly, for example, in the renewed attacks across public education institutions against the study of aesthetics—and the humanities in

general—via defunding, canceling programs, and removing students' financial support. These measures are presented as the only possible response to shrinking budgets (the rationale behind that shrinking is nonetheless never up for discussion, as if it were a spontaneous phenomenon) and under the pretext that a humanistic education is not the best way to prepare students, who instead must be first and foremost trained professionally. This is an outright attack on an important site where the collective political imagination can be cultivated.

20. For two sharp treatises on the theoretical problems of electoral politics, see Simone Weil, *On the Abolition of All Political Parties,* trans. Simon Leys (New York: New York Review of Books, 2013); and Jacques Rancière, *Hatred of Democracy,* trans. Steve Corcoran (London: Verso, 2006).

21. For a critique of these and other often overlooked elements of electoral and representative politics, see Emily Apter, *Unexceptional Politics: On Obstruction, Impasse, and the Impolitic* (London: Verso, 2018).

22. Jacques Rancière, *Disagreement: Politics and Philosophy,* trans. Julie Rose (Minneapolis: University of Minnesota Press, 1999), 11–12.

23. Rancière, 29.

24. See, for instance, Swyngedouw, *Promises of the Political.* For an approach from a literary perspective, see Meneses, *Resisting Dialogue,* 99–147 ("Deflection: Neoliberalism and the Affective Regulation of Citizenship").

25. David Harvey, *A Brief History of Neoliberalism* (Oxford: Oxford University Press, 2005), 33.

26. For important analyses, see Luc Boltanski and Eve Chiapello, *The New Spirit of Capitalism,* trans. Gregory Elliott (London: Verso, 2007); Wendy Brown, *Undoing the Demos: Neoliberalism's Stealth Revolution* (New York: Zone, 2017); Wendy Brown, *In the Ruins of Neoliberalism: The Rise of Antidemocratic Politics in the West* (New York: Columbia University Press, 2019); Quinn Slobodian, *Globalists: The End of Empire and the Birth of Neoliberalism* (Cambridge, Mass.: Harvard University Press, 2018); Pierre Dardot and Christian Laval, *Never Ending Nightmare: How Neoliberalism Dismantles Democracy,* trans. Gregory Elliott (London: Verso, 2019); and Maurizio Lazzarato, *Capital Hates Everyone: Fascism or Revolution,* trans. Robert Hurley (South Pasadena, Calif.: Semiotext(e), 2021).

27. Margaret Thatcher, "Speech to Conservative Women's Conference," Margaret Thatcher Foundation, May 21, 1980, www.margaretthatcher.org/document/104368.

28. Francis Fukuyama, "The End of History?," *National Interest* 16 (1989): 4; and Francis Fukuyama, *The End of History and the Last Man* (New York: Free Press, 1992).

29. Slavoj Žižek, *The Ticklish Subject: The Absent Centre of Political Ontology* (London: Verso, 1999), 236, 198.

30. Fisher expresses this as "the widespread sense that not only is capitalism the only viable political and economic system, but also that it is now impossible

even to imagine a coherent alternative to it." Mark Fisher, *Capitalist Realism: Is There No Alternative?* (Winchester, Eng.: Zero/Collective Ink, 2009), 2.

31. This is the case, for instance, in the depoliticization of dialogue as a vehicle to cause change via the expression of dissent. See Meneses, *Resisting Dialogue.*

32. As Hardt and Negri have maintained, "refusal certainly is the beginning of a liberatory politics, but it is only the beginning. The refusal in itself is empty. . . . [It] leads only to a kind of social suicide." Michael Hardt and Antonio Negri, *Empire* (Cambridge, Mass.: Harvard University Press, 2000), 202.

33. Frédéric Gros, *Disobey! A Philosophy of Resistance,* trans. David Fernbach (London: Verso, 2021), 157.

34. Jonathan Crary, *Scorched Earth: Beyond the Digital Age to a Post-capitalist World* (London: Verso, 2022), 12, 13. See also Evgeny Morozov, *To Save Everything, Click Here* (New York: PublicAffairs, 2014).

35. Ruha Benjamin, *Race after Technology: Abolitionist Code for the New Jim Code* (Cambridge: Polity, 2019), 77–96. For representative texts touching on the other themes mentioned, see Jonathan Crary, *24/7: Late Capitalism and the Ends of Sleep* (London: Verso, 2013); David Golumbia, *The Politics of Bitcoin: Software as Right-Wing Extremism* (Minneapolis: University of Minnesota Press, 2016); Adam Greenfield, *Radical Technologies: The Design of Everyday Life* (London: Verso, 2017); John Cheney-Lippold, *We Are Data: Algorithms and the Making of Our Digital Selves* (New York: NYU Press, 2017); Shoshana Zuboff, *The Age of Surveillance Capitalism: The Fight for a Human Future at the New Frontier of Power* (New York: PublicAffairs, 2019); and Mark Shepard, *There Are No Facts: Attentive Algorithms, Extractive Data Practices, and the Quantification of Everyday Life* (Cambridge, Mass.: MIT Press, 2022).

36. Tufekci, for instance, has shown how social media have played in part a positive role in certain prodemocracy movements across the world. See Zeynep Tufekci, *Twitter and Tear Gas: The Power and Fragility of Networked Protest* (New Haven, Conn.: Yale University Press, 2017).

37. For instance, the advocacy for accelerationism by certain voices on the left disregards crucial political questions, such as the extractivist, exploitative, and cannibalistic nature of the technofuturist practices at the core of such an agenda. See, for example, Aaron Bastani, *Fully Automated Luxury Communism: A Manifesto* (London: Verso, 2019). For a critique of accelerationism, see Benjamin Noys, *Malign Velocities: Accelerationism and Capitalism* (Winchester, Eng.: Zero/Collective Ink, 2014).

38. On the latter point, the war on perception has proven a perfect method to exploit the historical vacuum left by consensus governance. In 2005, Mouffe anticipated the dangers of a reactionary kind of populism that would take the world by storm ten years later. Chantal Mouffe, "Current Challenges to the Post-political Vision," in *On the Political* (London: Routledge, 2005), 66–69.

39. Sophia Rosenfeld, *Democracy and Truth: A Short History* (Philadelphia: University of Pennsylvania Press, 2019), 176.

40. See Aurelien Mondon and Aaron Winter, *Reactionary Democracy: How Racism and the Populist Far Right Became Mainstream* (London: Verso, 2020); and Mikkel Bolt Rasmussen, *Late Capitalist Fascism* (Cambridge: Polity, 2021).

41. Karl Marx and Friedrich Engels, *The Communist Manifesto,* ed. David McLellan, trans. Samuel Moore (Oxford: Oxford University Press, 1998), 7; and Antonio Gramsci, *Selections from Cultural Writings,* ed. David Forgacs and Geoffrey Nowell-Smith (London: Lawrence and Wishart, 1985).

42. Walter Benjamin, "The Work of Art in the Age of Its Technological Reproducibility: Second Version," in *Walter Benjamin: Selected Writings, 3: 1935–1938,* ed. Howard Eiland and Michael W. Jennings, trans. Edmund Jephcott et al. (Cambridge, Mass.: Belknap, 2006); Theodor W. Adorno, *Aesthetic Theory,* ed. Gretel Adorno and Rolf Tiedemann, trans. Robert Hullot-Kentor (London: Bloomsbury, 2013); Roland Barthes, *Mythologies,* trans. Annette Lavers (New York: Hill and Wang, 1972); Hélène Cixous, *The Newly Born Woman,* trans. Betsy Wing (Minneapolis: University of Minnesota Press, 1986); Gloria Anzaldúa, *Borderlands/La Frontera: The New Mestiza* (San Francisco: Aunt Lute, 1987); Paul Virilio, *War and Cinema: The Logistics of Perception,* trans. Patrick Camiller (London: Verso, 1989); Toni Morrison, *Playing in the Dark: Whiteness and the Literary Imagination* (Cambridge, Mass.: Harvard University Press, 1992); and Edward W. Said, *Culture and Imperialism* (New York: Vintage, 1993).

43. One could choose from a number of works by these theorists. See, for instance, Alain Badiou, *Handbook of Inaesthetics,* trans. Alberto Toscano (Stanford, Calif.: Stanford University Press, 2005); Jacques Rancière, *The Politics of Aesthetics: The Distribution of the Sensible,* trans. Gabriel Rockhill (London: Bloomsbury, 2013); Slavoj Žižek, *Living in the End Times* (London: Verso, 2010); and Giorgio Agamben, *The Fire and the Tale,* trans. Lorenzo Chiesa (Stanford, Calif.: Stanford University Press, 2017). For an analysis of Agamben's comments on the pandemic, see Adam Kotsko, "What Happened to Giorgio Agamben?," *Slate,* February 22, 2022, slate.com/human-interest/2022/02/giorgio-agamben-covid-holocaust-comparison-right-wing-protest.html.

44. Michel Foucault coined the term agonism to describe "less of a face-to-face confrontation that paralyzes both sides than a permanent provocation." Michel Foucault, "The Subject and Power," in *Power: Essential Works of Foucault, 1954–1984,* vol. 3, trans. Robert Hurley (New York: New Press, 2000), 342. In its configuration as agonistics, it has featured prominently in much of Mouffe's work, including in aesthetic terms. See, for instance, Chantal Mouffe, "Agonistic Politics and Artistic Practices," in *Agonistics: Thinking the World Politically* (London: Verso, 2013): 85–105. On antagonism, see Oliver Marchart, *Thinking Antagonism* (Edinburgh: Edinburgh University Press, 2018).

45. Jacques Rancière, *Dissensus: On Politics and Aesthetics,* ed. and trans. Steven Corcoran (London: Bloomsbury, 2010), 69, 139. For other, related ways in which the aesthetic manifests a radical conception of politics, be it in a "conflictual," "unexceptional," or "investigative" modes, to name a few, see, respectively,

Oliver Marchart, *Conflictual Aesthetics: Artistic Activism and the Public Sphere* (London: Sternberg Press, 2019); Arne De Boever, *Against Aesthetic Exceptionalism* (Minneapolis: University of Minnesota Press, 2019); and Matthew Fuller and Eyal Weizman, *Investigative Aesthetics: Conflicts and Commons in the Politics of Truth* (London: Verso, 2021).

46. Thomas Docherty, *Aesthetic Democracy* (Stanford, Calif.: Stanford University Press, 2006), 87.

47. Ernesto Laclau and Chantal Mouffe, *Hegemony and Socialist Strategy: Towards a Radical Democratic Politics* (London: Verso, 1985), 159–60.

48. Lois Beckett, "Mike Davis, California's 'Prophet of Doom,' on Activism in a Dying World: 'Despair Is Useless,'" *Guardian,* August 31, 2022, www.theguardian.com/us-news/2022/aug/30/mike-davis-california-writer-interview-activism.

CHAPTER 1

The Infrastructural Aesthetic

Materialist Politics in Karen Tei Yamashita's I Hotel

CHRISTOPHER BREU

Politics Is Dead; Long Live Politics

We live in strange times. The times feel too political and not political enough. The neoliberal consensus seems to be breaking apart, with the return of both right and left antiliberal discourses and social visions. From one perspective, the attenuation of neoliberalism as a social discourse is promising. For those of us who came of age under its depoliticizing force, or what Japhy Wilson and Erik Swyngedouw call postpolitics, the emergence of real socialist and anticapitalist politics is a welcome development. Any political movement away from neoliberal business as usual feels like it holds promise.[1] If, as Fredric Jameson argues, part of the postmodern condition is that it is easier to imagine the end of the world than the end of capitalism, then the present suggests that we may be moving beyond this fetter on our imagination.[2] We are able again to posit visions of an equal, just, and ecologically sustainable future. We no longer exist in the half-life of postmodernism. Although what Mark Fisher terms capitalist realism may not yet have vanished as a dominant discourse, it is safe to say that it is not the only game in town.[3]

If such stirrings on the left are promising, then a newly revitalized and antiliberal right wing—one organized around explicit fascist and biological racist rhetoric—is profoundly disheartening. Neofascisms and racisms are powerfully emergent, when not dominant, in the United States, Brazil, India, Poland, and the Philippines, to mention only a few. Whereas the left continues to be largely fragmented and atomized, the right has found a unifying populist rhetoric, one seeded with paranoia, conspiracy, nationalism, exclusion of gender and sexual diversity, and affirmation of racial or religious supremacy. Thus, if the right feels too political, the left does not feel political or collectivist enough.

Yet there is another way our times feel postpolitical. This contradictory affect, where the times feel both too political and not political enough, is perhaps the shape the postpolitical takes on in our late neoliberal present. The left both longs for a collective politics and has lost the large-scale forms of organization and thought that would enable such a politics. Instead, the political is experienced on a resolutely individual level.

On one level, for the left, everything seems thoroughly political. Judging by internecine battles within the left on social media, we can read all aspects of culture, including identities, representations, cultural practices, and even bodily comportment through the lens of the political. In this context, the struggle of 1990s-era cultural studies to read every aspect of culture, even the most seemingly commodified or compromised, in relationship to struggles around cultural hegemony has emerged victorious. As Eleanor Courtemanche argues, the work of cultural studies, what she terms Cultural Studies 2.0, has shifted locations from the classroom, where it is a staid discipline at this point, to locations in popular culture and specifically social media.[4] Students no longer need to be taught how to read popular culture politically. They are already debating any range of cultural topics, from feminism in Marvel movies and racial appropriation at Coachella to the proper way to talk about and understand sexual identities—all before they have entered their first cultural studies class. We should appreciate how much of a victory this is. It is certainly an improvement over the old models of depoliticized humanism and the unquestioned reign of high art, which characterized discourse in the humanities (and specifically literary studies) before the advent of cultural studies. Certainly the aim of any leftist theoretical project is to become part of the fabric of popular culture and achieve something like a genuine cultural transformation. It would be a rather cutting irony if cultural studies, with its championing of popular culture, turned against its uptake in popular culture.

On another level, though, the version of cultural studies that has been enshrined in popular culture lacks the reflexivity and broad political address of the academic version, particularly in the best versions of it as practiced by, say, Raymond Williams, Stuart Hall, or Angela McRobbie. Instead, the version of cultural critique practiced online tends toward the micropolitical, moralizing, and identarian. If Bourdieu's critique of cultural capital was central to the cultural studies reevaluation of the canon in the 1990s and early 2000s, then the online version of cultural critique seems to be more about amassing cultural capital than interrogating it.[5] It is in this latter context that it feels like our moment is too political, in the sense of rendering all relationships in terms of micropolitical antagonism. Factionalism, purity politics, and microidentities proliferate, and any type of collectivist or unifying discourse is rejected for the way in which it excludes the particular. Even theory has become primarily concerned with the personal and increasingly leery of larger claims or arguments. Take, for example, the explosion of autotheory, with its centering of the individual, who functions at best as a micropolitical actor and at worst as an egoic and apolitical monad. Good dialectical thinking always attends to the way in which the particular is in contradiction with the universal, but dialectics does not champion the particular at the universal's expense.

In this sense, we are living in a time that does not feel political enough. Issues of representation, identity, and discourse have been thoroughly politicized, in ways both productive and unproductive. As a collective category, identity can be a powerful organizing rubric, functioning to unify collectivities around a given conception of race, gender, sexuality, and/or class, and indeed, much of the political force of collective struggles in the United States in the 1960s and 1970s, such as the Asian American movement depicted in Yamashita's *I Hotel*, and in our own present (such as Black Lives Matter) take a politicized and collective understanding of identity as a source of genuine political articulation. Yet too much identity formation in the present has become individualized and micropolitical. Similarly, when institutionalized within the neoliberal academy and other corporate contexts, multicultural and antiracist discourses quickly become defanged techniques of bureaucratic management. Meanwhile, the larger material, economic, and ecological context that enables representation—and indeed human and nonhuman flourishing as such—has not been politicized enough. Given the seriousness of the material problems facing us in the present, including the climate emergency, an endlessly mutating pandemic, profound economic inequality, and immiseration, we need a collective discourse that can address large-scale material changes and political-economic transformations. To the degree that we lack the political forms to address these macropolitical dynamics, we are living in a postpolitical context. We have powerfully politicized identity and culture, but we remain largely silent about the kinds of materialist politics and forms of collective identification necessary to achieve large-scale social transformation.

Toward a Politics of Infrastructure

This broader politics is one of infrastructure. It is about politically engaging and transforming the material organization of everyday life. Central to such a conception of infrastructure is attending not only to what Jason Moore has called world ecology but also to the political-economic organization of the "worldsystem."[6] As I have argued elsewhere, representation matters, but what enables representation and what representation obscures matter more.[7] Such a politics of infrastructure would also involve forms of collective organizing, rather than ones that emphasize both micropolitics and microidentities. This is fundamentally an argument against commodity fetishism, particularly because the commodities have become ourselves. For all the ways in which we argue about representation on TikTok, Twitter/X, Facebook, Tumblr, and Instagram, we need more work that addresses and politicizes the forms of complexly racialized and gendered labor, infrastructure, and ecologies that are central to contemporary life. We also have little sense of infrastructure's ecological or economic costs as well as benefits. The good news is that the growing field of infrastructure studies has emerged to address this shortcoming.[8] Perhaps more important, activism such as the #NoDAPL movement, which was led by Indigenous environmental activists, has emerged to directly politicize infrastructure and challenge the suicidal global dependency on fossil fuels.

A politics adequate to the present, then, would not merely engage issues of representation and identification (as important as these are) but would also engage the material structuration of such categories as they intersect with the forms of infrastructure (including those of labor and social reproduction) that enable collective existence. Such a politics would be more attentive to the class divisions that structure categories of difference, understanding the profound differences in experience between, say, a well-off trans person in New York City versus an underclass one in Port-au-Prince. It would also provide a framework for understanding the large-scale issues of ecocide and inequality that are the most pressing global issues in the present.

A politics that is attentive to the material underpinnings of our lives would be organized around what Hannah Appel, Nikhil Anand, and Akhil Gupta describe as "the promise of infrastructure."[9] While they also attend to the failures, forms of violence, and inequalities that can and often do characterize capitalist and colonial versions of infrastructure, they articulate a political vision of the infrastructural that is organized around a politics of "aspiration, the prospective, and futurity."[10] The infrastructural can function to catalyze forms of collective utopian imaginings. Such large-scale visions can produce forms of political solidarity on the left, enabling us to successfully counter the already more unified and politically effective right. It produces a politics that is less oriented around interpersonal antagonisms and more toward collective political-economic, ecological, and social transformation and flourishing. In this way, such a politics of infrastructure would negate the forms of post-politics that become dominant when atomization rules the day.

The politics of infrastructure are about the need to produce a new, more materialist politics in the present. They might thus be considered a rejection of neoliberal postpolitics as it is described by Juan Meneses: "Through its grip on language, the postpolitical is a hegemonic mode that celebrates democracy, free speech, and multiculturalism and defends tolerance, mutual understanding, and collaboration. At the same time, however, it spuriously impedes the emergence of dissenting responses in the name of the very principles it extols by labelling them disruptions of the 'normal' functioning of politics."[11] Meneses's definition emphasizes the spurious production of managed consent and the way in which ostensibly progressive categories (such as multiculturalism) have come to function as part of the maintenance of neoliberal hegemony. I agree with his account of hegemonic and state-sanctioned forms of the post-political, but I find that postpolitics is not reducible to officially sanctioned discourses but rather can be defined by an excess of atomizing and purely representational political struggles and an attenuated engagement with material transformation. Even leftist movements like Occupy Wall Street, Black Lives Matter, and the Arab Spring fell short of producing the material transformations they were aiming for. Much of this had to do with the resistance they encountered, but, as Jodi Dean and others have noted, it also had to do with their refusal to articulate a singular radical vision.[12]

To produce a politics of infrastructure, we need a symbolic politics that can reorient political struggle toward the material and the infrastructural. It is also crucial that we do not negate political struggles that are about forms of symbolic hierarchy, exclusion, and violence. Racism, sexism, homophobia, and transphobia (not to mention social class, as distinct from economic class) all have crucial symbolic and representational dimensions to which we need to attend. Yet if we only conceptualize these struggles as representational, they are easily appropriated by the state and neoliberal rhetoric of "there is no alternative." Capitalism is quite comfortable appropriating identity rhetoric to advance its own ends. To take just one example, the corporate sponsorship of Pride marches happily affirms a contained and capitalized conception of queerness, one in which the economic inequalities that characterize queer communities remain unaddressed. Thus, my argument is not about muting representational struggles so much as articulating them in relationship to a form of collective politics that can move across symbolic formations to produce a sense of collective solidarity around material transformation. Such material transformations would also address the material dimensions of racism, sexism, homophobia, and transphobia—arguing, for example, for socialized medical rights for all, including the right to medically transition, the right to free and legal abortions, the right to childcare, and the right to live in spaces that are not ecologically contaminated or deadly. It would be about reckoning with the ways in which race, class, gender, and sexuality shape different material life chances and to actively intervene in the ways in which such unequal life chances are produced and routinized. Such a politics is not about jettisoning collective categories of race, gender, and sexuality for class; instead, it is about attending to the material basis and structuration of each category and demonstrating that they have a shared investment in material transformation.

Yamashita's Materialist Vision

To imagine a material politics more fully, I turn to one of the most ambitious and groundbreaking novels of the twenty-first century, Karen Yamashita's *I Hotel*.[13] The novel is remarkable for several reasons. The term novel does not do it justice. It is an experimental assemblage that recounts through various media a polyvocal history of the Asian American movement of the 1960s and 1970s as it intersects with other histories of leftist organizing in the United States and beyond. The centering of Asian American here may seem to affirm a kind of representational politics, but it is crucial to distinguish the collectivist and materialist vision of identity put forward in *I Hotel* from the individual articulations of identity under neoliberalism. As Don T. Nakanishi describes it, the movement was organized around "pan-Asian Pacific American unity and collective action, and the founding of a multitude of community-based organizations from Boston to Los Angeles."[14] In addition, as Lai Ying Yu, quoting Daryl J. Maeda, argues, "the Asian American movement was 'fundamentally committed to the ideologies of interracialism and internationalism' in its struggles."[15] Yu also notes the material struggles undertaken by the movement: "Activists in the Asian American movements were united by a radical democratic vision that promoted affordable housing, workers' rights, and community health resources." Moreover, "they founded a new generation of community-based organizations, formed a garment cooperative, organized labor unions, joined residents in anti-eviction protests in Japantown and Manilatown, and published community newspapers."[16] They also built alliances with African American, Latinx, working-class, and Indigenous political organizations and struggles. Their vision was as much Marxist and socialist as it was radical democratic. The book itself focuses primarily on the West Coast and transpacific manifestations of the movement and is centered around the struggle to save the novel's titular hotel, which served as a key locus of organizing and residence for movement participants in San Francisco's Chinatown and Manilatown. The hotel was destroyed by developers in 1977.

The book is thus centrally concerned with large-scale political struggle and organizing. It is also invested in large-scale material transformation, situating the Asian American movement in domestic struggles that are primarily about representation but linking it to larger anticolonial struggles that were central to this moment of global decolonization and, as Christopher Leigh Connery demonstrates, the global reach of different versions of international Marxism, including Maoism.[17] Thus, in opposition to national or pluralist conceptions of identity and difference, Yamashita suggests that a genuinely political solidarity can be produced; this solidarity is organized around defending and developing collective forms of infrastructure, represented most forcefully in the novel's detailing of the movement to save the International Hotel. This, then, is Yamashita's infrastructural aesthetic. It suggests that we need to privilege the infrastructural and the material in constructing a political way forward that can unify disparate experiences of identity and difference. Yet as a materialist novel, it also indicates how hard it is to produce such a unity, however strategic or provisional.

AN INFRASTRUCTURAL AESTHETIC

Yamashita's aesthetic, like her emphasis on infrastructure, is rigorously materialist. As Jennifer Glaser persuasively puts it, the novel is organized around a kind of "intermedial architecture."[18] *I Hotel* is made up of material fragments from the past, including a comic book, the written transcription of a jazz performance, a film script, an FBI briefing that mixes photos, film, and transcripts, the written form of a play, ekphrases of murals, poetry, drawings, fiction, nonfiction, various first- and third-person narratives, fragments of soul music lyrics, a compendium of different quotations from Lenin, Mao, Yoko Ono, Imelda Marcos, Confucius, and more. On the level of form, the materiality of the archive structures the novel. This emphasis on documentary fragments and materials suggests that the novel itself is organized around a kind of historiographic infrastructure, one that is organized around the neglected materials of the past and that refuses the amnesia of the dominant U.S. interpretations of the 1960s and 1970s, which leave little room for the history of the Asian American movement or third world Marxism.

Like any historical novel, *I Hotel* has a double focus.[19] It is not only an account of the recent past, but it also reflects the moment of its writing: it was published in 2010, after the economic crash of 2008 yet during the period when neoliberalism seemed nearly impossible to topple. Such a double focus is standard for historical novels. The explicit focus of the narrative is about producing a believable re-creation of the past; the ways this vision is shaped and constrained by the present's historiographic frame become its subtext. Yamashita reverses this framework. In emphasizing documentary and media materials and foregrounding the technical mediation of all events that the novel chronicles, it insists that there is a material history here, but one that we can access only through the epistemological frames and limitations of various media accessed in the present. The novel thus foregrounds the historiographic work of reconstructing the past. We do not have direct access to the events depicted in the narrative. Instead, like historians or novelists, we need to sift through these materials to begin to do the work of reconstructing the past and uncovering what it suggests for our present. Yet unlike a postmodern reflexive novel like John Fowles's *The French Lieutenant's Woman,* this is not mere subjective or narratological reflexivity. The reflexivity is on the side of the material and emphasizes the need for subjects (including historians or novelists) to recognize the affordances and distortions of the archive, to see the materiality of form that filters our access to the past. Unlike postmodern metafiction, which tends to reduce history and subjectivity to the fictional, Yamashita's novel suggests that we need to recognize the domains of history and historicism embedded in our fictions.

As this description already suggests, Yamashita's novel is not only historiographically reflexive but also rigorously materialist. It emphasizes the material fragments and documents that make up the primary material for producing narrative history. The material histories and practices of different populations are captured by the material textual fragments that make up the text itself, even as the text also stresses the need to move beyond the fragment and synthesize a collective history. In this sense, the novel echoes Rachel C. Lee's argument that the fragmentary and "unanchored quality to Asian America's constituent parts has been a *prima facie* tenet of the field" of Asian American studies. Rather than bemoaning this aspect of the field, Lee encourages us to "relish the fragment."[20] In a similar spirit, Yamashita's fragments become the record of a series of lived histories, countercultural practices, and common endeavors that are only part of the history of Asian America; yet they also imagine ways of partially unifying these fragments (without smoothing over their sharp edges) into a larger political, economic, and ecological whole.

While presenting a polyphony of different, often conflicting perspectives, *I Hotel* does not stay on the level of the fragmentary but imagines a form of collective transnational solidarity. Such a vision works to articulate these struggles together as part of and a positive form of large-scale collectivity—one that does not silence dissent and difference but transcends the level of the fragment. *I Hotel* does so by enacting the interrelationship between different forms and registers of the material to point toward an affirmative and revolutionary conception of solidarity (even as the text is about the eventual failure of this struggle). This solidarity incorporates different Asian American, Asian Pacific, and other political visions in order to imagine the possibility of constructing a just and sustainable, if also still conflictual, collectivity.

Spaces of Collectivity

The possibility of an alternative, collectivist historiography manifests, for Yamashita, in the narratives and practices that form around the site of the International Hotel on the border between San Francisco's Manilatown and Chinatown, which was a single-room-occupancy hotel that housed working and underclass Asian Americans, as well as a number of radicals, in the late 1960s and early 1970s. Its storefronts were also home to radical organizations, including the Asian Community Center, Asian Legal Services, Chinatown Cooperative, Chinatown–North Beach Youth

Council, Chinese Progressive Association, and Kearny Street Workshop (an arts organization that continues to this day). As Ana María Manzanas Calvo and Jesús Benito Sánchez argue in relationship to the hotel, "infected spaces of segregation become repossessed spaces of congregation and longing."[21] The hotel was a locus of struggle during this period, with tenants and activists fighting for a stay on the planned destruction of the hotel in the name of gentrification and the growth of the financial district. The text thus narrates the growth of finance capital that has been central to neoliberal hegemony of the last forty years and the way it has destroyed forms of collective and public culture and has worked instead to seal us into postpolitical identities and social visions. Community activists stayed the destruction of the hotel for nine years and fought against riot police and snipers before finally being evicted in 1977.

In Yamashita's novel, this central space opens outward to multiple narratives, indicating the ways in which the story of the I Hotel reaches beyond any singular narrative and beyond the space of the nation-state itself to indicate the multiple times and spaces that make up the collective vision the novel is working toward. Each section is named by a different year but also contains events from earlier years. Thus, we get multiple, temporally overlapping narratives creating a kaleidoscopic understanding of any given moment in time. Each section is also presented visually at the beginning as an unfolded origami version of a three-dimensional room that contains characters, locations (such as UCSF, Japantown, Tule Lake, Chinatown, China, and Vietnam), and different times, as well as the dominant style used in the section (such as narrative voice, cinema verité, myths and tales, history, and aphorism). What one gets is thus a multitemporal, multispatial, and multistylistic history of the same period told from different perspectives. This folded-out room (representing one of the rooms of the I Hotel—both the San Francisco institution and the book) can be imagined as something that can literally be cut out of the text and assembled, producing a material entity that moves beyond the two-dimensionality of text and becomes a three-dimensional material construction. The book itself is thus infrastructural. It not only calls attention to the importance of infrastructure but also literalizes infrastructure in its very writing. This is a central part of Yamashita's infrastructural aesthetic, one that works as a material site that unifies the different actors in the narrative.

Framing the Postpolitical

One version of the postpolitical in the present is the reduction of notions of difference and identity to an implicitly or explicitly national context. American exceptionalism is central to conservative and white supremacist understandings of the nation-state, but it is also present in less overt forms in much liberal and even leftist discourse in the United States. Central to much identarian discourse in the United States is a resolutely individualist framework that is organized around gaining rights and symbolic recognition from the nation-state itself and from the culture at large. Struggles for rights are crucial, and recognition is the first part of producing a more transformational politics (even as struggles for individual recognition intersect with the production of human capital under neoliberalism); Yamashita's narrative demonstrates what such notions exclude. If American exceptionalism emphasizes affirmative national distinctiveness and assimilation, then *I Hotel* underscores transnational tensions and solidarities as well as refusals and rejections of assimilationist narratives. In contrast to assimilationist narratives, Yamashita presents narratives of migration that refuse assimilationist norms:

> We have always arrived, they say, in waves, waves of yellow people splashed against the American shores. A very few of us can say we made the trip out of curiosity, but everyone else must probably admit we've been forced across the Pacific, caught in the shifting consequences of war. That war might be violently active or violently passive, hot or cold, political or economic, but nevertheless war. They've called us sojourners, immigrants, FOBs, refugees, exiles, even the brain drain, but we are all the ordinary and extraordinary veterans of cycle upon cycle of global conflict. (602)

Here, Yamashita counters the narratives of assimilation and voluntary immigration that are central to the liberal version of American exceptionalism with an account of the production of immigration out of material necessity. Such necessity is produced by various forms of violence, including political, economic, imperialist, military, and/or ideological (and often from a mix of all of them, as in the displacements produced by the Korean and Vietnam wars). Thus, in contrast to the exceptionalist rhetoric of the nation-state as democratic and inclusive, Yamashita presents a vision of the United States as an imperial power deeply embroiled in global conflict and violence. These acts of violence play a large part in producing the very immigrants whom it then restricts and treats as a cheap source of labor. Indeed, from this perspective, immigrants are less estranged from the material conditions that enable the existence of the United States than those whose racial and national privilege allows them to believe in exceptionalist America. They are the citizens of a different collectivity—one that is transnational, dynamic, conflictual, unstable, and yet crosshatched by solidarity, and one that emerges out of spaces of travel and affiliation throughout what Arif Dirlik and Rob Wilson call the Asia/Pacific.[22] To extend this notion, the immigrants are likened, in their collectivity, to the waves of the Pacific crashing against the American shore. Here the centrality of the nation-state is radically decentered in relationship to the ocean in which it is immersed. Immigration reveals itself to be part of a transnational infrastructure of economic, military, and geopolitical movement, violence, and possibility. In this oceanic metaphor, exceptionalism and nationalism associated with the United States are negated by revealing the larger continental and finally transpacific ecosystem in which it is embedded.

Yamashita not only negates the violent and ideological positivity of exceptionalism but also uses negation to figure the conflicts between different political, ethnic, and class affiliations, groups, and subjectivities. Indeed, the text often works through dialectical juxtaposition in which negation is coupled with the possibility of its partial or strategic overcoming. Take, for example, this passage describing a Marxist reading group in which Karl Kang, Ben San Pablo, and Olivia Wang participate:

> 9.4 Olivia said, *I see it like the scientific method, that you analyze empirical data and actual phenomena. It's a technique to observe the real world and real people.*
>
> 9.5 Ben asked, *If you follow that idea, then Marxist ideas would be like hypotheses.*

9.6 Karl Kang said, *Marx worked out a theory of history that should embody social experiments or, as you say, proposed hypotheses.*
9.7 Olivia said, *In other words, we should be able to create an experiment to test the theory with predictable results.*
9.8 Ben said, *I'm worried about the predictable part.*
9.9 Olivia gritted her teeth.
9.10 Karl said, *Marx said that men make their own history but not necessarily as they please. He predicted the inevitable failure of the capitalist mode of production, and you yourselves can see the contradictions that make continuous acquisition of the earth's resources and the exploitation of everyone to do so a finite proposition, but when it will fail and how, that's . . .*
9.11 Olivia inserted, *up to us.* (323–24)

Imitating the form of the *Analects of Confucius* as well as the aphoristic style of Mao's *Little Red Book,* the passage stages definitional debates about materialism—debates that shaped both the possibilities and the limits of Marxist struggle in the twentieth century. Thus, the passage metacritically reflects on *I Hotel*'s central preoccupation: materialism. It illustrates both the incompatibility and necessity of thinking different forms of materialism together. Olivia attempts to make Marx's historical materialism equivalent to scientific materialism, but Ben nicely complicates this by challenging the predictive dimensions of historical materialism. Karl, meanwhile, tries to reconcile this latter complication by providing Marx's definition of historical constraint and possibility in which material conditions mix with human actions. He also demonstrates that for the predictive dimensions of Marxism to have any force, they will have to be put into dialogue with ecological materialism. Olivia (while risking volunteerism) finally invokes the centrality of material action and commitment to any politics that hopes to produce change—the kind of change the book itself chronicles. Thus, while each of these materialisms exists in contradiction, on a theoretical level, they are all necessary to think together in their contradiction. A similar complex negativity frames the relationship between Ben and Olivia, the one a Filipino son of a *manong* and the other an ethnically Chinese daughter of a "high-ranking family" (296).

Their combustible relationship and marriage condense the ethnic, class, and gender antagonisms as well as unexpected alliances that characterize the rest of the book.

While the disagreements present in the passage point to the necessary work of theoretical debate and discussion for any leftist struggle (and it also suggests the dangers of too quickly smoothing out disagreements or structural differences), it also suggests, in a manner that resonates with our own moment, the ways in which intellectual and embodied differences can harden into antagonisms that close down rather than open up the possibility of solidarity and collective praxis. As Nathan Ragain persuasively demonstrates, the novel is fundamentally organized around the dialectic between the universal and the particular.[23] Both poles of the dialectic need to be emphasized in their contradiction. Yamashita demonstrates both the necessity of attending to the multiplicity of different embodied, economic, gendered, sexual, and social experiences and the need to find ways of linking these disparate histories, which share a common experience of exclusion around both class and race—specifically race as a modality in which class is lived, as Stuart Hall has famously put it.[24] Asian American labor was racialized, but this racializing was also a class formation, as Colleen Lye demonstrates.[25] Historically, Asian (American) laborers were not entitled to the same protections or recognitions attached to the white working class. Yamashita suggests both the historical limits of the period she represents and suggests the possibilities of what could have been in the 1960s and 1970s for Asian Americans, and others as well. She indicates why perhaps the more revolutionary and transformative possibilities were not realized. This understanding of the limits of 1960s and 1970s radicalism (even as the text rubs history against the grain to suggest what might have been) also points toward the atomization of the left in our political present.

In making this argument, I do not wish to minimize other axes of collective struggle, such as gender and sexuality. Rather, I am arguing that the left needs to find ways of coming together around specific sites of exploitation to form a collective politics that can produce a radically different infrastructural and material organization of life in the twenty-first century. Just because a struggle does not address all aspects of our subjectivity or experience does not mean that we should not join it. We should be struggling for others (including others from other oppressed or exploited populations) as well as ourselves. By definition, solidarity must transcend personal experience. Moreover, such struggles are not merely undertaken out of ethical commitment. Material transformations that benefit the most excluded or exploited benefit everyone except the elite. For example, a recognition of the ways in which both race and gender have historically been the sites of unpaid labor under capitalism would create a context in which both unpaid and paid labor are recognized and supported by an infrastructural commons as well as socialized state structures.

Elements of Infrastructure

The complex, overlapping, yet divergent media presented by the novel has an indexical function. The media point, in the dense counterpoint of their aesthetic juxtapositions, toward other forms of materiality that are central to the narrative. Take, for example, the following passage, focalized via a choreographer Sandy, which frames a dance she has authored: "But what is Asian American dance? Sandy wants to know. Does the body have a memory? What's the memory of the Asian-American body? She says she choreographs as if blind. Choreographs as if deaf. Choreographs in silence. Sandy says you got to feel the body's energy, Watch for texture and density and intensity. Fill the space like the pictographs splashed across rice paper. Now, listen to the bodies' movements" (279). This passage indexically points to the body's materiality, both in its energy and in its racialization and specificity in historical memory. This racialized body also invokes the cultural materialism associated with cultural studies figurations of race, except here, the materiality of the body is not merely a product of social construction and inscription (although its racialization is certainly that) but also an energetic and physical entity, one that can be framed in terms of physical disabilities. The disabilities, rather than constraining, become productive, allowing Sandy to conceptualize interrelations between the body's movement and the composition. The disabled body and the racialized body here are defined by positive possibilities rather than limitations. The very limiting conditions produced by racism and ableism enact specific energetic, mnemonic, and artistic practices that become part of an alternate materialist politics, which is grounded in the body but also reaches past it to larger material structures.

The body and its needs are central to Yamashita's radical infrastructural vision. Rather than grounding this infrastructure primarily in identities, it grounds it in the needs, affordances, labor, and desires of different bodies. As I have argued elsewhere, the materiality of the body needs to be theorized as central to any materialism worthy of the name.[26]

Central to the maintenance of the material body is of course nutritional sustenance, and another crucial aspect of materiality in Yamashita's novel is the bioinfrastructural production of food. The section entitled "1974: I-Migrant Hotel" provides a Marxist-inflected history of class formation and agricultural production; it has an ecological and materialist emphasis on the shared production and consumption of food. Food as a biological necessity and its organization via agriculture are ground zero for imagining a collective, socialist vision of infrastructure. Bodies and subjectivities cannot thrive without material sustenance. The chapter focuses on the largely forgotten history of Filipino and Filipino American farm workers in California who were some of the founding members of the United Farm Workers. Central to the narrative is not only the struggle for better (i.e., less immediately deadly) working conditions but also the consciousness and practice of the production of food provided by a lifetime of both working in agriculture and preparing food for workers.

Manong (and it is important to note Yamashita's emphasis, in this naming, on the absence of a fetishized individual identity but rather one produced through labor), one of our narrators for this section, describes it this way:

> You think about it. Food is the basis for everything. Without food, it's all over. Kaput. They don't lie when they say you are what you eat. If you can't get nothing to eat, you are nothing. Nothing. They also don't lie when they say that you eat to live. And you live to eat. What's someone's culture but the way he eats? Everybody living from meal to meal, even if it takes somebody three days to get to the next one. Call that the culture of poverty. . . . Who grows it? Cultivates it? Sells it? Cooks it? Who gets fed and does not

> get fed? Who throws it away? Who eats the leftovers? . . . Once you know this principle of the world, then everything becomes clear. You take Marx. You take Freud. You take Einstein. You take Suzuki. The politics of food. The ex of food. The relativity of food. The Zen of food.
>
> I tell these radical kids, eventually all the answers can be found in food. Are they listening? Follow the food, I say. You born in the city. You forgot your connection to the earth. And I don't just mean Watsonville or Delano. That's what guys like me have, the knowledge. (441)

This long passage captures the richness and complexity of the novel's materialist invocations of both food and labor. Manong's meditations on food are also meditations on sustenance, infrastructure, economics, and survival. The passage stages the production of food in fundamentally Marxist terms: humans producing sustenance and social relations by transforming the earth through labor. This is Marxist materialism at its most basic and straightforward. This basic quality becomes part of the passage's vision of a collectivist infrastructure. Under everything else is food. Before everything else is food. It is what sustains cities, intellectual abstraction, and structures of wealth and poverty alike. It is also a question of labor. Manong asks foundational Marxist questions: "Who grows it? Cultivates it? Cooks it? Who gets fed and does not get fed? Who throws it away? Who eats the leftovers?" These are questions not only of production but of circulation, consumption, and access. They are thus also fundamentally infrastructural questions. How does a population sustain itself? How does the labor of one racialized population sustain the consumption and pleasure of another? How do those that do this work of sustenance build a politics and a way of life that allow them to survive and challenge the unequal conditions of production? Thus, the passage alludes to the necropolitical conditions of agricultural production in the midcentury United States for a racialized labor force (conditions that persist into the twenty-first century), in which workers may go three days before their next meal and were routinely exposed to carcinogenic pesticides.[27] These are the conditions against which the labor organizing detailed by this part of *I Hotel* is directed.

Infrastructural Possibility

In all these contexts, but underscored most thoroughly by the passage on food, the book's emphasis is not just on struggles for recognition and collective challenges to oppression and exploitation, but also on the production of a positive conception of infrastructure and the political possibilities it enables. Organizing the food workers echoes other scenes of labor and political organizing throughout the text: organizing an all-female textile workers' cooperative, students' taking over San Francisco State, and the organizing of various leftist groups. All these are detailed by the novel and are often headquartered in the novel's titular structure. This affirmative conception of infrastructure is echoed throughout Yamashita's narrative. Indeed, it runs as a dialectical counterpoint to the moments of negative dissolution, failure, and dissention that also punctuate the text. However, while detailing the sometimes productive but often self-destructive factionalism that plagued social movements of the 1960s and 1970s (and pointing toward the unproductive factionalism of the present of the book's writing and publication), it also interweaves an ode to the historical moment's possibility. The titular International Hotel is the novel's key material site, the dwelling where all these diverse groups and struggles meet. The text chronicles the battle to preserve the International Hotel as a countercultural and oppositional space in the face of the city of San Francisco's attempts to demolish it. The longevity of the hotel even after being slated for destruction and the ways in which it housed so many different leftist organizations and residents of different nationalities and backgrounds enable it to become the novel's most capacious symbol of a sustaining infrastructure, one centered on an affirmative valuation of materiality in its different registers. The hotel and its defenders become the locus of the lyrical "we" that emerges in the novel's last section, "1977: I-Hotel." The section chronicles the struggle to halt the demolition of the hotel and the eviction of its residents. The failed struggle to save the hotel works as the text's capstone (to use an architectural metaphor) to all the activism, organizing, and struggle that have been chronicled by the rest of the novel. It becomes both epitaph and redemptive account of future possibility for the forms of collective organizing narrated by the novel.

The collective voice that emerges in this section is produced in relationship to the material space of the I Hotel itself and through the activity of becoming "radical-activist revolutionaries" (599). Yamashita emphasizes the material connections between infrastructure and action. The "we" emerges as a historical possibility conjured in part by the physical dwelling that is the hotel itself. This collectivity is both present and unstable, one that can disintegrate back into the individualities out of which it is constructed: "Our transformation from individuals into collectivities was precisely the thing that gave us power, but power has many sides to it, especially the power of a group. Perhaps it could be said that four mighty fists emerged from the four doors to confront a common enemy, to fight in concert the foes of the I-Hotel, but we admit that very often the left fists did not follow the right fists . . . we could not agree on our tactics and strategies" (599). Here the physical space of the hotel becomes the locus in which the power of the people becomes manifest. In her anthropomorphic yet thoroughly materialist metaphor, the people become the fists of the hotel; their collective power is realized at this site. This struggle manifests on the level of the body: "In the final hours we join this great gathering of human bodies, our bulwark of flesh surrounding an old brick hotel" (605). Here flesh and brick merge and become a single material barrier. Yet this collective power is also never fully realized precisely because of the way the "we" never fully coheres—if only for the moment of confrontation—into a singular entity.

As she puts it in the novel's last paragraph, "And in time we may remember, collecting every little memory, all the bits and pieces into a larger memory, rebuilding a great layered and labyrinthine, now imagined international hotel of many rooms" (605). Here memory itself becomes material, the little pieces and fragments of the past echoing the fragments of the ruined hotel.[28] Through the novel's double temporality, memory finally points to future possibility, represented by the building of a new, if still imaginary, hotel.

Building the I Hotel of the Future

This vision of present and future political possibilities is central to Yamashita's infrastructural aesthetic. Her novel, via its redemptive and materialist historicism, points toward the possibility of moving past the postpolitics of the present. Central to her vision of a renewed collectivist politics is the primacy of infrastructural and material transformation. If politics remains entirely on the level of identity formations, it cannot help but ignore the material and produce a politics that is all about symbolic antagonisms and material stasis. Representation matters, but it is not sufficient to produce genuine material change. Instead, we need to look to building a new (national and transnational) infrastructure, one organized around equality, justice, and long-term ecological sustainability and flourishing.

Turning to infrastructure grounds and structures politics. It opens the possibility for alliances that may be lost when we remain on the level of representation and increasingly micrological and agonistic conceptions of identity. Think, to take just one example, of what a genuinely just and socialized health care system would represent not only for working and underclass subjects, but also for women, trans subjects, and intersex subjects who desire medical intervention and support, whether it be access to reproductive services (including free and legal abortion), technologies of transitioning, or the insistence that medical intervention only takes place with the consent of the subject (even as we may need to change ages of consent in the cases of intersex and trans kids). Think of similar transformations around access to free and clean water, good housing, valuation of all labor whether paid or unpaid, and a socialized economy that makes human, ecological flourishing central. Such an economy can be organized around need and flourishing rather than around the whims of the market and the need for exponential growth at all costs that characterize global capitalism. In the face of the neoliberal claim that there is no alternative, what Mark Fisher aptly describes as the ideology of capitalist realism, Yamashita's vision can finally be described as imagining an infrastructural commons.[29] In opposition to Hardt and Negri's conception, which is organized primarily around and catalyzed by what they term "immaterial production," Yamashita structures her commons around a collectively produced infrastructure and the just and sustainable distribution of material goods and access.[30] It would work, in the formulation of Christian P. Haines and Peter Hitchcock, to "deprivatize social relations and material resources."[31] Such a commons would undo class inequalities as well as the forms of appropriation and exclusion that shape race, gender, and sex. It is to such a collectivist vision that Yamashita's redemptive vision of a future hotel is dedicated. It is toward such a vision that we must work to produce a politics worthy of the name.

NOTES

1. Japhy Wilson and Erik Swyngedouw, "Seeds of Dystopia: Post-politics and the Return of the Political," in *The Post-political and Its Discontents: Spaces of Depoliticization, Specters of Radical Politics,* ed. Japhy Wilson and Erik Swyngedouw (Edinburgh: Edinburgh University Press, 2014), 1.

2. Fredric Jameson, *The Seeds of Time* (New York: Columbia University Press, 1994), 76.

3. Mark Fisher, *Capitalist Realism: Is There No Alternative?* (Winchester, Eng.: Zero/Collective Ink, 2009), 4.

4. Eleanor Courtemanche, "The Peculiar Success of Cultural Studies 2.0," *Arcade: The Humanities in the World* (blog), Stanford University, September 19, 2016, shc.stanford.edu/arcade/interventions/peculiar-success-cultural-studies-20.

5. For Bourdieu's definition of cultural capital, see Pierre Bourdieu, *Distinction: A Social Critique of the Judgment of Taste,* trans. Richard Nice (Cambridge, Mass.: Harvard University Press, 1984), 12.

6. Jason W. Moore, *Capitalism in the Web of Life: Ecology and the Accumulation of Capital* (London: Verso, 2015), 179.

7. Christopher Breu, "The Humanities as Contradiction: Against the New Enclosures," *Humanities* 7, no. 3 (2018): 1–16.

8. For an excellent account of the field, see Hannah Appel, Nikhil Anand, and Akhil Gupta, "Introduction: Temporality, Politics, and the Promise of Infrastructure," in *The Promise of Infrastructure,* ed. Nikhil Anand, Akhil Gupta, and Hannah Appel (Durham, N.C.: Duke University Press, 2018), 3–38.

9. Appel, Anand, and Gupta, 7.

10. Appel, Anand, and Gupta, 7.

11. Juan Meneses, *Resisting Dialogue: Modern Fiction and the Future of Dissent* (Minneapolis: University of Minnesota Press, 2019), xiii.

12. Jodi Dean, *Crowds and Party* (London: Verso, 2016), 1–29.

13. Karen Tei Yamashita, *I Hotel: A Novel* (Minneapolis: Coffee House, 2010).

14. Don T. Nakanishi, "Preface: Moving the Historical Movement Forward," in *Asian Americans: The Movement and the Moment,* ed. Steve Louie and Glenn Omatsu (Los Angeles: UCLA Asian American Studies Center Press, 2014), viii.

15. Lai Ying Yu, "'Capturing the Spirit': Teaching Karen Tei Yamashita's *I Hotel,*" *Asian American Literature: Discourses and Pedagogies* 1 (2014): 69–70.

16. Yu, "Capturing the Spirit," 70. On the alliance between the American Indian Movement (AIM) and the Asian American Movement in relationship to the

occupation of Alcatraz (something depicted by Yamashita's novel), see Catherine Fung, "'This Isn't Your Battle or Your Land': The Native American Occupation of Alcatraz in the Asian-American Political Imagination," *College Literature* 41, no. 1 (2014): 152–73.

17. Christopher Leigh Connery, "The World Sixties," in *The Worlding Project,* ed. Christopher Leigh Connery and Rob Wilson (Berkeley: North Atlantic, 2007), 77–108.

18. Jennifer Glaser, "Comics, Race, and the Political Project of Intermediality in Karen Tei Yamashita's *I Hotel,*" in *Comic Studies Here and Now,* ed. Frederick Luis Aldama (New York: Palgrave, 2018), 72.

19. On the idea of the double focus of the historical novel, see György Lukács, *The Historical Novel,* trans. Hannah and Stanley Mitchell (Boston: Beacon, 1962), 19–88.

20. Rachel C. Lee, *The Exquisite Corpse of Asian America: Biopolitics, Biosociality, and Posthuman Ecologies* (New York: NYU Press, 2014), 8.

21. Ana María Manzanas Calvo and Jesús Benito Sánchez, *The City in American Literature and Culture* (Cambridge: Cambridge University Press, 2021), 93.

22. Arif Dirlik and Rob Wilson, *Asia/Pacific as a Space of Cultural Production* (Durham, N.C.: Duke University Press, 1995).

23. Nathan Ragain, "A Revolutionary Romance: Particularity and Universality in Karen Tei Yamashita's *I Hotel,*" *MELUS* 38, no. 1 (2013): 137–54.

24. Stuart Hall, "Race, Articulation, and Societies Structured in Dominance," in *Selected Writings on Race and Difference,* ed. Ruth Wilson Gilmore, Paul Gilroy, and Bill Schwarz (Durham, N.C.: Duke University Press, 2021), 239.

25. Colleen Lye, *America's Asia: Racial Form and American Literature, 1893–1945* (Princeton, N.J.: Princeton University Press, 2005).

26. Christopher Breu, *Insistence of the Material: Literature in the Age of Biopolitics* (Minneapolis: University of Minnesota Press, 2014), 7–10.

27. On necropolitics, see Achille Mbembe, *Necropolitics* (Durham, N.C.: Duke University Press, 2019): 66–93.

28. For an evocative reading of this passage in relationship to memory and political possibility, see A. Robert Lee, "House of Memory: Imagining Karen Tei Yamashita's *I Hotel,*" in *Karen Tei Yamashita: Fictions of Magic and Memory,* ed. A. Robert Lee (Hawai'i: University of Hawai'i Press, 2018), 143–54.

29. Fisher, *Capitalist Realism.*

30. Michael Hardt and Antonio Negri, *Commonwealth* (Cambridge, Mass.: Harvard University Press, 2009), 132.

31. Christian P. Haines and Peter Hitchcock, "No Place for the Common," introduction to special section, "Is There a Place for the Commons?," ed. Christian Haines and Peter Hitchcock, *Minnesota Review* 23 (2019): 55.

CHAPTER 2

Irrational Exuberance

The Politics of Start-up Futurism

SHERRYL VINT

My interest in this topic begins with Jed Rothstein's documentary *WeWork, or The Making and Breaking of a $47 Billion Unicorn.*[1] Two things fascinated me about this story of the rapid rise and spectacular crash of the WeWork start-up. First were the repeated testimonials by former employees and members about their investment in the rhetoric offered by founder Adam Neumann: he positioned WeWork as a utopian project of reinventing how people live and work—a project "to elevate the world's consciousness," as per the slogan coined by Neumann's wife, Rebekah. Second was the insistence that WeWork was a technology company: what it offered was a new way of leasing office space, but the claim was that it would create a collaborative community, not just permit pooling of resources. This conflation of financial success with political revolution and social betterment is key to why WeWork wanted to be seen as a technology company: its corporate ethos—and funding model—imitated the Web 2.0 start-up culture of Silicon Valley, a blend of countercultural ambiance with massive valuation.

Silicon Valley is emblematized by the word "disrupt," which perfectly captures the ironies between its surface image and its structural effects. While the image claims to disrupt moribund industries and outdated methods to create a utopian future, the reality—especially in social media companies reliant on advertising algorithms that promote extreme content—has been to disrupt stable employment in many industries (from journalism to taxicabs) and liberal democratic norms.[2] Silicon Valley is also known for its interest in science fiction (sf), evident in the reasons billionaires Elon Musk and Jeff Bezos articulate for being interested in funding private space travel,[3] in the name Palantir had chosen for Peter Thiel's surveillance company, and in the entwined history of sf readers and computer geeks, especially during the 1990s dot-com era. The sf genre is demarcated in part by its relationship to narratives of futurity, and the genre is often considered part of the tradition of utopian writing. My interest in WeWork's fantasy of world transformation is linked to my commitment to the project of utopian thinking as a site of political engagement. Specifically, I seek to map the triangulation among Silicon Valley's patina of countercultural and sf futurism, the reality of Silicon Valley's material effects on economics and politics in the era of platform capitalism, and the restructuring of public discourse about governmentality, collectivity, and wealth that has unfolded since the end of the Cold War.

Through the influence of Silicon Valley on the economy overall, a certain kind of science-fictional thinking I call start-up futurism has become endemic, embraced even by those who have never read a word of sf. It conflates the future of capitalism with the future of the human species, drawing on utopian and speculative aesthetics but orienting them toward the end of accumulating wealth. Start-up futurism exemplifies the context that many have described as postpolitical, and I argue that is crucial to disentangle its feigned utopianism from its embrace of neoliberalism to resist its allure, thereby to create counterimaginaries that enable different futures.

THE POSTPOLITICAL AS ECONOMIC FORMATION

Before continuing with my analysis of Silicon Valley, it is necessary to outline what I mean by the postpolitical. Central to my way of thinking about politics is the widespread influence of Francis Fukuyama's "end of history" thesis, which mistakenly took the collapse of the Soviet Union for a global consensus that liberal democracy was universally accepted and would continue uninterrupted into a triumphant future. The conflation of capitalism with democracy was a central strategy of U.S. Cold War politics, given the need to demonstrate that capitalism was a system of universal social betterment, as the United States repeatedly claimed. This resulted in a brief period during which the country redistributed wealth to a greater degree than before or since.[4] Yet as the past forty years have shown, not only does capitalism not need democracy, but its neoliberal, market fundamentalist version views democracy, particularly governance related to redistributive tax policies or industry regulation, as antagonistic. As Quinn Slobodian outlines in his indispensable intellectual history of this ideology, neoliberalism is reliant on a specific form of governmentality: preventing democratic preferences from interfering with the freedom the market needs to embody its fabled efficiency. The neoliberal political project thus built institutions and policies to "encase" financial institutions to protect them from the democratic choice.[5]

The current hegemony of neoliberalism, in which market freedoms are mistaken for democratic ones, and in which deliberative debate about the purposes and ends of governance are replaced by managerial approaches to continue capitalist business as usual, is defined as postpolitics by Japhy Wilson and Erik Swyngedouw. They draw a distinction between the "political" as a space of contestation and "politics," which they define as "technocratic mechanisms and consensual procedures that operate within an unquestioned framework of representative democracy, free market economics, and cosmopolitan liberalism."[6] The Silicon Valley fantasy of positively transforming the world through lucrative disruption exemplifies how our political imagination has become truncated such that we cannot imagine outside of this framework. Mark Fisher describes this as "capitalist realism," which he defines as "the widespread sense that not only is capitalism the only viable political and economic system, but also that it is now impossible even to *imagine* a coherent alternative to it."[7] My interest in the WeWork start-up, and similar tales of "unicorn" valuations, emerges from how a faux countercultural imaginary has been cultivated within Silicon Valley, particularly as it contrasts with the structural reality of these industries' market and social effects.[8] What does it say about the social imaginary today that our ability to imagine a better world is frequently channeled through this Silicon Valley filter?[9]

The story of Silicon Valley is in many ways the story of the rise of neoliberal ideology to preeminence, a shift that is related to this specific location in two ways: first is Silicon Valley's origins in public monies spent on defense projects that were soon transmuted into private wealth, a story that runs in parallel with shifts in the structure of U.S. capitalism from the late 1970s to the present; the second is the specific ethos that has attached to the public image of Silicon Valley, associated with vaguely left-wing, countercultural ideals despite its economic foundation in capitalist business as usual. The start-up futurist effect I seek to diagnose here is made possible by the ongoing public belief in a narrative of Silicon Valley as progressive, even revolutionary. Most central to this myth is the strongly held belief that it is a meritocratic culture, despite overwhelming evidence that success depends on having the right connections, which often are available only to those who share identity characteristics with the already successful (masculinity and whiteness).[10] Ultimately, the idealization of individual achievement, particularly an Ayn Rand–influenced libertarian celebration of rational self-interest as the central moral principle, dominates Silicon Valley. Rand's thought was influenced by the Austrian (later Chicago) school economic theorists organized around the Mont Pelerin Society, who promoted neoliberal economic policies and overtly sought to shape public opinion to promote a culture that preferred individualism over collectivism.[11]

Start-up futurism embodies the irony of Silicon Valley's political influence: while its discourse remains wedded to liberal notions of democratic inclusion and collective betterment, its funding structure fuels the worst excesses of market volatility in ways that contribute to the redistribution of wealth upward.[12] Yet start-up futurism simultaneously promotes a narrative of utopianism, drawing on a repertoire of sf icons that diverts attention away from the harm created while reinforcing a capitalist realism sensibility. Evgeny Morozov describes this as "technological solutionism"—that is, "recasting all complex social situations either as neatly defined problems with definite, computable solutions or as transparent and self-evident processes that can be easily optimized—if only the right algorithms are in place."[13] He points out the limitations of solutionism, which "presumes rather than investigates"[14] problems and reduces the complexity of the world to the simplicity of its framings. This is how Silicon Valley culture contributes to the postpolitical understood as both the reduction of all political alternatives to the fine-tuning of capitalism and as a truncation of our imaginary such that more radical transformations of the social order become impossible to conceive.

As Morozov points out, the identification of anything that fails to align with neoliberal efficiency and accumulation as a "problem" is a central method by which solutionism stymies the possibility of real politics: "a deeper investigation into the very nature of these 'problems' would reveal that the inefficiency, ambiguity, and opacity—whether in politics or everyday life—that the newly empowered geeks and solutionists are rallying against are not in any sense problematic. Quite the opposite: these vices are often virtues in disguise."[15] Here I work through the implications of this tension between the solutionism and libertarianism that drives contra its continued presence as a site of affective, utopian investment shaping dreams of a better future. Its countercultural patina has always papered over an investment in wealth accumulation, and I consider how the changes it ushered in via sf rhetoric ironically pushed the overall economy toward financialization and neoliberal militancy—the most central dystopia forces of our era.

Irrational Futures: The Dot-Com Boom and Economies of Belief

Alan Greenspan in 1996 gave a speech, "The Challenge of Central Banking in a Democratic Society," delivered at the height of the dot-com boom when it seemed that the new knowledge economy might be the answer to slowing economic growth. Greenspan used the phrase as he attempted to distinguish between real promise and market hype that may have "unduly escalated asset values."[16] The larger thrust of his comments was to praise what we might call the "properly escalated" value generated by what was dubbed the New Economy, made possible by the computer industry. This New Economy emerged at a time when shifts in U.S. political power associated with Ronald Reagan brought neoliberal economic doctrines into the mainstream, but these shifts persisted because neoliberalism was equally embraced by Bill Clinton as he reoriented the Democratic Party. The New Economy was central to the postpolitics of capitalist realism: the tacit agreement that the needs of the market necessarily structured any policy debates. Elsewhere, Greenspan—who, not incidentally, was part of Ayn Rand's intellectual circle at an earlier point in his life[17]—contended that the economic gain from innovation is "not just a cyclical phenomenon or a statistical aberration, but reflects, at least in part, a more deep-seated, still developing, shift in our economic landscape."[18] We must take note especially of the title of Greenspan's speech, which stresses the tension between the needs of the neoliberal economy and those of democracy. His project was to find ways to secure financial stability should market exuberance prove irrational.[19]

Economist Robert Shiller later used the term to analyze market irrationality through a framework closer to what I seek to unpack here: the feedback loop between narrative hype and investor frenzy, wherein news of a high price further pushes it up to irrational levels.[20] Shiller's focus was stories circulated to rationalize such massive valuations. Irrational exuberance was a feature of the stock market during the dot-com bubble, but during the 2010s era of unicorn valuation, irrationality became core to the start-up business model itself. The immense success of a few Web 2.0 initial public offerings (IPOs)—that is, the price at which stock sells when first available on public markets—drew more venture capitalists (and their money) to Silicon Valley, hoping to fund the next big thing. In this context, the *story* became the central product, and this too had reverberating effects: the more a few unicorns succeeded, the more the story of the lucrative future via disruption compelled belief, and the more money flowed into Silicon Valley. This story has recently faltered with revelations of some stunning failures attributed to the malfeasance of their founders—not only Neumann's WeWork but also Theranos, the biotech health company founded by Elizabeth Holmes. My point, however, is that Neumann and Holmes operated from the same playbook that grounds the entire industry, not some fraudulent version of it.[21] This playbook—permeated by the image of Silicon Valley as an sf-infused site of progressive futurism, funded by a venture capital structure in which *the story is the product*—is the politics of start-up futurism, one that enriches the investor class by siphoning away both money and utopian energies into a fantasy that disavows the material results of this structure.

The term unicorn was coined by Aileen Lee in 2013 to describe companies with valuations over $1 billion.[22] The desire to find and profit from these fabled investments shifted the flow of investment capital sharply toward Silicon Valley, not only inflating its valuations but also blocking this capital from being invested elsewhere, particularly in the kinds of corporations romanticized about in discourse regarding how tax breaks for the rich will create opportunities and jobs for all.[23] Kim Phillips-Fein, writing in May 2022, notes: "Today, there are more than 1,000 such 'unicorns' around the world, compared to fewer than 200 in 2016. Venture capital equaled 11 percent of all nonresidential fixed investment in 2021, significantly more than the 7 percent it equaled in 2000, the height of the dot-com frenzy, let alone the average of under 2 percent per year between 1980 and 2007."[24] The consequences of this economic shift toward financialized investment are not solely down to Silicon Valley. Yet Silicon Valley, with its extremely low ratio of employees to market valuation compared with other industries, plays an oversize role in the rise of financialization. Ken-Hou Lin and Megan Tobias Neely contend that financialization is *the* engine of growing inequality today, and moreover that "the expanding profits and ballooning compensation in finance are not driven by this sector's contributions to the economy, but by the concentration of market power, the entanglement of finance into politics, and the private intermediation of public policies."[25]

While the name "unicorn" might have made sense in 2013, its contagious narrative shifted start-up culture such that the goal of any company was valuation—a goal more important than, say, making a product or providing a service. The distortions of the unicorn narrative are related to the dominance of shareholder value in corporate culture today, an ideology that shifted management priorities during the 1980s such that the main purpose was understood to be generating revenue for shareholders.[26] With unicorn start-up culture came another shift. The priority was to increase users, fueling absurd levels of growth without profitability, aimed at monopolization of an industry. The more V.C. capital a firm attracts, the longer it operates in start-up mode, meaning any economic payoff for most employees is deferred until the IPO—and the possibility of never securing adequate compensation should the IPO fail. A start-up mode that relies on private investment instead of trading on the open market also allows companies to avoid making disclosures about their profitability and the like required of publicly traded entities. Start-up culture operates via the logic of financialization, not manufacture. Through the 2010s this model enabled a groundless ethos in which many companies operated at a loss yet had high valuations, with their domination of user numbers promising future profitability through monopoly status or being bought out by a giant competitor to protect its existing monopoly. Neumann perhaps embodied this charlatan capacity better than his competitors, but he was hardly alone in focusing on valuation above all else.[27]

Today's unicorns are different from the dot-com start-ups largely because they delay their IPOs for a much longer period, relying on private funding for as much as a decade. There are multiple factors that explain the growth in unicorns, including low interest rates that make more traditional investments less profitable than in prior decades and the 2008 crash, which prompted investors to pull out of real estate and look for other opportunities.[28] The economic impacts of financialization, and the increased polarization that it causes, are both important to the entanglement of politics, economics, and Silicon Valley fantasies in reshaping the U.S. political landscape. I want to focus on the tension between the story Silicon Valley tells about its impact on the world and the structural reality of its political effects. Such companies insist that they are not just making money but also making the world a better place; indeed, this ideology is integral to the valuation process—investments of both venture capital and utopian desire. On the financial side, the desire to believe that this story could possibly be true frequently eclipses the knowledge that most start-ups fail. The desire to believe in this story, propagated through self-congratulatory narratives of individualist success via carefully curated public personas, works to shift the entire political spectrum toward the libertarian values Silicon Valley champions.[29] On the affective/utopian side, this rightward shift toward individual achievement truncates the possibilities for a collectivist politics while offering winners in this all-or-nothing struggle a consoling fantasy that their success proves their worthiness. Taken together, these financial and affective investments stymie our capacity for structural understandings that could ground a collectivist politics.

Start-up Politics, Neoliberal Futures

The start-up futurist narrative is based on more than risky bets driven by a fear of missing out on the next Google or Apple. In fact, it restructures public discourse about the relationship among industry, government, and the good future. Our desire to believe in Silicon Valley utopianism prevents us from recognizing the degree to which it participates in the upward redistribution of wealth, a problem that emerged alongside the enthusiasm for the New Economy. In July 1997's *Wired* magazine, at the time *the* venue for the dot-com era, published its Long Boom issue, proudly announcing on the cover, "We're facing 25 years of prosperity, freedom, and a better environment for the whole world"—based, of course, on the New Economy. Inside, Peter Schwartz and Peter Leyden argue that advances in I.T.—and those soon to come in biotech and nanotech—would enable environment-saving technologies such as alternative energy, while networking would create new forms of economic activity and a new "ethos of openness" that would transform social life. Most amusing in retrospect is their confident claim, "We are riding the early waves of a 25-year run of a greatly expanding economy that will do much to solve seemingly intractable problems like poverty and to ease tensions throughout the world. And we'll do it without blowing the lid off the environment."[30]

Certainly online culture has proven to fuel new modes of economic life, what Nick Srnicek names "platform capitalism." As he points out, while platforms present themselves as "empty spaces" in which already existing market forces simply reside, they "in fact embody a politics" that "shapes the appearance of a market."[31] Social media companies' need for network effects (by which the value of the service increases the more a single platform can enclose the entire market) leads toward monopolization, and the oligarchical tendencies of monopolies are a major driver of inequality, as Lin and Neely have shown.[32] Schwartz and Leyden were correct that they were on the cusp of a massive shift, but entirely wrong about its direction. The turn toward neoliberalism in U.S. culture, with its tax breaks for the rich and emphasis on deregulation to reduce governance to the protection of property, is deeply linked to the rise of Silicon Valley, and especially its narrative of countercultural progressivism. The manifest falseness of New Economy promises seems to have had little effect on the persistence of the dreams they articulate. Not only have we not lived through twenty-five years of prosperity since 1997, but the dot-com bubble collapsed only a few years after the article appeared. To return to the case of WeWork, testimonials of former employees and members in Rothstein's documentary repeatedly link their desire to change the world for the better with their hope to become rich in the process. How and why did we reach a point where utopian desire has become so entangled with capitalism that the fantasy of changing the world cannot be imagined outside of technological solutionism and capitalist accumulation? Silicon Valley wants to change the world, but without changing its political economy—a truism that names its most sinister postpolitical effect. Adrian Daub captures this best with his witty remark, "There is a tendency in Silicon Valley to want to be revolutionary without, you know, revolutionizing anything."[33]

Fred Turner's *From Counterculture to Cyberculture* documents how Silicon Valley mobilizes the language of 1960s counterculture without promoting its politics. He shows how Stewart Brand and his work to promote the *Whole Earth Catalog* as a business was crucial in transforming the image of I.T. culture from its post–World War II associations with big business and the military-industrial complex to the consumerist ethos of freedom and choice associated with Apple. The role of sf in promoting this shift is captured by Ridley Scott's massively influential advertisement for the first Macintosh, which famously concludes by announcing that Apple will be the reason that the year 1984 will not be like George Orwell's eponymous dystopia. Turner points out that Brand was associated predominantly with a homesteader group of countercultural "back to the land" practitioners, who are distinct from their activist peers. Both shared a desire to reject the workplace values of their parents' generation, but these New Communalists, as Turner dubs them, did not aim at the radical transformation of society. Rather, they "turned away from political action and toward technology and the transformation of consciousness as the primary sources of social change."[34] The *Whole Earth Catalog* included articles about futurism, new forms of consciousness, and alternative community, but it was mainly a business that marketed products to people who were establishing communes. The emphasis on community was also central to the new style research culture taking root in Silicon Valley in spaces such as Xerox Park and in informal gatherings such as the Homebrew Computer Club, which began to develop a language for talking about their improvised tech via "an ethos of information sharing, of peer-to-peer collaboration, and of information technology as something around which to build a community."[35] Readers of the catalog formed community through exchange of magazines and letters—activities similar to earlier practices of sf fandom, which created a sense of a shared identity and a shared social project rooted in inhabiting the same speculative spaces of narrative.

Yet much like the counterculture was discourse rather than praxis in this milieu, so too was the idea of a community, which emerged deeply tinged with consumerism and profit, paving the way for the Web 2.0 social media platforms that have turned community into a revenue-generating project. The New Economy marked a moment when entrepreneurial networks became generalized as a new approach to the social overall. Government attempts to regulate were cast as blockages against the utopian future these technologies would produce, if only they could be left to grow as their founders deemed fit. This translation of community into a revenue stream intensified the effects of translating publicly funded research into private capital, a process Margaret O'Mara details in *The Code*.[36] Even as they relied on the government-funded internet precursor Arpanet, the culture of individualism disavowed the collective material support that enabled entrepreneurial I.T. pursuits. In this ethos, a distinctly Californian version of the counterculture transmuted distrust of government embedded in the civil rights and antiwar movements into the belief that "perhaps business was the more natural, spontaneous form of human self-organization, and was actually less prone to abuse and tyranny than government."[37] Turner contends that Brand's product-shaped version of distributed community was crucial to online spaces becoming referred to as virtual communities, a term coined by Howard Rheingold in 1987.[38] The idea of online communities enabled a corporation to "convince its customers that they were engaging in social rather than economic activity,"[39] or at least to blur any distinctions between the two, thereby transmuting community into brand allegiance.

By the time people begin to talk about the New Economy in the 1990s, the rhetoric of utopianism had become entirely fused with the technology itself. Although they used terms taken from the discourse of their countercultural peers, Silicon Valley was never antistate, just antitaxation, and their distrust of government was the neoliberal desire to protect market forces from democratic oversight, not anything remotely countercultural. Yet the myth of Silicon Valley as progressive lived on, and this despite the fact that their probusiness version of social change was enabled by active lobbying against regulation of the industry, in favor of tax breaks for capital gains, and suppression of unionized labor as a political force. Elements of the Silicon Valley counterculture mixed seamlessly with older businesses such as H.P. and, more important, with their V.C. funders, the established banks and families in control of generational wealth. The New Economy continued to enrich those privileged by the old. A chief architect of this new order was Newt Gingrich, who, during his term as House speaker pioneered the performative and polemical style of governance now all too familiar on Fox news. This substitution of style for content also has strong links to Silicon Valley start-up culture, embodied in its exaggerated TED talk modality: Stewart Brand was at the first TED talk in 1984, part of his project of bringing together the remnants of the New Communalists with emerging tech leaders.

In 1994, the Progress and Freedom Foundation, a right-wing think tank, furthered this work of repurposing leftish ideas into right-wing platforms in a paper coauthored by Gingrich, Esther Dyson, George Keyworth, and Alvin Toffler, whose *Future Shock* (1970)—coauthored without crediting his wife, Adelaide Farrell—might now retrospectively be understood as part of this co-optation of the future by capitalism.[40] The shock of Toffler's rhetoric now appears increasingly like the strategies Naomi Klein dubs the "shock doctrine" in her eponymous book about the way neoliberalists exploit disaster to force through market-friendly legislative and policy reforms.[41] This paper, dubbed the Magna Carta for the knowledge age, anticipates Long Boom utopianism, even more directly conflating neoliberal ideology with the project of social betterment, as it shapes the public sphere such that supporting technology deregulation becomes the only way to ensure a good future.[42] The preface dizzyingly asserts that opportunities for wealth accumulation are unlimited because "the powers of mind are everywhere ascendant over the brute force of things": the new knowledge age is no longer subject to material limitations to production.[43] Yet it also warns that "the Third Wave, and the Knowledge Age it has opened, will not deliver on its potential unless it adds social and political dominance to its accelerating technological and economic strength." Key to this social and political dominance is the elimination of regulation and other governance that stands in the way of its accumulative potential. This will require, they warn, remaking the "meaning of freedom, structures of self-government, definition of property, nature of competition, conditions for cooperation, sense of community and nature of progress."

While cloaked in the rhetoric of technological solutionism, this manifesto's real targets are political: eliminating protections for workers, choices by democratic populations, and tax regimes to ensure social services—precisely the neoliberal dream of encasing the market. The new Magna Carta's preamble stirringly concludes with a call to rewrite the American dream—that is, to reinvent what we view as "the promise of American life." Morozov suggests that the recoding of political life under technological solutionism has reached the point of proposals "to ditch politics altogether and hope that technology—especially 'the Internet'—can rid us of problems that politics can no longer solve or, in a milder version, that we can replace politicians and politics with technocrats and administration."[44] In this way, we can see a direct line between New Economy regulation and start-up futurists' contentions that only new apps, not political deliberation and public policy, can solve the most pressing problems today.

Through this intermingling of neoliberal deregulation, Randian libertarianism, and sf-fueled utopianism, the internet was branded a utopian space of freedom and promise.[45] Although it is often suggested that the true promise was somehow co-opted by bad actors who came later, this history shows that I.T. liberation was libertarian from the start. It is not so surprising, then, that the second generation of aspiring unicorn founders imagined friends as things to be monetized and sociality as best served by polarizing algorithms that promote tribalism. A central observation in Alice Marwick's ethnography of the early days of Web 2.0 start-ups is that its entire ethos naturalizes a hierarchical, neoliberal subjectivity by "position[ing] the entrepreneur as the mythic hero and venture-backed start-ups as the epitome of high status."[46] Thus, she argues, these technologies embed inequality in their design since they are created in a context that "position[s] capitalism to be an agent of social change without challenging underlying inequalities."[47] Combining this reward structure with the belief that "simply introducing social technology to a community will result in greater participation and democracy"[48] means that the overall result of social media is that they tend to "promote inequality rather than counter it."[49]

From Counterculture, through Science Fiction, to Libertarianism

In this final section, I want to return to the role of sf narrative and the imagination in this remaking of the economic and political possibility. Science fiction has been central to Silicon Valley since the dot-com days, including work by a generation of sf writers central to the experimental culture emerging in the early days of the public internet. Influences are not difficult to find, from the industry's embrace of the term cyberspace to the much-told tale of Neal Stephenson's *The Diamond Age* being distributed to coders at Second Life, to the more recent name change of Facebook's parent company to Meta, derived from that novel's term for online communities, the metaverse. Yet this is not simply a question of the overlap in Venn diagrams between those who are sf enthusiasts and those who developed the programming skills to be the architects of this brave new world. Indeed, at times the confluences between sf and Silicon Valley seem more like noise than signal, such as the fact that Peter Thiel's CIA-serving surveillance system, Palantir, takes its name from Tolkien's seeing stones. Such companies have taken their emblems from sf but often ignore these images' thematic contexts. The relationship between sf and Silicon Valley ideology, then, is a matter of both recoding certain icons or images into new connotations and of amplifying the voices of the libertarian authors within the sf canon. It often operates in lockstep with the reactionary racial politics that can be found—or sometimes made via counterintuitive readings—in sf as well.

Even Palantir insists that its mission is about the good. Indeed, it is more polemical, announcing that it works to protect what its website names "our way of life" against unknown antagonists. Of course, "our way of life" is a not so subtly coded signal to white supremacists who have been finding one another online since the bulletin board system, or BBS, days. Thiel's overtly supremacist beliefs are documented, including his role in the *Stanford Review* during his time as a student. Thiel founded it to provide what he framed as a voice of reason to counter ongoing diversification of the Western canon as education sought to become antiracist.[50] Thiel later coauthored *The Diversity Myth* (with David O. Sacks), which contends that multicultural education is "the intellectual equivalent of junk food."[51] Max Chafkin suggests that Thiel's well-publicized hostility toward higher education as a waste of resources (compared with starting a company) is related to his fear of the liberal influence of universities on American thought.[52] Space precludes a detailed analysis of gender and racial biases in Silicon Valley, but it is worth noting that it is a very small community composed almost entirely of white men who came from privilege. Researching influential technological and financial partnerships, one sees the same names and connections time and again in these histories. As Chafkin, O'Mara, and Marwick have shown, Silicon Valley works structurally to prevent anyone other than this elite from gaining access, even as it continually credits itself with being a meritocracy. As Daub acerbically puts it, "Silicon Valley loves the words 'everyone,' 'universal,' and 'people,' but what they usually mean is 'people I went to school with,' 'my housemates in East Palo Alto,' or 'my four immediate subordinates.' The universality that their business model pushes them toward exists in tension with the fact that they actually know very few people."[53]

More pertinent to the conjunction of ideas I wish to explore here, as this countercultural rhetoric fused with the economics of highly competitive start-up economics, proselytizers for this better-through-technology future began to write a mode of tech journalism in venues such as *Wired* that might best be understood as its own kind of science fiction.[54] This techno-optimism transmogrified into business plan has always been a strain within the genre of sf, exemplified in its early days by Hugo Gernsback's work to create a community around *Amazing Stories* in ways very similar to Brand's later creation of a community linked to the *Whole Earth Catalog*. Both men encouraged readers of their publications to write in with feedback, recommendations, and editorial observations, creating an ethos in which readers regarded themselves as part of a shared community fostered by the magazine rather than just as customers buying a commercial product. In some of his earliest editorials, Gernsback extoled the versions of the new genre of "scientification," as he originally named it, to suggest the fiction itself contributed to scientific advance simply by imagining the new technologies that would inspire research. He dedicated as much of his time to seeking patents on things he imagined as he did to promoting sf. This Gernsbackian idea of sf as a mode of projecting, thereby to manifest, a technophilic future is culturally dominant today, even though most of its adherents have never read a pulp magazine and many would resent and reject any association with genre fiction. Yet start-up futurism has one foot in science fiction and the other in libertarian fundamentalism.

Grant Wythoff suggests that Gernsback is better understood as someone pioneering a theory of how to engage new media as a social technology, not as the inventor of a fictional mode, albeit what was new in Gernsback's day was the radio and pulp magazines:

> Gernsback's inventions blurred the lines between the real and the imaginary. While some were awarded patents and available for sale to consumers, others seem more like open invitations for a community of tinkerers to "fork" [a radio tuning metaphor] his hardware and continue development on an as-of-yet unrealizable idea. These amateurs and their work in the aggregate may not have been entirely responsible for the technologies Gernsback loved to claim he had predicted, but they were part of a collective endeavor to imagine the future by slowly, painstakingly, feeling their way toward it.[55]

Gernsback celebrated and created a community around a very specific way of understanding sf as part of a sociotechnical ideal that was part boosterism, part policy lobby, and part purely imaginative projection based on a belief that articulating the vision will manifest the result. This tinkering ethos, straight out of pulp sf, found its way into the famed start-ups of the first generation of Silicon Valley entrepreneurs to ground their now well-mythologized origins in home garages, not corporate headquarters.

In other words, Gernsback's marketing is the template from which the founder role has descended. Unlike their Homebrew Computer Club ancestors—who, closer to Gernsback's own visions, did tinker with technology—in the unicorn era, the role of the founder is often not that of coder. Rather, founders come up with the social vision that will inspire the next product, identifying predominantly as disruptors whose mode of invention is narrative rather than material. They then hire staff who will create technology that realizes the vision (they hope). This is evocative of how Gernsback believed the relationship between scientists and sf might work back in the 1920s, which included the suggestion that patents might be shared between those whose stories inspired new technologies and those who actually built them. Silicon Valley has shifted this somewhat preposterous suggestion into the cult of the founder, most prominently in the widespread celebration of Steve Jobs as a technical genius, although most of the engineering was done by Steve Wozniak; the all-important marketing of the vision of the world transformed fell to Jobs. Jobs is the figure most celebrated by later founders.[56] The central role of hype in the economic underpinnings of Silicon Valley is the chief way in which there is something foundationally science fictional about it. While the cases of Theranos and WeWork make these rhetoric foundations easier to perceive, it would be a mistake to see them as aberrations rather than intensified examples.

The consequences of this style of showman/narrative/solutionist politics are why I find the example of Adam Neumann so fascinating: it points to the generalization of Silicon Valley ideology to the economy as a whole.[57] Neumann and his partner, Miguel McKelvey, developed a business plan to lease buildings, divide them into office and communal spaces, and rent them to small businesses. In addition to providing the office services, WeWork marketed itself as futuristic; Neumann suggested that the shared space would not only contribute to a sense of joy and purpose in an environment that blurred the distinction between work and leisure time, but also that this environment would create collaborations that would enrich and improve all business in the shared space. WeWork became known for its Summer Camp music festival, which mixed frat-party events with visionary seminars about the company's future. These are central tenets of every Silicon Valley start-up: capitalist accumulation posing as community and world-changing mission; refusal of a distinction between life and work. It is impossible to overstate the importance of Neumann's own charisma to WeWork's valuation, a point that emphasizes the centrality of aesthetics—style and the affect it produces—to this reinvention of public engagement as economic project. Both the documentaries and the narrative dramatizations about WeWork and Theranos reinforce this point repeatedly: the pitch is all, and the conviction with which it is delivered shapes IPO success far more than the underlying product.

As WeWork's valuation grew, along with Neumann's ambition, he and Rebekah began to envision it as only the first in a set of We Companies, at least two of which they briefly launched: the shared living space WeLive and the private school WeGrow. Neumann began to talk about being president of the world one day, and announced this expanded company mission at a festival summit in Los Angeles. WeWork, he insisted, would deliver on the communal promises made—but never delivered—by social media companies: WeWork was "a community, a company, a family,"[58] eliding the differences among these kinds of collectives. In his conversations with investors, Neumann framed the technological elements of his company differently, via surveillance capitalism: the office environment would generate data about how people worked that could be monetized and used to implement efficiencies. Given the valuation structure of start-ups, the fact that this data gathering never worked was beside the point, because the user numbers continued to grow based on Neumann's invocation of the imaginary of company as community. He suggested that WeWork was a 3D version of social media, "a physical social network" or "physical Facebook," frequently drawing contrasts between the "i" of Apple technologies and the "We" supposedly central to WeWork.[59] The inspiration for the company was attributed to Neumann and McKelvey's shared upbringing on experimental communes; Neumann even described WeWork as a "capitalist kibbutz."[60] Yet although he frequently evoked fond memories of his time on a kibbutz in Israel, others testify that from a young age Neumann had the ambition to be enormously wealthy.[61]

Understood within the historical context outlined above, there is something appropriate about Neumann's insistence that WeWork is a tech company—although it offers nothing technological. The Silicon Valley start-up futurism embodied in the hunt for the unicorn and promulgated in the Long Boom discourse of the New Economy conflates profitability and utopianism. WeWork had virtually no option *but* to claim to be a tech company—a strange extension of the frequently diagnosed aspect of the postpolitical in which we cannot imagine any alternative to capitalism: WeWork cannot imagine success other than as a tech start-up. Yet as financial analyses in the wake of its crash have made clear, WeWork could never be a tech company, and this is because real estate (as an asset) cannot scale and generate profits in the way that software can. Once developed and adopted, software has few cost increases associated with massive distribution, whereas the fixed costs of managing real estate rise alongside the amount of real estate managed. Here returns the materiality that the knowledge age's Magna Carta claimed to have transcended, as it inevitably must. But WeWork simultaneously is a knowledge age company in that what it *actually* sold was a countercultural vision that it is possible to improve the world via capitalism—indeed, WeWork suggests that it is *only* via the right company that change is possible. WeWork marketed branded merchandise with slogans such as "Do What You Love" and "Making a Life, Not Just a Living"—invocations familiar in this era of the gig economy that are among the best exemplars of capitalism's ubiquity, and its success in naturalizing its own operations as simply the state of the world.

WeWork was especially popular among millennials, a generation that was also celebrated by Schwartz and Leyden in their "Long Boom" article. It prophesized that the millennial generation would be the leaders in a better world that would arrive by 2020, arguing that "kids who have spent their entire lives steeped in the new technologies, living in a networked world" would be poised to understand and manifest the powers of these new technologies to solve all the world's problems. Schwartz and Leyden continue: "These are higher-level concerns, the intractable problems—such as eradicating poverty on the planet—that people throughout history have believed impossible to solve. Yet this generation has witnessed an extraordinary spread of prosperity across the planet. They see no inherent barrier to keep them from extending that prosperity to—why not?—everyone."[62] This is start-up futurism at its finest, especially if we recall that in addition to extolling the benefits of the New Economy just a few short years before the massive dot-com crash, advocates of the New Economy also insisted that neoliberal deregulation was the only pathway to ensure that a better world could happen at all.

My purpose is not simply to point out this hypocrisy. Rather, I am interested in what is visible from the vantage point of understanding Neumann's desire for a capitalist kibbutz as perhaps the purest manifestation of the faux counterculture endemic to Silicon Valley—and, I would argue, to public discourse overall today. The prediction was correct that millennials would grow up to be a generation who believes in this vision of the world made better through capitalism. Yet it is also a generation that has lived through significant displacements and disruptions to financial stability and employment, and it is a generation less able to accumulate wealth than those before it.[63] The 2014 Millennial Impact Report, conducted by the Case Foundation and about the relationship between social engagement and employment, found that, overwhelmingly, millennials want their jobs to be linked to the social causes that they care about, and that most see a continuum between work and activism.[64] This is precisely the desire that Adam Neumann so adeptly exploited as he urged people to contribute countless unpaid or minimally paid hours to building his company and to take stock options instead of providing an adequate salary—all so that they could be part of something transformative. When WeWork finally crashed after a disastrous attempt at an IPO, Neumann walked away with a $1.7 billion exit package while most employees were left with worthless stock options. Many of them also lost their jobs as new management aggressively sought to make the company profitable. Among the people interviewed in the WeWork documentary is Megan Mallow, Neumann's former assistant, who speaks of her need for therapy in the aftermath: she felt "not that I lost a job but that I lost my purpose," and wonders how she can help make the world a better place without WeWork.

For all Silicon Valley's claims to utopian purpose, the documented truth is that social media companies contribute to rising tribalism and violence. Further, they continue to resist regulation that might hurt their profitability and fund lobbyists to help them evade taxes, which starves the state of the capacity to provide social services, further deteriorating the capacity for liberal politics. To the extent that Silicon Valley is influenced by Randian libertarianism, it even sees this avoidance of taxation as a right-wing utopian project, arguing that taxation is theft from the productive by those who do not truly contribute to society. Even as they also strive to burnish their public image through charitable donations and polished statements about community and public service, the billionaire class, especially those who accrued their wealth through the New Economy, give less in charitable donations than they would pay as their tax burden under systems of taxation that preceded the neoliberal tax breaks to the rich.[65] In its branding of such charitable giving, Silicon Valley often evokes technological solutionism as an alternative to democratic governance, suggesting that their success in accumulating massive amounts of wealth somehow better qualifies them to understand how to direct resources and solve society's problems. Were they to pay taxes at an appropriate rate, it is implied, this money would simply be wasted by inefficient bureaucracy. The result eliminates in one stroke the economic foundations of the liberal state and any pretext that democratic oversight should play a role in resource distribution. Marwick also reports that the strong belief in libertarian individualism "may explain why wealthy technology workers are far less philanthropic than their 'high society' counterparts": if Silicon Valley is a meritocracy, as it believes of itself, then "the mythology certainly implies that those mired in poverty are similarly deserving of their lowly status."[66]

Neoliberal Fundamentalism, Silicon Fascism

Ruha Benjamin reminds us that the massive influence of technology companies on our economic life and on public discourse means that "private industry choices are in fact public policy decisions."[67] We need to recognize and contend with the degree to which many of these public policy decisions are fueled by a libertarianism disguised as utopianism with a countercultural, sf veneer. The social and economic consequences of start-up futurism can be grasped only when we look simultaneously at the public affect they mobilize through their utopian technological solutionism (including the promotion of extreme content) and the increased inequality they promote via their funding model, disruption of established jobs, and lobbying efforts to ensure their profitability remains.

Lin and Neely point out that the shift toward neoliberalism and financialization over the past forty years, especially choices to expand access to personal credit that enabled middle-class buying power to maintain consumption even as wages fell, has created a situation in which governance cannot be understood outside of the economic settlements that privileged the investment sector. They point out that "the state relies on private financial institutions to achieve its policy goals," because it has embraced a model by which the middle-class can continue to access services (health care, education, homes, pensions) through financial instruments created by banks. Inevitably, however, "financial institutions prioritize their interests over the government's," and the government is thus forced to concede to policies that do not serve the public or risk losing access to needed credit entirely.[68] Goodman concurs with this analysis, contending that such entanglements of political efficacy with economic power is a crisis for democratic governance. Goodman asks, "How can democratic societies attack inequality when democracy itself is under the control of the people who possess most of the money?"[69] Until we develop alternative economies, he concludes, we must "accept the continued degradation of democracy."[70] Mark Zuckerberg, who was enriched by the very structures critiqued here—describes the future of democracy differently. In his view, gone are the days of the fourth estate, when news agencies and professional reporting shaped the public discourse. Facebook offers a more democratic alternative, a "fifth estate" comprising "the unedited voice of the people."[71] According to Zuckerberg, moderation that bans hate speech or disinformation would be akin to hurting democracy: "the cacophony of voices would of course be discomfiting, but debate was essential to a healthy democracy."[72] In Silicon Valley, it seems, democracy is just another story one tells to protect profitability.

Democracy-eroding economies have not been shaped by Silicon Valley start-up futurism alone, but billionaires who made their fortunes through technology are increasingly prominent in corporate lobbying efforts, in what jobs remain within platform capitalism and widespread automation, and in public discourse via both the influence of their own statements and their structural control of infrastructure of public debate. What distinguishes these new robber barons from the old is that they have convinced us that their mission is utopian, not simply accumulative. This prevents us from understanding their role as capitalists, not futurists. Among the figures Jane Mayer discusses in her history of the use of private wealth to shape U.S. politics is William Simon, appointed as secretary of the treasury under Nixon, author of *A Time for Truth* (1978).[73] It warns that the nation is "careening with frightening speed towards collectivism," calling for a "counter-intelligentsia" to refute the critique of capitalism in contemporary colleges and universities: "Ideas are weapons—indeed the only weapons with which other ideas can be fought."[74] Silicon Valley's ability to disguise its upward redistribution of wealth as a utopian project of futurism has been one of the most successful weapons in this war against collectivism, but unlike Simon, this new generation of billionaires has succeeded in convincing us that they build rather than destroy community. We need to see more clearly, and we need another politics. This starts with another story.

Notes

I thank Joe Street for comments that were extremely helpful in sharpening this chapter intervention. I also thank Juan Meneses, who introduced me to the discussion of the postpolitical and who has helped me understand how my work is legible in this framework.

1. *WeWork, or The Making and Breaking of a $47 Billion Unicorn* (dir. Jed Rothstein, 2021).

2. The role of Facebook in particular in spreading misinformation during the 2016 election is well documented by Frenkel and Kang; as they note, the company chose to include paid political advertisements under the umbrella of "political speech" that was exempt from typical moderation rules under the

contention that the "newsworthiness" of candidate statements justified more lenient measures regarding hate speech and false information. Sheera Frenkel and Cecilia Kang, *An Ugly Truth: Inside Facebook's Battle for Domination* (New York: Harper, 2021), 13, 116, 250. Elements of the role that monetization played in pushing Facebook to court conservatives and refuse to moderate content are also documented in Antonio García Martínez, *Chaos Monkeys: Obscure Fortune and Random Failure in Silicon Valley* (New York: Harper, 2018).

3. Musk claims to be committed to ensuring that humanity is a multiplanetary species. Bezos is interested in saving the earth/environment by outsourcing polluting industries to space stations. See Tim Fernholz, *Rocket Billionaires: Elon Musk, Jeff Bezos, and the New Space Age* (New York: Mariner, 2018). We must be cautious about taking these claims at face value, of course, because there is also profit to be made in private space travel since the signing of the U.S. Commercial Space Launch Competitiveness Act of 2015, which reduces government regulation of the industry and grants companies the rights to resources taken from space.

4. There are other factors involved in the shift of policy from the 1980s onward related to the tendency for the rate of profit to fall under capitalist structures, shifts in global economic policy, the OPEC crisis, and the end of the gold standard.

5. Quinn Slobodian, *Globalists: The End of Empire and the Birth of Neoliberalism* (Cambridge, Mass.: Harvard University Press, 2018), 270.

6. Japhy Wilson and Erik Swyngedouw, "Seeds of Dystopia: Post-politics and the Return of the Political," in *The Post-political and Its Discontents: Spaces of Depoliticisation, Spectres of Radical Politics,* ed. Japhy Wilson and Erik Swyngedouw (Edinburgh: Edinburgh University Press, 2014), 6. My own approach to this problem focuses more on the need for changes to the underlying structure of the economy, particularly redistribution of material resources and political power. I am less convinced that a return to the political as a space of debate and contest marks a significant difference without a commitment to structural change, including those in campaign finances.

7. Mark Fisher, *Capitalist Realism: Is There No Alternative?* (Winchester, Eng.: Zero/Collective Ink, 2009), 2; italics in the original.

8. The satirical HBO drama *Silicon Valley* (2014–19) takes this rhetoric (and the structural contradictions it elides) to absurd levels, suggesting the rhetoric is only ever performative; see especially season 1, episode 7, "Proof of Concept," which aired May 18, 2014.

9. Seymour suggests that the "subterranean" effects of social media, their influence on "the infrastructures of daily life," are so significant that we should describe these technologies as "sub-hegemonic" because they do not need to compel belief, just shape action. Richard Seymour, *The Twittering Machine* (New York: Verso, 2020), 172.

10. Unsurprisingly, the other industry that follows a similar profile of endorsing meritocracy while relying on social capital is the hedge fund industry. On the importance of personal connections in Silicon Valley, see Adrian Daub, *What Tech Calls Thinking: An Enquiry into the Intellectual Bedrock of Silicon Valley* (New York: Farrar, Straus and Giroux, 2020); and Alice Marwick, *Status Update: Celebrity, Publicity, and Branding in the Social Media Age* (New Haven, Conn.: Yale University Press, 2013). For similar analyses of the hedge-fund world, see Megan Tobias Neely, *Hedged Out: Inequality and Insecurity on Wall Street* (Berkeley: University of California Press, 2022); and Karen Ho, *Liquidated: An Ethnography of Wall Street* (Durham, N.C.: Duke University Press, 2009).

11. Peter Thiel and Marc Andriessen, respectively involved with creating PayPal and Mosaic/Netscape, promote Randian ideas. Seen as founders in the popular imagination, both have had more influence via their venture capital projects. As Frenkel and Kang put it, "As two of the most powerful men in Silicon Valley, they did more than just create and invest in new start-ups: they shaped the ethos of what it meant to be a tech ingénue. That ideology was rooted in a version of libertarianism that embraced innovation and free markets and scorned the overreach of government and regulations. At the core was a belief in individual autonomy." Frenkel and Kang, *Ugly Truth*, 25.

12. Multiple scholars discuss this consequence of deregulation and financialization. Piketty offers the most thoroughgoing analysis of overall trends: Thomas Piketty, *Capital in the Twenty-First Century* (Cambridge, Mass.: Belknap, 2014). Lin and Neely offer a pointed argument of how financialization is the key driver on ongoing inequality: Ken-Hou Lin and Megan Tobias Neely, *Divested: Inequality in the Age of Finance* (Oxford: Oxford University Press, 2020).

13. Evgeny Morozov, *To Save Everything, Click Here: The Folly of Technological Solutionism* (New York: PublicAffairs, 2013), 5.

14. Morozov, 6.

15. Morozov, 6.

16. Alan Greenspan, "The Challenge of Central Banking in a Democratic Society," speech delivered at the annual dinner and Francis Boyer Lecture of the American Enterprise Institute for Public Policy Research, December 5, 1996, www.federalreserve.gov/boarddocs/speeches/1996/19961205.htm. Greenspan was chair of the U.S. Federal Reserve from 1987 to 2006 and set the monetary policy that has influenced the global economy over the last thirty years. For a more detailed analysis of the interplay between belief and market valuation as a science-fictional mode, see Sherryl Vint, "Promissory Futures: Reality and Imagination in Finance and Fiction," in special issue, "Speculative Finance/Speculative Fiction," ed. David M. Higgins and Hugh C. O'Connell, *CR: The New Centennial Review* 19, no. 1 (2019): 1–36.

17. See Adam Tooze, *Crashed: How a Decade of Financial Crisis Changed the World* (New York: Viking, 2018), 293; and Matt Taibbi, *Griftopia: Bubble Machines, Vampire Squids, and the Long Con That Is Breaking America* (New York: Spiegel &

Grau, 2010), 38–43. Taibbi notes the gap between Rand's claims about central banks versus Greenspan's actions while the Federal Reserve chair, suggesting that ultimately Greenspan was mainly influenced by Rand's individualist philosophy in terms of his ethical choices, which were repeatedly to cut social programs to enable tax cuts to the rich, under the assertion that a high-performing stock market signified a healthy economy.

18. Qtd. in Fred Turner, *From Counterculture to Cyberculture: Steward Brand, the Whole Earth Network, and the Rise of Digital Utopianism* (Chicago: University of Chicago Press, 2006), Kindle loc. 3193.

19. To secure markets against the consequences of overextension, he developed a series of monetary policy choices referred to as the "Greenspan put." This "put" seeks to reverse drops in stock market values to the shocks of market crashes. The net result was to encourage more reckless speculation given that bankers had no disincentive not to pursue the higher returns of risky investments, given the government backstop. These choices led directly to the 2008 crash.

20. Robert Shiller, *Narrative Economics: How Stories Go Viral and Drive Major Economic Events* (Princeton, N.J.: Princeton University Press, 2019).

21. There are multiple parallels between their stories, which are beyond the scope of my analysis but which are documented elsewhere in books, such as John Carreyrou, *Bad Blood: Secrets and Lies in a Silicon Valley Startup* (New York: Knopf, 2018) (about Theranos); and Eliot Brown and Maureen Farrell, *The Cult of We: WeWork, Adam Neumann, and the Great Startup Delusion* (New York: Crown, 2021); documentaries, such as Rothstein's *WeWork* and *The Inventor* (dir. Alex Gibney, 2019) (about Holmes); and narrative dramas, such as Hulu's *The Dropout* (2022) (about Holmes); and, from Apple TV+, *WeCrashed* (2022) (about Neumann). There are also overlaps in the successful (by some standards) story of Uber, dramatized by Showtime in *Super Pumped* (2022). This public interest is another mark of the fascination these figures continue to hold, although they also operate as critique. *Super Pumped* is the most effective in this respect because it understands Kalanick's story to be emblematic of the industry, not a special case. Even successful companies do tremendous damage to the social fabric: thanks to Uber, funds for civic projects that once came to cities in the form of taxis and licensing fees now flow to the private wealth of Uber stockholders; moreover, the platform capitalist employment model allows companies to avoid paying benefits and meeting minimum wage standards.

22. Aileen Lee, "Welcome to the Unicorn Club: Learning from Billion-Dollar Startups," *TechCrunch*, November 2, 2013, techcrunch.com/2013/11/02/welcome-to-the-unicorn-club.

23. As Goodman acerbically points out, this too is a matter of narrative: "As he campaigned for Trump's tax cuts in 2017, Jamie Dimon trotted out the usual argument—that corporations relieved of their tax burdens would use the extra money to build factories, expand operations, and increase pay. 'That connection is real,' Dimon told the journalist William D. Cohan. 'It's indirect. I can't prove it

to you, but I know it's true.'" Dimon is a major player in the venture capitalist space and, not incidentally, the banker central to WeWork's rise. Peter S. Goodman, *Davos Man: How the Billionaires Devoured the World* (New York: Custom House, 2022), 455.

24. Kim Phillips-Fein, "The World that Venture Capital Made," *New Republic,* May 11, 2022, newrepublic.com/article/166330/world-venture-capital-made.

25. Lin and Neely, *Divested,* 7.

26. See Lin and Neely, *Divested;* Goodman, *Davos Man;* Grace Blakely, *Stolen: How to Save the World from Financialization* (London: Repeater, 2019); and Costas Lapavitsas, *Profiting without Producing: How Finance Exploits Us All* (New York: Verso, 2014). The origin of this doctrine is usually traced to a 1970 editorial by Milton Friedman of the famed Chicago School: Milton Friedman, "The Social Responsibility of Business Is to Increase Its Profits," *New York Times,* September 13, 1970, www.nytimes.com/1970/09/13/archives/a-friedman-doctrine-the-social-responsibility-of-business-is-to.html.

27. This business model has worked in the past for companies that are now massively profitable, such as Meta and Amazon. For equally valuable companies such as Google, profit came only with a shift toward advertising revenue, a change that also began in the 2010s. As Zuboff shows, what such companies sell is their users' data and attention to advertisers, making the goal to ensure that people spend as much time as possible on their platforms. The role of extreme content is another chapter in Silicon Valley's manipulation of politics, as it generates more engagement and hence more revenue. Shoshana Zuboff, *The Age of Surveillance Capitalism: The Fight for a Human Future at the New Frontier of Power* (New York: PublicAffairs, 2019). Frenkel and Kang demonstrate that profit concerns factored into Facebook's decision to allow Trump to spread misinformation during the 2016 U.S. election. See Frenkel and Kang, *Ugly Truth.*

28. See Tooze, *Crashed;* Lin and Neely, *Divested;* and Nick Srnicek, *Platform Capitalism* (Cambridge: Polity, 2017).

29. See Max Chafkin, *The Contrarian: Peter Thiel and Silicon Valley's Pursuit of Power* (New York: Penguin, 2021); and Frenkel and Kang, *Ugly Truth.* Also relevant are Goodman, who focuses on how the venture capitalist class similarly manipulates public discourse to support neoliberal values, and Mayer, who charts a well-organized network to promote neoliberal ideals funded by the elite: Goodman, *Davos Man;* Jane Mayer, *Dark Money: The Hidden History of the Billionaires behind the Rise of the Radical Right* (New York: Doubleday, 2016).

30. Peter Schwartz and Peter Leyden, "The Long Boom: A History of the Future, 1980–2020," *Wired,* July 1, 1987, www.wired.com/1997/07/longboom.

31. Srnicek, *Platform Capitalism,* 46, 47.

32. Lin and Neely, *Divested.*

33. Daub, *What Tech Calls Thinking,* 42.

34. Turner, *From Counterculture to Cyberculture,* Kindle loc. 115.

35. Turner, Kindle loc. 1733.

36. Margaret O'Mara, *The Code: Silicon Valley and the Remaking of America* (New York: Penguin, 2019).

37. Daub, *What Tech Calls Thinking,* 50.

38. Howard Rheingold, *Virtual Reality* (New York: Simon and Schuster, 1991).

39. Turner, *From Counterculture to Cyberculture,* Kindle loc. 2405.

40. Alvin Toffler, *Future Shock* (New York: Random House, 1970).

41. Naomi Klein, *The Shock Doctrine: The Rise of Disaster Capitalism* (New York: Metropolitan, 2007).

42. Esther Dyson, George Gilder, George Keywork, and Alvin Toffler, "Cyberspace and the American Dream: A Magna Carta for the Knowledge Age," Progress and Freedom Foundation, *Future Insight,* release 1.2 (August 1994), www.pff.org/issues-pubs/futureinsights/fi1.2magnacarta.html.

43. This statement seems designed to counter the earlier Club of Rome report, *The Limits to Growth* (1972), which argued precisely the opposite—namely that ecological concerns required resisting the endless growth demanded by capital. This report, gains by unions, and political victories to expand the welfare state prompted overt organization by the ownership class to shift public opinion in their favor, as extensively documented by Jane Mayer. The elite thus shifted political discourse overall toward the extreme right by naturalizing neoliberal ideology while also fueling economic policies that enriched their class at the expense of the working class, leading to the extreme rage we see in the alt-right today. She also notes attempts to discredit her research via false information, the post-truth strategy so successful to destroying the public sphere. Her focus is on the oil industry, but there are overlaps with Silicon Valley, including interest in Ayn Rand's anti-communalism and funding private think tanks to influence public discourse.

44. Morozov, *To Save Everything, Click Here,* 128.

45. One pertinent element here is the fact that Grateful Dead lyricist John Perry Barlow became an avid user of the early *WELL (Whole Earth 'Lectronic Link)* online forum organized around Brand's catalog community. Around the same time as the Knowledge Age Magna Carta and the *Wired* Long Boom issue, he wrote the cyberlibertarian Declaration of Independence of Cyberspace (1996), a widely disseminated manifesto (originally published from Davos, home to the World Economic Forum) that declared the internet a space of freedom beyond the jurisdiction of any government. Drawing language from the U.S. Declaration of Independence, another document of economic rights masquerading as political freedoms, Barlow's Declaration was a response to the U.S. Telecommunications Act of 1996, which sought to incorporate the internet into existing telecommunications law. Barlow's insistence of the sovereignty of the internet and its denizens' capacity to manage needed regulation among themselves set the ground for the continued content moderation struggles so pertinent to today's polarization of politics. Elon Musk's overt libertarian stance and purchase of Twitter/X mark an intensification of this damage: previously, Twitter/X, unlike Facebook, was willing to label political lies as such.

46. Marwick, *Status Update,* Kindle loc. 451. Frenkel and Kang also point to the hypocritical foundations of Facebook, a company that profits from encouraging its users to embrace openness (thereby creating data from which Meta can profit) while enacting an internal corporate culture of secrecy and restrictive nondisclosure agreements; Frenkel and Kang, *Ugly Truth,* x. Marwick notes these ideas date back to the dot-com era, further pointing to the coconstruction of neoliberal hegemony, Silicon Valley solutionism, and the erosion of democracy.

47. Marwick, *Status Update,* Kindle loc. 451.

48. Marwick, Kindle loc. 408.

49. Marwick, Kindle loc. 81. Reinforcing this point, Frenkel and Kang detail an experiment in shifting the Facebook news feed algorithm toward posts that are "good for the world" over those "bad for the world." The result was that people spent less time on Facebook (session metrics), and thus Zuckerberg demanded that the algorithm be changed. In the end, a version was approved that allowed for de-emphasizing what was "bad for the world" only to the extent that this shift in the feed did not entail a shift in the session metrics. Frenkel and Kang, *Ugly Truth,* 286.

50. Chafkin, *Contrarian,* 31.

51. Qtd. in O'Mara, *Code,* 253.

52. Relatedly, the Kochs and other wealthy industrialists also see universities as an enemy to their worldview, according to Mayer's research. They deliberately set up a counterdiscourse emphasizing neoliberal perspectives by funding independent research centers on university campuses, promoting and funding research consistent with their political beliefs through entities such as the Olin Foundation and the Cato Institute, and funding grassroots organizations to popularize these ideas. Among those funded by the Olin Foundation is Charles Murray, one of the authors of the notorious *Bell Curve* (1994), which contends that intelligence correlates with race, with Black people the least intelligent. The Olin Foundation also funded right-wing newspapers on college campuses. Richard J. Herrnstein and Charles Murray, *The Bell Curve: Intelligence and Class Structure in American Life* (1994; reprint, New York: Free Press, 1996).

53. Daub, *What Tech Calls Thinking,* 13.

54. Schwartz and Leyden's "Long Boom" article is itself a kind of journalistic sf: published in 1997, it offers the history from 1980 to 2020. Science fiction authors, including William Gibson, have published in *Wired.* Esther Dyson, a V.C. investor, is the daughter of physicist Freeman Dyson, whose theory of the Dyson sphere (advanced technology that encloses a civilization's star within artificial structures to maximize energy extraction) inspired several sf narratives of artificial worlds as habitats, including *Ringworld,* written by a libertarian: Larry Niven, *Ringworld* (New York: Ballantine, 1970). There is significant overlap between sf and Silicon Valley ventures such as life extension, cryptocurrency, and "seasteading," the last a libertarian fantasy of creating an island to establish a society free from any government jurisdiction. These overlaps are explored

extensively in Finn Brunton, *Digital Cash: The Unknown History of the Anarchists, Utopians and Technologists Who Created Cryptocurrency* (Princeton, N.J.: Princeton University Press, 2019). As if to emphasize the point about the smallness of these circles, seasteading was briefly funded by Peter Thiel, and its main promoter is Patri Friedman, grandson of Chicago School neoliberalist Milton Friedman.

55. Grant Wythoff, *The Perversity of Things: Hugo Gernsback on Media, Tinkering, and Scientification* (Minneapolis: University of Minnesota Press, 2016), 43.

56. A large part of the Elizabeth Holmes story recounts her conscious patterning of herself on Jobs, but she is far from alone in seeing him in grandiose terms.

57. There is also much to say, beyond my scope here, about the diverging fates of Neumann and Holmes. Both misled investors and created economic harm for those they employed as a result of the failures of their companies to deliver what was promised. As Brown and Farrell show, Neumann manipulated the board, which voted him out but gave him a massive buyout—a move necessary to prevent his further devaluing what remained of their investment through his eccentric behavior. Holmes, in contrast, was tried for fraud and sentenced to prison. In my view, gender—and the opportunities it affords or precludes—is a central part of this divergence. Brown and Farrell, *Cult of We.*

58. Qtd. in Brown and Farrell, *Cult of We,* 8.

59. Neumann makes these statements in footage included in the documentary *WeWork, or The Making and Breaking of a $47 Billion Unicorn,* including in footage initially intended as a video accompaniment to the IPO. In some ways, Adam's claim that WeWork is a "physical Facebook" is simply the reversal of Brand's trajectory: the *Whole Earth Catalog* turned a print commodity for geographically dispersed homesteader communities into virtual community; Neumann promises to virtualize the physical office.

60. Brown and Farrell, *Cult of We,* 34.

61. A similar anecdote comes up in the story of Elizabeth Holmes documented by Carreyrou. This affective invention in making money as a life ambition—without much concern with the project by which one makes that money—is further evidence of how centralization of neoliberal ideology has fundamentally shifted the public imaginary and thus the political. Accumulation is now openly embraced not only as an end in itself, but also an end that somehow also signifies the moral worth of the wealthy person, a central tenant of Randianism. Carreyrou, *Bad Blood.*

62. Schwartz and Leyden, "Long Boom."

63. In complete contrast to the vision of millennial life celebrated by Schwartz and Leyden, Malcolm Harris demonstrates that millennials have instead been trained to be the perfect neoliberal human capital required by the platform capitalist economy. His predictions for their growing role in politics name them as a generation that will either continue to embody the worst of these tendencies,

thus bringing a return to fascism, or one that will make a revolutionary break to something better—but only if they reject the New Economy in which they were nurtured. Malcolm Harris, *Kids These Days: Human Capital and the Making of Millennials* (New York: Little, Brown, 2017).

64. Millennial Impact Report, 2014 reports, www.themillennialimpact.com/past-research.

65. Goodman extensively traces this cost to the state; in one example, about Marc Benioff, famed for promoting corporate philanthropy, Goodman notes, "So-called profit shifting has been costing the American Treasury $60 billion a year in lost taxes. Compared to this legalized form of tax evasion, the $10 million that Benioff had helped secure to attack homelessness in San Francisco amounted to a rounding error." He continues, "Part of why individuals like Benioff could crow about giving back was because of how comprehensively they had taken to begin with. They had benefited from public goods financed by taxpayers—the schools that educated their employees; the internet, developed by publicly funded research; the roads, the bridges, and the rest of modern infrastructure, which enabled commerce—and then deployed their lobbyists, accountants, and lawyers to master legal forms of tax evasion that starved the system." Goodman, *Davos Man,* 35, 244. Mayer traces similar strategies of tax evasion by industrial billionaires who use their funds to start charitable foundations that support pro-neoliberal scholarship and otherwise work to shape the public sphere. Through the availability of 501 exemption status for some of these entities, as well as inheritance tax policies that allow trusts to transfer assets without taxation to the next generation so long as interest is donated to charities, billionaires can tax-deduct much of what they spend on advocacy for their own worldview. Mayer also lays much of the blame for the influence of private wealth on political discourse at the door of the *Citizens United* Supreme Court decision. Mayer, *Dark Money.*

66. Marwick, *Status Update,* Kindle loc. 4106.

67. Ruha Benjamin, *Race after Technology: Abolitionist Tools for the New Jim Code* (Cambridge: Polity, 2019), 12.

68. Lin and Neely, *Divested,* 82.

69. Goodman, *Davos Man,* 339.

70. Goodman, 339. Mayer similarly notes the political consequences of political spending by the wealthy made possible by the *Citizens United* decision. She claims that the Kochs built an institute to influence the Republican Party—an institute that has now taken over that party. Mayer, *Dark Money.*

71. Qtd. in Frenkel and Kang, *Ugly Truth,* 254.

72. Frenkel and Kang, 264.

73. William Simon, *A Time for Truth* (New York: McGraw-Hill, 1978).

74. Qtd. in Mayer, *Dark Money,* 102.

CHAPTER 3

Un violador en tu camino

Reimagining the Political through Mediated Feminist Street Performance

JACQUELYN ARCY AND ALLISON PAGE

On November 25, 2019, the International Day for the Elimination of Violence against Women, members of the Chilean feminist art collective LASTESIS gathered in central Santiago to perform *Un violador en tu camino* (A rapist in your path). As onlookers watched and occasionally cheered, blindfolded performers danced, sang, and chanted over a throbbing and insistent drum beat that matched the performance's minimalist choreography. Through lyrics like "El violador eras tú / El violador eres tú / El estado opresor es un macho violador" ("The rapist was you / the rapist is you / the oppressive state is a macho rapist"), the performers articulated sexual violence as state violence. *Un violador en tu camino* was filmed by LASTESIS, uploaded to YouTube, and subsequently went viral, sparking similar actions in more than two hundred locations worldwide. Performances spanning locales from Central and South America to Europe took up LASTESIS's powerful feminist contestation of rape culture, state violence, and survivor blaming.[1] Two years later, in December 2021, near the end of a second year of the global Covid-19 pandemic, Chile elected as president a thirty-five-year-old leftist, Gabriel Boric, the youngest leader in the country's history. Boric's election bucked a worldwide trend toward authoritarianism as seen in the election of leaders like Viktor Orbán in 2010 (his second term after serving from 1998 to 2002), Donald Trump in 2016, and Jair Bolsonaro in 2019. Critically, Boric campaigned on radically changing the economic policies installed in the country during the 1970s by Augusto Pinochet. Those neoliberal policies, which demonstrators have objected to for years, wrought devastating inequality and incommensurable harm. As scholars and activists have detailed, Chile is considered the early locus of neoliberalism, with Pinochet relying on Chilean economic advisers known as the Chicago boys, so called because they trained at the Chicago School under Milton Friedman, a central architect of neoliberal economics.[2] A former activist himself, Boric proclaimed, "If Chile was the cradle of neoliberalism, it will also be its grave."[3]

As authoritarianism and fascism rise, so too do movements that reimagine a more just world. We begin with Boric and *Un violador en tu camino* to map the simultaneous flourishing of progressive and collective political activity, from global racial justice and antiausterity protests to feminist and climate justice action. We focus on *Un violador* because it offers a compelling case study for theorizing the relationship between postpolitics, feminist activism, and aesthetics, given its affective and corporeal engagement. Performers use synchronized and choreographed movement to contest sexual violence. We theorize that these movements, performed as a collective, produce feelings like pain, rage, and solidarity, which move in unpredictable ways. In a collection on aesthetics and the postpolitical such as this one, this chapter about *Un violador* provides a feminist rejoinder to how we understand what constitutes the political and what is efficacious in the face of staggering violence and inequality.

To this end, theories of the postpolitical typically identify ways that resistance movements, including rights-based struggles, are subsumed into electoral politics, thereby neutralizing their efficacy in changing the status quo. This business-as-usual political order depends on the illusion of participatory democracy and global consensus—seemingly intrinsic paradigms that many in putatively liberal democracies now perceive as precarious.[4] From this perspective, Boric's election could represent a further entrenching of electoral politics as the primary site of struggle. Although Boric was not a return to politics as usual, he still remains within the realm of the electoral politics apparatus. LasTesis demonstrates how the corporeal and affective offer a site for political intervention outside of the electoral system. We argue that the bodily capacities both produced and engaged by the *Un violador* performance generate a fissure in the status quo by bringing to the fore the realities of sexual violence that are typically invisibilized, including visualizations of pain and humiliation and the state's implication therein. Our interest in *Un violador* stems in part from the performance's use of synchronized and choreographed movement to contest state violence. This differs from other denunciations of gender-based violence (such as #MeToo) in that *Un violador* expressly centers the body and the corporeal as well as the generative possibility of literal movement. We therefore take our cues from *Un violador,* theorizing emotions and bodily sensations as transformative elements of the performance that contribute to the formation of new (and agentic) subjects and collectives. As we suggest, feelings and bodily sensations aren't as readily absorbed by power's grasp. Rather, they linger and have unpredictable effects. Below, we analyze the performance to trace some of these effects.

In this sense, we view *Un violador* as a generative case study that challenges the ready incorporation that is part of what characterizes the postpolitical. Yet it is not just the unpredictability of emotions and movement that makes *Un violador* an instance of political action. The performance also points us to political imaginaries that center rather than dismiss or ignore the body. For Joshua Chambers-Letson, performance "is a vital means through which the minoritarian subject demands and produces freedom and More Life at the point of the body."[5] As we suggest, *Un violador* generates an affective response both for the dance's participants and for its viewers *through* collective movement, repetition, and vocalization. This in turn produces embodied knowledge and an alternative vision, even if momentary, of different ways of being.

Our understanding of the postpolitical is informed by scholarship that highlights the relationship between neoliberalism (as a political-economic system) and politics.[6] Scholars like Jodi Dean have suggested that neoliberalism has expanded capitalism's capture of the political such that any critique is commodified and thus neutralized—particularly evident in communicative capitalism's insistent grasp on digital realms. Contra scholarship that celebrates the putative democratic promise and possibility of social media, Dean instead details how speech is in fact immensely profitable for a digital economy that relies on user engagement. Although we concur with Dean's theorization of communicative capitalism as a reentrenchment of neoliberalism in digital space, we are struck by the question of the body and what affective politics it might offer.[7] As such, we are compelled by types of struggle that center the body and the affective through aesthetic forms as possible sites that expand political imagination. In light of our current moment, where the bodies of minoritized subjects are under increasing control from state surveillance (newly evident in U.S. abortion bans that seek to limit movement across state lines), it is urgent to consider what tools are available to circumnavigate new forms of control—and upend them. In this way, we view *Un violador* as a critical action that shows how the collective movement of bodies can produce emotive connections to politics (and collectives) that challenge the postpolitical status quo.

We closely read aspects of the original *Un violador* performance alongside its online response to theorize how feminist outrage and aesthetic categories deepen our understanding of the postpolitical. We seek to address a gap in the literature by drawing attention to the relevance of the body and the affective to considerations of what constitutes the political, particularly as this relates to gender. In what follows, we argue that the emotions and bodily sensations that emerge from participating in *Un violador* and watching the performance online exceed their total capture. Along these lines, connecting to and through other bodies via choreographed movement offers a powerful rejoinder to the social isolation that characterizes so much of contemporary life under neoliberalism. Our aim is to center affect and the body in the discourse on postpolitics, and to explore the political potential of feelings and movements that transcend accepted norms for women's bodies and the bodies of gender-nonconforming people in the fight against sexual violence.

AN "INTERNATIONAL FEMINIST ANTHEM": POSTPOLITICS AND NEUTRALIZING CRITIQUE

In much of the scholarship on postpolitics, theorists consider how post-political forms of governance "ensure that the framework of debate and decision-making does not question or disrupt the existing state of neoliberal political-economic configuration."[8] Although our focus is on the political possibilities of *Un violador* rather than the ways its critique of state-sanctioned violence was neutralized, we acknowledge that the framing of the performance within popular media and governmental responses supports depoliticizing efforts. In newspaper headlines across the world, *Un violador* was heralded as an "international feminist anthem" that unites women in the "common demand: to be respected."[9] News coverage suggested that the similarities between various women's movements spurred the global circulation of the video and the restaging of the performance in different countries, including Mexico, Colombia, France, Spain, and the United States. But in celebrating the commonalities between women, these reports elided the specific claims of violence addressed in the Chilean performance. In popular media, the viral circulation of the performance was, in itself, constructed as a triumph for women's rights.

Similarly, government officials from all sides of the political spectrum, in Chile and abroad, publicly supported aspects of *Un violador*'s message and thus neutralized the performance's critique by incorporating it into electoral politics. Right-wing Chilean politician Isabel Plá said she "recognize[d] the impact [the song and performance] has had both in Chile and in the world and how it has made visible sexual violence against women," proposing policy changes as the solution.[10] In Turkey, social democratic women lawmakers made a direct appeal for the government to address femicide by performing the song and displaying photos of murdered Turkish women in front of the national assembly.[11] These performances made visible the scale of violence against women; at the same time, within mainstream discourse, the ability to stage these protests was held up as proof of gender equality. Together, governmental and mainstream media narratives implied a consensus on the ills of violence against women, shifting focus away from the call for more radically transformative political action.

We also consider the viral circulation of *Un violador* as an example of the commodification of leftist movements, wherein critique is minimized via the construction of the political as something to be purchased and consumed.[12] Within postpolitical governance practices, the political has been so thoroughly enmeshed with consumerism that political imaginations have been reduced to working almost exclusively within these frames. As Jodi Dean explains, "The individualization of politics into commodifiable 'lifestyles' and opinions" means that rather than collective struggle, politics is merely "consumer choices, that is, individuated responses to individuated needs."[13] The potential of collective political contestation is thus evacuated. In contrast to digital optimism about the democratic possibility of social media, scholars like Dean underscore how corporate platforms like Twitter/X and Facebook promulgate the commodification and individualization of politics. Further, theorists like Jonathan Crary and Dominic Pettman demonstrate how the push for constant media engagement renders our capacity for political action tenuous at best.[14]

The above perspectives provide a compelling framework that highlights the ways that activist movements become subsumed by politics as usual.[15] At the same time, this framework risks obscuring alternate lenses that can show how movements contribute in unanticipated ways to social transformation, including theoretical frameworks that attend to emotion and the body. As such, we read scholarship on postpolitics alongside affect theory and feminist theory to uncover tools for theorizing the political potential of the body, emotions, and movement.

Rupturing the Status Quo: Generating New Bodily Capacities

Our analysis builds on Jacques Rancière's discussion of politics as an activity that causes a rupture in the status quo by bringing to the fore that which is typically rendered invisible and unsayable. For Rancière, politics *(le politique)* is an orientation that "calls into question the divisions of common and private, visible and invisible, audible and inaudible."[16] Political action *(le politique)* challenges the established political order *(la police)* by operating outside the boundaries of accepted forms of governing, behaving, speaking, and moving.

We focus here on Rancière's theorization that politics engages participants in "new forms of collective enunciation, and in doing so invents 'new subjects' with new bodily capacities."[17] The aesthetic and sonic elements of *Un violador*—costumes, chanting, physical movement, and staging performances in front of governing institutions—transform participants into active subjects in the fight against sexual violence. As participants enact (and later reenact) the political performance, their synchronized movements challenge the gendered expectations of bodies in public space. As Deborah Martin and Deborah Shaw observe in their analysis of *Un violador,* the performance not only challenges "a systematic form of patriarchal, state-sanctioned rape culture" but also constitutes a break from "regimes that consign certain bodies to specific spaces and positions."[18] This generates a rupture in the status quo by bringing to the fore that which is typically invisibilized and rendered unsayable.

As we explore in our analysis, the particular gestures included in the choreography make visible participants' pain from sexual violence and anger toward the complicit state. These emotions and bodily sensations are central to constructing "new bodily capacities," and they emerge from moving in—and even from viewing—political art performances. Like Martin and Shaw, we see the "intense corporeality" of the performance as central to facilitating new configurations of the body and the collective that have the potential to resist dominant structures. Our analysis adds emotion to this figuration by connecting the ways bodies and feelings intertwine through movement. Together, corporeality and emotion extend as performers across the world replicate the original performance for local contexts.[19]

Emotions and embodiment are powerful tools in manifesting an alternative vision of the world. Drawing on Rancière, we view political art as a way to bring forth new ways to imagine the social order. Although he notes that art traditionally identified as political—that is, made with the express purpose of intervening in political discourse and practices—has limited power to enact change because of the divergence between an artist's intent and individual spectator reactions, he sees possibility in the ways that political art can reorient our sense of the world. By creating alternative views of society, he writes, political art can invoke new ways to achieve what he terms "radical equality," which involves the overturning of social hierarchies.[20] The possibilities of choreographed performance are particularly striking. Such performance evokes ways of feeling and moving that can shift participants' understanding of established identities, actions, and interactions in ways that are unpredictable and potentially emancipatory in their imagining of new ways of being.

We bring Rancière's theorization of "new bodily capacities" and political art into conversation with affect theory to consider how corporeal intensities might inspire investment in movements that envision a different future. In the next section, we draw on affect theory and movement studies to explore how coordinated and collective performance creates affective flows. We are especially interested in how these emotions can be mobilized toward future radical collectivities that center a critique of state violence in the struggle against sexual violence.

The Politics of Aesthetics, Affect, and Bodies/Movement

The so-called affective turn in the humanities has occurred partly as a response to the centrality of the text within much humanities scholarship. Focusing primarily on language to the detriment of materiality and the body has resulted in areas of study ripe for exploration. Affect theory asks us to theorize "beyond the perceived, the discrete, the formulised, to offer the potential to feel, to relate, and to move."[21] Within this broad assemblage of work, scholars have differentiated between feelings, emotions, and bodily sensations. Describing the distinction between key terms within affect theory, Eric Shouse notes that "feelings are *personal* and *biographical,* emotions are *social,* and affects are *prepersonal.*"[22] Along these lines, scholars like Brian Massumi suggest that affect refers to bodily sensations and intensities that are prelinguistic—goosebumps, for instance, or the rising of hairs on one's arm. In this sense, infants or those without language can experience affect.[23] By contrast, theorists including Sara Ahmed, Teresa Brennan, and Clare Hemmings define affect as social and cultural rather than a psychological or prediscursive state.[24] These scholars suggest that affects are forged within social environments and that they pass between bodies. Further, feminist scholars draw our attention to the ways that the affect/emotion binary is racialized and gendered. As

Linda Åhäll explains, the separation of affect and emotion reinforces a "binary, gendered logic between a mobile, impersonal, masculinized affect and a contained, feminized, personal emotion."[25] Moreover, such a dichotomy works to neatly contain and define what are complex and elusive phenomena that are not so readily pinned down.

Our use of the term affect aligns with the meaning delineated by Ahmed, for whom there is a blurriness between emotion and affect rather than a hard-and-fast distinction. Ahmed compares the popular separation between affect and emotions to an egg's yolk and white: "That we can separate them does not mean they are separate."[26] To avoid making analytical distinctions between bodily sensation, emotion, and thought, Ahmed uses the idea of the impression. When bodies interact with other bodies—or, for our purposes, with art—they form an impression that creates an affective association. She explains: "Emotions shape the very surfaces of bodies, which take shape through the repetition of actions over time, as well as through orientations towards and away from others."[27] In other words, emotions are social and cultural in the ways they are formed through repeated exchanges between people and various phenomena, including cultural artifacts. The more often impressions repeat, the more they resonate and become ingrained. By attending to emotions, Ahmed notes, we can "address the question of how subjects become *invested* in particular structures."[28] Critically, repetition is central to the political charge of *Un violador:* there is repetition in both the chanting and the movement, which contests the repetition of individualizing sexual violence. Simply put, *Un violador* uses *collective* repetition, in contrast to the insistent individualized repetition of victim blaming.

We see the political potential of affect and bodily sensations in the ways that feelings emerge from recurrent actions and how group performances can circulate and channel feelings among both physical and digital participants. For *Un violador* in particular, using the body collectively—becoming the body, the collective—directly challenges gendered and racialized state violence. This violence is structural, yet it is perpetuated in part by the aforementioned repeated insistence on individualizing antiviolence efforts. To contest such individualization and erasure, LASTESIS draws on women of color feminisms, including Latina feminisms, which center "practices of self and collective healing" in "deeply embodied" ways. Writes Mariana Ortega, "Latina feminism . . . is part of what Cherríe Moraga has aptly called a theory in the flesh."[29] For Moraga, the body is the site on which women of color experience the realities of racism, sexism, homophobia, and xenophobia. These experiences, she avers, must become the basis of feminist theory that pursues a vision of society that "can begin to heal our 'wounded knee.'"[30]

During *Un violador,* the bodily movement in and of itself defies "state-sanctioned rape culture" by virtue of the fact that it disobeys "regimes that consign certain bodies to specific spaces and positions."[31] The physical movement also generates an affective response for both performers and viewers. In tandem with the song's lyrics, which we analyze below, the vocalization of rage and collective choreographed movement function as a form of "muscular bonding."[32] This refers to the notion that moving together in unison as a collective generates "feelings of euphoria and connection to the group."[33] Whereas there are similar feelings of euphoria generated through collective street protest, muscular bonding suggests that there is something unique about moving in unison, in choreographed ways. Moreover, emotions function here as a bonding mechanism, with the choreography interpellating participants into a structure of feeling, one that generates collective rage and grief but also euphoria, solidarity, and connection. Traditional forms of protest certainly produce collective embodied feelings. Drawing on the work of French sociologist Émile Durkheim, Zeynep Tufekci describes how protests generate a "transcendent feeling of being part of something larger than oneself," or what Durkheim calls "collective effervescence."[34] We are compelled, however, by how simultaneous choreographed performance intensifies emotional movement such that participants and viewers are moved in multiple senses of the word.

By disrupting and destabilizing expected norms of behavior and movement, *Un violador* demonstrates the power of moving and movement, both literally and figuratively. It is this aspect—moving and being moved—that especially interests us, particularly when we consider what political possibilities emerge through mediated responses to the viral circulation of the performance.

Moving Bodies: Coordinated Movement and Embodied Knowledge

This section explores the connection between *Un violador*'s choreography and the specific emotions that are evoked by gesture, including feelings like pain and humiliation (squatting), solidarity (marching, fist pumping), and rage directed at the state (pointing). The choreography creates an affective structure of feeling, defined by Raymond Williams as a "pattern of impulses [and] restraints" that invites participants and viewers to imagine emergent political and cultural formations.[35] Repetition and movement, when performed as a group, connect participants to one another and to particular emotional intensities. This builds a collective structure of feeling that in turn shapes what that collective can imagine and enact.

One of the stated goals of LASTESIS is to articulate feminist theory through art, and particularly through choreographed bodies in motion. The founders write: "Art is the trench of struggle and resistance we have chosen. . . . We believe in the transformative potential of art and performance, of art *from* bodies and *for* male and female bodies, collectivised art, appropriated through common experiences."[36] For LASTESIS, corporeal movement both creates and translates the embodied knowledge of systemic oppression. *Un violador* in particular draws on the work of Argentine feminist anthropologist Rita Segado, whose research on violence against women in Latin America challenges the perception of sexual violence as an individual crime, reframing it as a socially sanctioned tool leveraged across institutions, from the political system to the police, to discipline women.[37] The original public performance of *Un violador*, with motions symbolizing both sexual violence and accusation, was staged in front of a courthouse, thereby shifting the site of encounter from the private realm to the political sphere.[38]

Moreover, when protesters who are read as women perform in public, they pose a challenge to the social order by complicating assumptions about how women should behave and how they take up space. In *Agency and Embodiment*, Carrie Noland describes repeated movements and gestures as "learned techniques of the body" that are "the means by which cultural conditioning is simultaneously embodied and put to the test."[39]

In the context of gender performativity, gestures reinforce patriarchal structures that teach women to shrink their bodies, minimize their movements, and stay quiet while, alternatively, teaching men to take up space and assert their voices. This is manifested in gestures such as hunched shoulders and crossed legs versus "manspreading" (sitting with legs far apart), for example. Staging the first performance of *Un violador* in downtown Santiago in front of government buildings underscores the historic marginalization of women in the public sphere. Moreover, reclaiming public space contests the layered nature of violence, first in terms of the act itself (rape, disappearing) and then the subsequent erasure of survivor experiences. As LASTESIS member Sibila Sotomayor Van Rysseghem explains: "[The streets] are spaces which have never fully belonged to women. They largely represent sites of vulnerability, and these vulnerabilities are intersectional and are linked to different forms of oppression. . . . Therefore it was important for us to use different strategies to make our demands visible in these public spaces and sites of violence."[40] For Sotomayor Van Rysseghem, there is power in being visible and taking up space in the public arena, especially one that enacts and obscures violence against women. Like Rancière, LASTESIS sees the political in acts that make explicit that which is foreclosed by the presiding order. As LASTESIS members made clear in an interview, their performance art works as a "barricade" meant to halt movement and interrupt the status quo, including the status quo of spatial regulation. By actively shifting the typical flows of presence and behavior in public space, LASTESIS draws our attention to how space is most often ordered, governed, and regulated.[41] This rearticulation of space transforms the public sphere from a site of gender-based violence such as public shaming and policing into a site for resistance. Choosing to do so through dance (as opposed to other types of public action designed to disrupt the flow of movement, such as sit-ins) underscores the power of repetitive and choreographed motion capable of bonding participants. Further, as Joshua Chambers-Letson has underscored, performance "can be a particularly rich site for minoritarian subjects to experiment with and produce new ways of being in the world and new forms of collective vibration, or resonance."[42] Through choreographed dance, *Un violador* brings into being, however evanescent, an embodied feeling of collectivity.

Because postpolitics often renders the public sphere politically futile, *Un violador* offers political potential by interrupting quotidian governing logics. By taking up space in public streets, chanting loudly, and moving their bodies in wide, sweeping gestures, participants in *Un violador* upend existing gender norms and fixed understandings of decorum and the democratic process. By disrupting the status quo and presenting a specific antagonism regarding the role of the state in perpetuating sexual violence, participants become what Rancière calls political or supplementary subjects. Such subjects "are not reducible to social groups or identities but are, rather, collectives of enunciation and demonstration surplus to the count of social groups."[43] These subjects enact politics by making visible the terror and pain of a common problem (in this case, sexual violence) that is shared between participants.[44] Through gestures and choreography enacted in public political spaces, participants make themselves visible as a collective of subjects who have been previously uncounted or unrecognized.

This kind of mutual recognition is a powerful rejoinder to the ways sexual violence survivors are accounted for by the state as individual victims. Patriarchal governing structures like the legal and carceral systems single out victims and obscure the commonalities that characterize experiences of sexual violence, including such victimization by the state. By banding together in a common performance, participants reject official documentation and instead count participants together to make visible shared feelings around sexual violence.

The repetitive gestures that comprise the minimalist choreography are designed to address the feelings and conditions associated with gendered violence. *Un violador*'s choreography begins with participants stepping and turning their bodies from left to right as they chant:

> El patriarcado es un juez
> que nos juzga por nacer,
> y nuestro castigo

es la violencia que no ves.
El patriarcado es un juez
que nos juzga por nacer,
y nuestro castigo
es la violencia que ya ves.

An English translation is as follows:[45]

Patriarchy is a judge
that judges us for being born,
our punishment
is the violence you don't see.
Patriarchy is a judge
that judges us for being born,
our punishment
is the violence you now see.[46]

The focus on visibility and what is seen and unseen is symbolized by the protesters' wearing of black blindfolds, which signify in multiple ways. The visual significance of blindfolds conveys the pain and humiliation of state-sanctioned violence against women in the Chilean national context; more broadly, they reference the ways sexual violence is concealed by the state (lyrics: "the violence you don't see" and "the violence you now see"). The blindfolds also refer to the hundreds of people who suffered eye injuries from rubber bullets and tear gas deployed by the Chilean riot police during the 2019–20 protests against increasing privatization (including the increase in public transportation fees) and growing social inequalities in Chile.[47] Moreover, LASTESIS uses blindfolds to represent the violence that took place at a torture site called Venda Sexy (Sexy blindfold) that was operated by Chilean secret police during the Pinochet dictatorship. Guards at the site blindfolded women detainees as they subjected them to rape and sexual violence.[48]

After the opening steps, the choreography shifts and the participants place their hands on their heads and squat down, a movement that is repeated after each line in the chant:

Es femicidio.
Impunidad para mi asesino.
Es la desaparición.
Es la violación.

In English:

It's femicide.
Impunity for my killer.
It's disappearance.[49]
It's rape.

The squatting movement is another reference to the abusive conduct by the Chilean national police, the Carabineros, during the 2019–20 protests. Although strip searching was banned in Chile in 2019, officers forced detainees to strip naked and squat while being searched at the police station. Human Rights Watch reports that during these encounters, there were cases of "police touching women's genitalia," rape, and murder.[50] When *Un violador* performers squat and chant about forms of state sexual violence disproportionally targeting female-presenting Chileans, they put it on display as an embodied trauma.

During *Un violador* performances, gestures that reference the abjected body—particularly the ways feminized bodies are systematically tortured and raped—invite participants and spectators into a painful structure of feeling. The collective participation and witnessing of gestures that signify the trauma of sexual violence breaks the individualized articulation of victim and perpetrator. Instead, the performance indicates the commonalities between survivors, particularly the corporeal and affective experience of violation. Watching reenactments of violations like being forced to squat and being strip searched can evoke feelings like pain and humiliation that bring spectators into a collective witnessing that makes visible that which has historically been hidden.

Further, the spectator ethics of *Un violador* transcend individual responsibility and place the burden of sexual violence on the state. This enables the performance to be read outside of the dynamics of trauma porn and instead as an entrance into the political. As Sara Ahmed writes, expressions of pain are "crucial not only to the formation of feminist subjects (a way of reading pain as a structural rather than incidental violence), but to feminist collectives, which have mobilised around the injustices of that violence and the political and ethical demand for reparations and redress."[51] Further, she explains that when testimonies about pain are brought into the public realm, the tenor shifts from feelings of individual hurt to a collective feeling that action is required. Though Ahmed warns that we should not "ontologise women's pain as the automatic ground of politics," we see feelings as powerful tools to create empathy and collective action that does not simply rely on identity and experience.[52] Jennifer Nash underscores this point in her historicization of Black feminist "love-politics," which insists on "transcending the self and producing new forms of political communities as a kind of affective politics."[53]

In the next verse of *Un violador,* the tempo picks up and performers march in place, pumping their arms while chanting:

> Y la culpa no era mía, ni dónde estaba ni cómo vestía.
> Y la culpa no era mía, ni dónde estaba ni cómo vestía.
> Y la culpa no era mía, ni dónde estaba ni cómo vestía.
> Y la culpa no era mía, ni dónde estaba ni cómo vestía.

In English:

> And the fault wasn't mine, not where I was, not how I dressed.
> And the fault wasn't mine, not where I was, not how I dressed.
> And the fault wasn't mine, not where I was, not how I dressed.
> And the fault wasn't mine, not where I was, not how I dressed.

During this segment, there is a tonal shift with quicker and more sustained coordinated movements. In the recording of the performance, encouraging shouts are heard from offscreen. Like the lyrics, the gestures here signify a change in focus from the experience of gendered violence to the collective power of moving in unison. The lyrical repetition offers a powerful rejoinder to victim blaming, and the coordinated arm and leg movements simulate marching, thereby underscoring the unity of the protesters who are taking up space in the public sphere. As LASTESIS member Lea Cáceres Díaz explains, the "performance allows us to make visible the combined power of our bodies."[54] Moreover, it is significant that the lyric here is singular—that is, the fault "wasn't *mine*"—despite the collectivity constituted through the movement. This inverts the typical formulation wherein sexual assault survivors are generalized with certain tropes (clothing, behavior) whereas perpetrators are often considered in relation to their individual circumstances, thus constructing them as sympathetic figures.[55]

After challenging survivor blaming, the performers implicate the spectator, social institutions, and systems of government in the proliferation of sexual violence:

El violador eras tú.
El violador eres tú.
Son los pacos,
los jueces,
el Estado,
el Presidente.
El Estado opresor es un macho violador.
El Estado opresor es un macho violador.
El violador eras tú.
El violador eres tú.

In English:

The rapist was you.
The rapist is you.
It's the cops,
The judges,
The state,
The president.
The oppressive state is a macho rapist.
The oppressive state is a macho rapist.
The rapist was you.
The rapist is you.

With each line, the performers reach out their arms and point. First, they point straight ahead at the audience with the lyrics "the rapist was you; the rapist is you," the change in tenses marking how sexual violence is ongoing. They point overhead to the left with "It's the cops," forward to the left at "the judges," and then circle their pointed fingers overhead while calling out "the state." They keep their hands raised while finally referencing "the president." During the next line, "the oppressive state is a macho rapist," the performers pump their fists in the air. To conclude, they return to pointing to the crowd during the refrain "the rapist is you." The audience is thereby implicated in state violence.

In one sense, the pointing in the performance could place spectators in the role of the *violador,* or at least as a passive participant within systems of violence against women. However, the structure of feeling cultivated in the performance involves collective guilt, pain, and anger. These complex feelings can pass between performers and spectators, invoking empathy and connection rather than detachment. Performance scholar Sophie Anne Oliver theorizes that the "corporeal politics of feminist performance art may . . . serve as a model for an ethics of seeing the traumatized body."[56] For Oliver, performances of trauma often elicit feelings such as guilt, disgust, and pain. These feelings encourage viewers to reflect on the ways they are complicit in dehumanizing practices.

The final gestures in the performance—pointing and fist pumping—exude rage. Critically, this feeling is directed outward at those complicit in the perpetuation of gendered violence. These expressions of anger are particularly generative as a basis for politics (as defined by Rancière) because outrage makes visible their collective demands and requires that something be done. In particular, the affective sensation of being angry is energizing and motivates movement toward a different kind of world. As Ahmed writes, "If anger pricks our skin, if it makes us shudder, sweat and tremble, then it might just shudder us into new ways of being; it might just enable us to inhabit a different kind of skin."[57]

Elsewhere, we have argued that the performance of feelings like pain, solidarity, and anger create a sense of "feeling in common" that can serve collective healing.[58] Describing the online work of #MeToo participants, we write, "By creating a public archive of emotional responses to trauma—

what Ann Cvetkovich calls a 'trauma culture'—participants forge 'ways of living' and 'structures of feeling' that provide emotional justice for sexual trauma . . . beyond incarceration and the state, privileging care and restorative forms of healing and justice."[59] Collective feeling, in other words, is a means toward healing and building coalitions that can challenge the postpolitical status quo. In addition to healing, the embodiment of feelings through coordinated movement provides avenues for a different way of imagining the relationship between the state and its citizens. As Carrie Noland explains, beyond the semiotic meaning of gestures, the texture and velocity of movement "exceeds communicative or instrumental projects."[60] Though gestures are socially conditioned, the embodied act of producing them inspires variation. For Noland, it is this potential for variation that can lead to broader interventions in cultural practice.

The state's inability to capture the variations of bodily movement and emotional excesses makes them difficult to neutralize and subject to the realm of the postpolitical. In this sense, it is not simply the subversive gestures in *Un violador* that pose a challenge to rape culture and state-sanctioned violence; the sensory experience of moving one's body can also alter and reorient the ways that participants perceive and navigate their relationship to the state in ways that are difficult to police. In *Living a Feminist Life,* Ahmed describes how years of gender socialization and heteropatriarchal violence sediment in the body: "Being girl is a way of being taught what it is to have a body: you are being told; you will receive my advances. . . . To become girl is to learn to expect such advances, to modify your behavior in accordance; to become girl as becoming wary of being in public space; becoming wary of being at all."[61] Collective movement in public space, then, can be a momentary means to interrupting the affective and corporeal impact of a lifetime of microaggressions and violence. Emotions shape the body, and bodily repetition shapes emotions. Further, somatic affects are heightened when performed in unison. It is significant that *Un violador* centers physical movement. With the performance, individual bodies enter into a collective that counters and transcends the physical violence of rape through the body's remobilization into collective choreographed movement. After the performers of

Un violador use coordinated dance steps to convey the pain, solidarity, and rage associated with institutionalized sexual assault, the feelings linger.

Residual affects provide an afterlife for protests that cannot easily be predicted or predetermined. In many ways, the performance and its critique could be easily subsumed into the dominant order. As Rancière notes, when collective identities are formed, they are often folded into existing societal norms and evacuated of their political potential through the act of naming.[62] In the case of sexual violence in Chile, the state neutralizes dissent by claiming consensus around the ills of rape while making little change to the patriarchal practices of police and politics that enable widespread sexual assault. But emotions linger, flowing from one body to the next in both physical and virtual spaces, making the issue of sexual assault more difficult to eclipse.

Moving Online: Virality and Social Media Circulation

Moving from the street performance to digital circulation, *Un violador*'s affective resonances underscore the political potential of emotions, particularly given that a common response to the video of the original *Un violador* performance—goosebumps—cannot be policed.[63] As noted above, scholars like Jodi Dean have challenged the fetish of digital space as inherently democratic. For her, the flow of affect on social media is indeed part of the flow of communicative capitalism, where everything can be folded back into a sweep of content made profitable for capital. Certainly *Un violador* and its digital uptake could be seen as simply being folded back into the dominant order. However, despite efforts to contain affect (or, in Dean's formulation, for it to meld back into the flow), it lingers and provides an afterlife that cannot be predicted or predetermined.

Without lapsing into an uncritical celebration of social media and its political possibilities, we are compelled by the mediation of affect in a feminist context. Describing the significance of affect to social media, Jussi Parikka writes, "Affect travels and is constantly rematerialized in different signifying and asignifying contexts. Affect mobilizes. Secondly, as it mobilizes, affect is constantly channelled, educated, intensified. We are one particular carrier of affect that becomes a motor of social actions, including politically meaningful ones."[64] The inability (at present) to completely capture and contain affect, even in the realm of social and digital media, marks it as a site of political possibility. As we have detailed, *Un violador* is collective, embodied political action that generates ways of knowing—bound up with affect—for both participants and spectators in real time. But what of those who watch the performance online—asynchronously and at a distance? Exemplifying Parikka's claim that social media provides an "afterlife for affect," the comments on the *Un violador* YouTube page underscore the strong emotional response to the performance. In particular, commenters describe feelings of pride, happiness, pain, and healing as well as physical sensations like shivers, lumps in throats, and goosebumps. Here we can see the limits of language to describe what Chambers-Letson writes "is incommunicable. . . . Freedom as just a feeling is fugitive from linguistic capture. In this way, it's not unlike sound."[65] Likewise affect.

Descriptions of feeling moved, with its attendant physical sensations, are prolific in the comments. For instance, one commenter writes, "cada que veo estos videos lloro automáticamente, gracias infinitas por todo lo que hacen" ("every time I see these videos I cry automatically, infinite thanks for everything you do").[66] Others note, "Se me eriza la piel. Me encanta" ("My skin bristles. I love it").[67] One wonders how the simplicity can be so impactful: "Como una performance tan 'simple' puede tener tanta fuerza. El vello de punta" ("How can such a simple performance be so powerful? Goosebumps").[68] "Qué tremendo lo que hicieron, fue extraordinario se me erizaron los pelos, es histórico y trascendente, es un orgullo de las mujeres que tenemos en Chile cómo luchan por sus derechos. Una sugerencia con respecto a las mujeres desaparecidas, hacer una perfomance por ellas contra la prensa y TV todas de derecha en Chile que callan ocultan y prohiben como lo hacían en la dictadura" ("What a tremendous thing they did, it was extraordinary, my hair stood on end, it is historic and transcendent, it is a source of pride for the women we have in Chile as they fight for their rights. A suggestion regarding the disappeared women, to make a performance for them against the press and all right-wing TV in Chile that keeps silent, hides and prohibits as they did in the dictatorship.") The global circulation of the video is evident in comments like this one from a Turkish viewer who also mentions a sensory response: "this is extremely powerful, i got goosebumps watching it. love from this turkish sister right here. hope all you beautiful people are doing well ♡."[69] "Sigo escuchando esta canción! Es un maravilloso himno, es tan potente que me vienen los escalofríos eschuchándolo. Abrazos desde Italia ♡" (Translation: "I keep listening to this song! It's a wonderful anthem, it's so powerful that I get chills listening to it. Hugs from Italy ♡)."[70] These comments are representative of viewer response, forming what Ringrose and Mendes call "mediated affective solidarities" wherein intensities forge connection.[71] As the comments underscore, the aesthetics of the performance (including its music) create an affective force that remains intact even as the performance circulates online.

Although feelings of anger and rage are evident in the performance, they are strikingly not prevalent in the comments section. Rather, viewers emphasize feelings of hope, solidarity, joy, and sadness, as well as feeling seen and supported. This transformation of rage into feeling moved underscores the political possibilities of emotion, particularly when feelings of identification and support are expressly counter to the isolation and invisibility (illustrated in the performance by blindfolds) that characterize sexual violence.

The Political Possibilities of Affect

Given the demands of social media's attention economy and its reliance upon continuous flows of content, the digital circulation of the performance is not altogether remarkable. A politics of visibility via social media attention is in fact one of the hallmarks of what Sarah Banet-Weiser terms "popular feminism," a highly mediated and individualized feminism that invests in rather than challenges communicative capitalism.[72] However, our focus on embodied movement and affective flows, both in person and on social media, highlights the political possibilities of collective feeling. As we have suggested, the performance and its circulation moved beyond digital space by generating emotions, and in turn by sparking further embodied action.

Un violador thus provides a vital case study of both feminist performance and media activism as well as an important addition to scholarship on the postpolitical. *Un violador*'s differences from #MeToo, which also made sexual violence widely visible but was not oriented as a systemic challenge of the status quo (nor did it articulate sexual violence as state violence), highlight how *Un violador* expands our notion of the political. Unlike #MeToo, which focused on individual responsibility and policy reform, *Un violador* provides a systemic critique that is embodied in collective emotional expression and movement. By attending to the political possibilities of emotion—specifically emotion generated in and through bodies in choreographed motion—we have sought to address a lacuna in the literature. *Un violador* prompts us to ask what possibilities are available when one is moved or moving; what, in other words, do the goosebumps prompted by the performance suggest for how we might move beyond the quotidian discipline not just of neoliberalism but also heteropatriarchy? Goosebumps are prelinguistic and also political; a nerve is being touched. As *Un violador* demonstrates, there is significant possibility in ungovernable sensation, which is inseparable from emotion.

Notes

1. Deborah Martin and Deborah Shaw, "Chilean and Transnational Performances of Disobedience: LASTESIS and the Phenomenon of *Un violador en tu camino*," *Bulletin of Latin American Research* 40, no. 5 (2021): 712.

2. See, for instance, Juan Gabriel Valdés, *Pinochet's Economists: The Chicago School of Economics in Chile* (Cambridge: Cambridge University Press, 1995); Naomi Klein, *The Shock Doctrine: The Rise of Disaster Capitalism* (New York: Picador, 2007); and David Harvey, *A Brief History of Neoliberalism* (Oxford: Oxford University Press, 2005).

3. BBC News, "Gabriel Boric: From Student Protest Leader to Chile's President," December 20, 2021, www.bbc.com/news/world-latin-america-59694056.

4. See Astra Taylor, *Democracy May Not Exist, but We'll Miss It When It's Gone* (New York: Metropolitan, 2019).

5. Joshua Chambers-Letson, *After the Party: A Manifesto for Queer of Color Life* (New York: NYU Press, 2018), 4.

6. See Julie Wilson, *Neoliberalism* (New York: Routledge, 2018), especially chapter 6, "Enterprising Democracy: Neoliberal Citizenship and the Privatization of Politics." See also Aihwa Ong, *Neoliberalism as Exception: Mutations in Citizenship and Sovereignty* (Durham, N.C.: Duke University Press, 2006).

7. See, for example, Jodi Dean, *Blog Theory: Feedback and Capture in the Circuits of Drive* (Malden, Mass.: Polity, 2010).

8. Japhy Wilson and Erik Swyngedouw, "Seeds of Dystopia: Post-politics and the Return of the Political," in *The Post-political and Its Discontents: Spaces of Depoliticisation, Spectres of Radical Politics,* ed. Japhy Wilson and Erik Swyngedouw (Edinburgh: Edinburgh University Press, 2014), 7.

9. Monika Cvorak, "'A Rapist in Your Path': Chilean Protest Song Becomes Feminist Anthem—Video," *Guardian,* December 6, 2019, www.theguardian.com/world/video/2019/dec/06/a-rapist-in-your-path-chilean-protest-song-becomes-feminist-anthem-video; Lara Gómez Ruiz, "*Un violador en tu camino,* la canción chilena que ya es un himno feminista mundial," *Vanguardia,* December 6, 2019, www.lavanguardia.com/cultura/20191205/472068241496/un-violador-en-tu-camino-cancion-chilena-himno-feminista-mundial.html; and Charis McGowan, "'Our Role Is Central': More than 1m Chilean Women to March in Huge Protest," *Guardian,* March 6, 2020, www.theguardian.com/world/2020/mar/06/chile-womens-day-protest.

10. Matías Vega, "Ministra Plá destaca performance de Las Tesis y recibe ola de críticas en redes sociales," *BiobioChile,* December 4, 2019, www.biobiochile.cl/noticias/nacional/chile/2019/12/04/ministra-pla-destaca-performance-de-las-tesis-y-recibe-ola-de-criticas-en-redes-sociales.shtml.

11. "Turkey's Women Lawmakers Stage 'Rapist Is You' Protest," *Deutsche Welle,* December 15, 2019, www.dw.com/en/turkeys-women-lawmakers-stage-las-tesis-rapist-is-you-protest/a-51684425.

12. See Sarah Banet-Weiser, *Empowered: The Rise of Popular Feminism and Popular Misogyny* (Durham, N.C.: Duke University Press, 2018).

13. Jodi Dean, *Democracy and Other Neoliberal Fantasies: Communicative Capitalism and Left Politics* (Durham, N.C.: Duke University Press, 2009), 11.

14. Jonathan Crary, *24/7: Late Capitalism and the Ends of Sleep* (London: Verso, 2013); and Dominic Pettman, *Infinite Distraction: Paying Attention to Social Media* (Malden, Mass.: Polity, 2016).

15. Here we are referring to "politics" primarily in an electoral sense, as in the watering down of more radical critique into existing structures that remain unchanged.

16. Jacques Rancière, "Introducing Disagreement," trans. Steven Corcoran, *Angelaki: Journal of the Theoretical Humanities* 9, no. 3 (2004): 6.

17. Jacques Rancière, *Dissensus: On Politics and Aesthetics* (London: Continuum, 2010), 139.

18. Martin and Shaw, "Chilean and Transnational Performances," 714.

19. Rose Minutaglio, "How a Chilean Chant Became the World's Most Powerful Feminist Anthem," *Elle,* February 13, 2020, www.elle.com/culture/career-politics/a30858742/las-tesis-chilean-chant-feminist-anthem.

20. Jean-Philippe Deranty and Alison Ross, eds., *Jacques Rancière and the Contemporary Scene: The Philosophy of Radical Equality* (London: Continuum, 2012).

21. Tony Sampson, Stephen Maddison, and Darren Ellis, "Introduction: On Affect, Social Media and Criticality," in *Affect and Social Media: Emotion, Mediation, Anxiety, and Contagion,* ed. Tony Sampson, Stephen Maddison, and Darren Ellis (New York: Rowman & Littlefield, 2018), 31.

22. Eric Shouse, "Feeling, Emotion, Affect," *M/C Journal* 8, no. 6 (2005), journal.media-culture.org.au/0512/03-shouse.php; emphasis in the original.

23. Shouse.

24. See Teresa Brennan, *The Transmission of Affect* (Ithaca, N.Y.: Cornell University Press, 2004); Clare Hemmings, "Invoking Affect: Cultural Theory and the Ontological Turn," *Cultural Studies* 19, no. 5 (2005): 548–67; and Sara Ahmed, *The Cultural Politics of Emotion* (Edinburgh: Edinburgh University Press, 2014).

25. Linda Åhäll, "Affect as Methodology: Feminism and the Politics of Emotion," *International Political Sociology* 12, no. 1 (2018): 36–52.

26. Ahmed, *Cultural Politics,* 210.

27. Ahmed, 4.

28. Ahmed, 12; emphasis in the original.

29. Mariana Ortega, "Speaking in Resistant Tongues: Latina Feminism, Embodied Knowledge, and Transformation," *Hypatia* 31, no. 2 (2016): 315.

30. Cherríe Moraga, "Entering the Lives of Others: Theory in the Flesh," in *This Bridge Called My Back: Writings by Radical Women of Color,* 3rd ed., ed. Cherríe Moraga and Gloria Anzaldúa (Berkeley, Calif.: Third Woman, 2002), 21.

31. Martin and Shaw, "Chilean and Transnational Performances," 714.

32. William McNeill, *Keeping Together in Time: Dance and Drill in Human History* (Cambridge, Mass.: Harvard University Press, 1995).

33. Stephen Johnson, "'Muscular Bonding': The Strange Psychological Effects of Moving Together," *Big Think,* November 18, 2020, bigthink.com/the-present/muscular-bonding.

34. Zeynep Tufekci, *Twitter and Tear Gas: The Power and Fragility of Networked Protest* (New Haven, Conn.: Yale University Press, 2017), 89.

35. Raymond Williams, *Politics and Letters: Interviews with New Left Review* (London: New Left, 1979), 159.

36. "The LASTESIS Collective. Practices for the Feminist Revolt," Museo Nacional Centro de Arte Reina Sofía, Madrid, October 23, 2021, www.museoreinasofia.es/en/activities/lastesis-collective-practices-feminist-revolt; emphasis in the original.

37. Eugénia Palieraki, "'The Rapist Is You': Origins of a Worldwide Feminist Movement," modified January 30, 2020, ideas4development.org/en/the-rapist-is-you-origins-of-a-worldwide-feminist-movement.

38. *Un violador* shares similarities with protests by Argentinian women that began in the 1970s during the military dictatorship of Jorge Videla. *Madres de La Plaza de Mayo* (Mothers of the Plaza de Mayo) protested their disappeared children *(desaparecidos)* in part by gathering in public space. See *Las Madres: The*

Mothers of Plaza de Mayo, dir. Susana Blaustein Muñoz Lourdes Portillo (1985), www.lourdesportillo.com/las-madres.

39. Carrie Noland, *Agency and Embodiment: Performing Gestures/Producing Culture* (Cambridge, Mass.: Harvard University Press, 2009), 2.

40. Canela Laude-Arce, "How Chilean Performance Collective Las Tesis Is Growing a Global Feminist Movement," *shado,* December 20, 2021, shado-mag.com/all/how-chilean-performance-collective-las-tesis-is-growing-a-global-feminist-movement.

41. Statz Tatsumi Saines, "Artist Profile: LASTESIS," *Artists at Risk Connection,* February 2020, artistsatriskconnection.org/story/lastesis.

42. Chambers-Letson, *After the Party,* 167.

43. Rancière, "Introducing Disagreement," 6.

44. Participants share concern over sexual violence, though not necessarily the experience of sexual violence.

45. English translation from Camilla Soldati, "'The Rapist Is You': The Chilean Protest Song against Gender Violence that Sparked a Global Movement," *Lifegate,* December 17, 2019, www.lifegate.com/the-rapist-is-you-un-violador-en-tu-camino.

46. The final line can also be interpreted as "the violence you already see."

47. "Santa Fe gritará 'El violador eres tú,' la canción feminista chilena que se volvió viral en el mundo," *Aire Digital,* December 2, 2019, www.airedesantafe.com.ar/santa-fe/santa-fe-gritara-el-violador-eres-tu-la-cancion-feminista-chilena-que-se-volvio-viral-el-mundo-n136937.

48. Martin and Shaw, "Chilean and Transnational Performances," 721.

49. In Spanish, this also signifies the *desaparecidos/as,* translated as "the disappeared," as a government tactic in the dirty wars in Latin America in the 1960s, 1970s, and 1980s, where dissenters were detained, killed, and thrown into mass graves. See Peter D. Rush, "Dirty War Crimes: Jurisdictions of Memory and International Criminal Law," in *The Hidden Histories of War Crimes Trials,* ed. Kevin Heller and Gerry Simpson (Oxford: Oxford University Press, 2013): 367–84.

50. Human Rights Watch, "Chile: Police Reforms Needed in the Wake of Protests," November 26, 2019, www.hrw.org/news/2019/11/26/chile-police-reforms-needed-wake-protests#.

51. Ahmed, *Cultural Politics,* 172.

52. Ahmed, 173.

53. Jennifer Nash, "Practicing Love: Black Feminism, Love-Politics, and Post-intersectionality," *Meridians* 19 (2020): 441. According to Nash, affective politics describes "how bodies are organized around intensities, longings, desires, temporalities, repulsions, curiosities, fatigues, optimism, and how these affects produce political movements (or sometimes inertias)" (441).

54. Laude-Arce, "How Chilean Performance Collective."

55. This is, of course, racialized, with white perpetrators accessing sympathy or support.

56. Sophie Anne Oliver, "Trauma, Bodies, and Performance Art: Towards an Embodied Ethics of Seeing," *Continuum* 24, no. 1 (2010): 120.

57. Ahmed, *Cultural Politics,* 175.

58. Allison Page and Jacquelyn Arcy, "#MeToo and the Politics of Collective Healing: Emotional Connection as Contestation," *Communication, Culture and Critique* 13, no. 3 (2019): 338.

59. Page and Arcy, 339.

60. Noland, *Agency and Embodiment,* 2.

61. Sara Ahmed, *Living a Feminist Life* (Durham, N.C.: Duke University Press, 2017), 26.

62. Rancière, "Introducing Disagreement," 7.

63. It is worth noting that emotional AI, where AI trains to recognize human emotion, is currently a site of immense corporate interest.

64. Jussi Parikka, "Introduction to Part II," in Sampson, Maddison, and Ellis, *Affect and Social Media,* 65–66.

65. Chambers-Letson, *After the Party,* 39.

66. Sofía Valdez, comment on Colectivo Registro Callejero, "Performance colectivo Las Tesis *Un violador en tu camino,*" YouTube, November 26, 2019, www.youtube.com/watch?v=aB7r6hdo3W4.

67. Giuliana Moscoso, comment on Colectivo Registro Callejero, "Performance colectivo."

68. TVC, comment on Colectivo Registro Callejero, "Performance colectivo."

69. Min Yoongi, comment on Colectivo Registro Callejero, "Performance colectivo."

70. Laura Capobianco, comment on Colectivo Registro Callejero, "Performance colectivo."

71. Jessica Mendes and Kaitlynn Ringrose, "Mediated Affect and Feminist Solidarity: Teens Using Twitter to Challenge 'Rape Culture' In and Around School," in Sampson, Maddison, and Ellis, *Affect and Social Media,* 174.

72. Banet-Weiser, *Empowered.*

CHAPTER 4

Thinking Jacques Rancière with Ursula K. Le Guin

Aesthetics and Politics in a Postpolitical Age

ROBERT P. MARZEC

This chapter explores the work of Jacques Rancière, specifically the affiliations he carves out between aesthetics and politics, and considers these affiliations in relation to Ursula K. Le Guin's short story "Direction of the Road." Le Guin's short story deals with the rise of modern technology in the Anthropocene and its impact on the environment. In tracing technology's gradual colonization of the spatial and temporal modes of existence, Le Guin illuminates in an uncanny fashion Rancière's engagement with the tensions that surround aesthetics and politics in a postpolitical world. More specifically, Le Guin's story aestheticizes Rancière's identification of the postpolitical as a phenomenon of the anti-ideological fantasy of unlimited growth. For Rancière, the postpolitical is identified in the form of what he names policing, and in terms of its renouncement of future promises—that is, of utopian gestures that point toward new orders and a new community telos that would suggest that the current conditions of existence are not what they should be. In place of these promises, governments assign themselves the single task of unending expansion. In this end-of-history moment, politics "henceforth view[s] itself as the art of steering the ship and embracing the waves" as "the natural, peaceful movement of growth, of that production which reconciles the Greek *phusis* with the everyday art of pushing forward one step at the time."[1] For Le Guin, this renouncement of future promises in favor of a wholesale commitment to growth appears in the form of a certain mode of technological development, specifically manifested in her story in the form of the automobile. Le Guin crafts a polemical aesthetic in which we see a self-destructive technological order unfold in a slow but violent process that fully reappropriates and transforms the realm of human perception. In this appropriation, politics ceases to exist and aesthetics is militarized in the process of being transformed into a mechanical tool of representation. To articulate the full significance of connecting these two thinkers to the question of aesthetics and politics in the face of postpolitical forces, I begin with a brief discussion of Rancière's critique of the postpolitical and his conception of politics and aesthetics, then move to an analysis of Le Guin's politicoaesthetic intervention.

In *On the Shores of Politics,* Rancière offers an extensive critique of the postpolitical regime. As articulated above, the postpolitical can be identified as the embrace of a present no longer divided by a promise that we need to break with the present in order to achieve a different future. This absence of a temporal division—that is, of a political recognition that the politics of the present have to change—is also "matched by a *space* freed of division."[2] In other words, because the present is no longer in need of any fundamental political transformation, those living in the present no longer need to be fundamentally divided from one another. Hierarchical divisions of inequality exist, of course, but the postpolitical regime lacks the kind of ontological division that would call for the reformulation of the very stage of existence. With this absence of a temporal division that would demand a different historical landscape thus comes a correlational absence of a spatial division that might have formerly been manifested in terms of radically different political parties. Though they might disagree on how to control the flow of wealth and resources, libertarians, Republicans, and Democrats, for instance, are not divided when it comes to their embrace of neoliberalism. Moreover, many of those concerned about climate change or species extinction, who might consider themselves to be more in line with a left green politics, still embrace the neoliberal growth models of "sustainable development." Even the apparent political struggles undertaken in the name of sexual and racial justice, as Todd May points out, are "passive politics" or a "passive equality" orchestrated by governments responding to "special interests."[3] Demanding those interests does not require any radical change in the political system itself, only that one may operate within the system more equitably. Such passive political demands for equality are ultimately "the creation, preservation, or protection of equality by governmental institutions."[4]

Put differently, the end of history (of the need for a transformation of what is into a different historical future) brings about an end to ideology (political divisions in the polis). Because the regime of what is (considered to be no regime) need only grow, its focus is wholly on the production and circulation of itself. As May points out, this is precisely why neoliberalism promotes the "end of politics": the "economic will attend to the needs formerly pressed in the political sphere."[5] Henceforth, the idea of "the center" begins to dominate as the new configuration of this post-political arena—the site where the new consensus is built.[6] The power of this new center lies in its characterization of anyone attempting to pose alternatives (promises of a different future), and any immense effort to offer a different space, to be impotent or mad. Any political candidate who might suggest an otherwise to what is, by offering promises for a better future, is both anachronistic and dishonest—dishonest in the sense that no one who is honest can live up to the massive, system-changing efforts required to make a different future possible. We have only to look to the inaction on climate change for an example. And we need only observe the reactions from both liberals and conservatives characterizing one another (and by extension all politicians) as manipulators that never live up to their promises. The postpolitical reigns because it pits "the men of the promise never kept [against] the men of dynamism who always move forward."[7] There is thus a defensive element in the postpolitical perpetuation of dynamic growth, manifest in the condemnation of the challenger advocating change.

Coupled to this postpolitical perpetuation of dynamic growth—of "potency"—is an authoritative power. To ensure that the dynamism of always moving forward not be challenged, the leader of growth must condemn anyone standing in opposition, and do so with the authority of the *auctor:* the "master of words," the "guarantor" who uses words "to unite people" and "pacify by virtue of a strength that precedes the exercise of power."[8] Rancière calls the *auctor*'s invocation of this power "the clinching moment": "the moment when the move from potency to power has to be made, when potency's mere display must be transformed into the proof of capacity and the right to power."[9] This power is of a very specific kind. It evinces itself as the "opposite of a promise": "the candidate-president promised nothing but the worst—namely upheaval and civil war."[10] In this moment, the new postpolitical politics is transformed into the "art of suppressing the political."[11] Its fundamental character is pacification: "To diminish politics is . . . to reduce it to its function as a pacifying procedure between individuals and collectivity. . . . It is to remove the symbols of political division in the interests of expansion, of society's inherent dynamism."[12] The *auctor*'s threat of civil war replaces the democratic politics of the *demos* with the angry mob of the *ochlos:* the "figure of the *ochlos,* which is not the disordered turbulence of the many but the hare-driven rallying around the passion of the excluding One."[13] *Ochlos* is "the howling of the pack," the chaotic, tumultuous, unpredictable angry mob as opposed to the common people of the democratic populace.

Conversely, the *demos* is "the people," "the gathering of men of no position" who, despite their lack of position, have the fundamental right to freedom like anyone else: "The people are nothing more than the undifferentiated mass of those who have no positive qualification—no wealth, no virtue—but who are nonetheless acknowledged to enjoy the same freedom as those who do."[14] As an essential claim of equality for all, *demos* thus names two essential elements: first, the refusal to be incorporated and unified according to a hierarchized state system, which attempts to assign everyone an identity based on rank; and second, the resistance to the call to a pure anger, which is the goal of the leader-*auctor* who wishes to incite the violence of the unified one against the other (an act that would split the demos and transform equality into the right only given to an "us" at war with a "them" undeserving of equality). The pure or primal anger of *ochlos,* in other words, has nothing at all to do with equality or democracy. The crowd of the *demos* is thus essentially different from the mob of the *ochlos,* for the *demos* is the claiming of freedom and equality for the entire community—a quality shared by anyone and everyone. The pursuit of democratic equality, therefore, is not an act of unifying around the one against the other but the act of leveling all assigned identities and hierarchies that allows for the equality of all. Following Rancière, we might say that the postpolitical is thus a smokescreen for the bringing to an end of the *demos*—that is, the end of democracy and the claim to equality.

How does this conception of the political connect to the realm of the aesthetic? First, for Rancière, politics and aesthetics, despite their heterogeneity, are singularly related. The two are linked in and through what Rancière calls "the distribution of the sensible" *(partage du sensible).*[15] The sensible refers both to what is made available to the senses and what is considered to make sense within a particular regime. But as Yves Citton articulates, the sensible also refers to a crucial element: the subject's "*capacity* to sense."[16] The human capacity to sense and take in new sensations is by nature an active process, and the more a subject "gain[s] in sensitivity" the more they gain "the power to act."[17] This, Citton argues, is "the founding moment of political subjectification": "whether I stand in front of a work of art or am involved in a social movement, the possibility of politics rests on [the] moment when I am led to reconfigure the *partage du sensible* I have inherited from the majoritarian norm."[18] In the expansion of sensibilities, one acquires the capacity to dissent from and reconfigure the established distribution of the sensible. The sensible thus names both an aesthetic formulation and a political resistance to established aesthetic formulations in and through the experience of different aesthetic formulations. The distribution of the sensible is where politics and art cross paths. A work of art, for instance, has the capacity to call normalizing hierarchies of language, storytelling, and representation into question and name them as unequal distributions of power—despite the fact that a work of art does not walk out into the streets and start a political movement. The distinctive power of a work of art lies elsewhere, in its ability to manifest inequalities in the "distribution of the sensible."[19] The work of politics involves the direct confrontation of power, but it does not invent speculative situations and characters on a journey exploring the ontological nature of reality and the creative imagining of alternative futures. Despite these differences, each meets in the act of confronting the limits of representation and representational orders.

We can sharpen the connection between the two by specifying that aesthetics and politics are both interventions in the order of things. Both make possible, from very different locations, a conception of politics as the act of an intellectual emancipation grounded in the nonpositive radical equality of all intelligences. In what I've articulated above, we see how Rancière identifies the postpolitical as essentially an erasure of politics. But what does Rancière mean by politics, precisely? In *Disagreement: Politics and Philosophy,* Rancière makes a stronger distinction between the pseudopolitics of the postpolitical and the democratic struggle for equality found in politics proper in the following manner. The pseudopolitics of the postpolitical he names, after Foucault, "policing" politics—that is, the surveillance and administration of identities in order to ensure that each identity is associated with doing a task at a specific time and in a specific place. The worker, for instance, is associated with the time and the place of the factory. The time and place of the factory, which gives the worker little time for anything else, constitutes the identity of the worker. Temporally, the worker has no time for getting involved in, let alone understanding, the complexities of policymaking; spatially, the worker is cut off from the location of policymaking, which takes place in sanctified capital buildings far from the worker's location.

In opposition to postpolitical policing politics, Rancière defines genuine politics as the refusal to be incorporated into a social collectivity "that assigns ranks and identities."[20] Genuine politics amounts to an undoing of all locating and assigning an identification. Put differently, it is the resistant claiming of an equality of any and all to do anything and everything. In *Disagreement,* Rancière will articulate politics as the naming of a "wrong," the lack of equality, by the "part of those who have no part."[21] The naming of a wrong is the act of calling out the assigning of identities as none other than the erasure of the equal capacity to resist assignation and to struggle for political transformation (working in a factory *and* demanding a livable life for all in Congress). Politics in this sense is a disruption of the positions people are assigned in their sociopolitical order.

Conversely, aesthetics disrupts the sensible and what is made sensible to a public. In that disruption, a properly aesthetic act undermines the common and generalized social distribution of how things are imagined, accomplished, and crafted. Aesthetics questions the nature of the realm of the sensible, its ontology, and its historicity. It involves a reimagining of the ontological composition of the sensible register of human material and cultural existence: "Artistic practices are 'ways of doing and making' that intervene in the general distribution of ways of doing and making as well as in the relationships they maintain to modes of being and forms of visibility."[22] Aesthetics relates directly to the ontological character of social existence—the relationships that exist, the being of these relationships, who relates to whom, how one is made visible, how one is seen by others. This is another way of saying that Rancière thinks aesthetics as an event that takes intervention as its single rationale. An aesthetic event intervenes in the distribution of the forms of visibility given to a community and disrupts how the general schema distributes certain forms of visibility differently and unequally across the arena of existence. In the same sense, a properly political act, according to Rancière, is an intervention that would change the very framework that predetermines how things are set up and made to work. It is in this fashion that Rancière argues that there is "an 'aesthetics' at the core of politics."[23]

However, this aesthetics still differs primordially from politics, for aesthetics maintains a unique relationship to creativity. The stage, Rancière suggests, is a site of public activity but also the "exhibition-space for 'fantasies'" meant to trouble accepted identities, the spaces to which these identities are assigned, and the duties, roles, and activities associated with these identities. Literature performs the same function, for it presents us with characters who may or may not perform their designated roles in the cultural and political order of reality, or characters who may inappropriately wander off without any identifiably reasonable justification. Art, therefore, "disturbs the clear-cut rules of representative logic that establish a relationship of correspondence at a distance between the sayable and the visible."[24] Politics and aesthetics therefore meet to the extent that art hopes to forge new forms of existence, and politics struggles to form a new distribution of bodies by overturning an entrenched, naturalized order of accepted sensibilities. Aesthetics has the power to delink us from the sensible ideas to which we cling. As such, it makes possible a space for a new community and a new sense of existence.

The "part of those who have no part" are the people of the *demos*, and the wrong they claim is the equality of all that is hidden within a system in which everyone is assigned a position and told to do only those tasks associated with those positions. As Davide Panagia phrases it, this *demos* is suppressed in and through a set of authoritative judgments defining political access that arises from a "prepolitical authority that qualifies the dividing line of political participation."[25] The "wrong" being done to this part of those given no part is the exclusion that keeps them in nonexistence when it comes to policymaking. Rancière thus fundamentally offers us an affiliative politics, one that occurs in and through the eruption of a part who have no part that challenges the oligarchical procedures of the institutionalized socioeconomic reality: "Politics exists when the natural order of domination is interrupted by the institution of a part of those who have no part."[26] It is in this sense that politics occurs with the appearance of this part of those who now enter the arena precisely by naming the wrong of not having been given a part. Those who already have a position, a part, and a role assigned to that part within the social realm are thus essentially committed to a postpolitical world, because it is in their interests to stay where they are and continue to access the wealth and privilege associated with the position they occupy. Thus, "the part of the rich," for instance, "has only ever said one thing, which is most precisely the negation of politics: there is no part of those who have no part."[27]

Aesthetics is a way of intervening in the given ontological stage on which reality is allowed to unfold. More specifically, art imagines new worlds, and the humanities, in relation to art, considers how those new imaginaries might influence a culture to build a new world. In and through this act of intervention, art meets the political at the crossroads of the established distribution of subjects and objects. In the case of literature, a work of fiction partakes, as Rancière argues, in an intransitive use of language that defines itself as anticommunicational (art for art's sake, for instance); but in and through that anticommunicational act, it enacts a different communication—one not available within the established confines of cultural and political existence. This tension between literature's own exclusive materiality and the communication of that uncustomary materiality forms the basis of what we might call an aestheticopolitical act. In *The Politics of Literature*, Rancière makes it clear that this anticommunicational or antirepresentational act is fundamentally different from the modernist paradigm, which sought to define genuine art as that which breaks art from every form of representation. An art that transcends any form of representation mystifies its complex historical, cultural, and political affiliations. Such a notion of art is itself an unacknowledged proleptic product of the very historical and particularly Western cultural phenomenon of the postpolitical. In what might be the ultimate paradox, the isolation of art from politics in the years after World War II in the United States was itself the product of substantially funded political efforts. As Frances Stonor Saunders reveals in *Who Paid the Piper? The CIA and the Cultural Cold War,* the CIA spent considerable money subsidizing humanities efforts in the Western world in an attempt to promote those artists and endeavors that understood the humanities to be a project carried out in the name of democratic values (read American liberalism and capitalism) and a specific notion of freedom as apolitical, which in turn was designed to counter the kind of direct political action art was thought to undertake in communist Russia.

Alternatively, for Rancière, the work of art, far from backing away from an encounter with the political, is a function that expresses the desire to fundamentally transform the nature of the political as currently staged. Rancière puts it this way:

> The historic distinctiveness of literature is not due to a state or specific use of language. It is due to a new balance of the powers of language, to a new way language can act by causing something to be seen and heard. Literature, in short, is a new system of identification of the art of writing. A system of identification of an art is a system of relationships between practices, the forms of visibility of such practices, and the modes of intelligibility. So it is a certain way of intervening in the sharing of the perceptible that defines the world we live in: the way in which the world is visible to us . . . and the capacities and incapacities that reveal themselves accordingly.[28]

Literature, or the use of literary language, enables something to be seen and heard that was not seen or heard before. A literary work confronts existing modes of intelligibility and challenges the customary nature of those modes in order to bring different relationships, practices, and forms of visibility to bear against that intelligibility—in the hopes of producing new forms of thinking and knowing. It identifies the limitations of our perceptibility by bringing into existing frameworks previously unimaginable. It identifies our structural problematics (if Rancière wouldn't mind my reference to Althusser's signature concept here) and brings forth new capabilities.[29] Literature, as an intervention in the realm of the perceptible and the capable, thus constitutes a political intervention in the realm of existing human capacities, and the roles we assign ourselves according to these capacities. As Peter Hallward puts it, politics is politically "staged" in theater-like moments when a people act "at a distance from themselves."[30] Such moments of mimesis confound "the order of function and place" and open "the door to what Rancière will . . . describe as the virtual program of politics as such."[31] Nowhere is this reorchestration of the perceptible, of human capacities and the roles we assign ourselves, and the frameworks we impose on human potential thematized more beautifully than in Ursula K. Le Guin's short story "Direction of the Road."

"Direction of the Road" is an exemplary literary artifact from the early contemporary period of social science fiction. It was published a mere six years after May 1968, after Rancière had begun to formulate his extensive critique of Althusser (his first major work, *Althusser's Lesson,* was published the same year as Le Guin's story). "Direction of the Road" tells the story of an old oak tree experiencing the gradual but violent rise of technological modernity from the early years of the 1900s into the later part of the mid-twentieth century. It is the story of growth—a certain technological growth orchestrated around speed and efficiency manifested in the form of the automobile and its eventual widespread adoption by humans. It is also a story of the rise of a form of human subjectivity that would come to rule the new technological world, in part making possible the rise of a postpolitical world. In the process, we witness how this technological growth eventually results in the transformation in the human distribution of the sensible, here in the triple sense of the term sensible: in what is made available to the senses, in what the senses can recognize, and in what makes sense on the register of intelligibility. In this redistribution of the sensible, we come to understand how a postpolitical world comes into existence. We also recognize in the process how the postpolitical comes to severely affect the environment and the futures of species' lives. The story lays bare the essential connection between an evolving system of meaning and a coevolving loss of visibility organically linked to the rise of the new distribution of the sensible brought about by the automobile.

The story is told not from the standpoint of a human but from the standpoint of an oak tree. In that simple shift of representation—which moves the authority over meaning outside of the human colonization of representation—Le Guin unhinges the established order of who has the right to speak and who is never considered for that right. In this sense, the story exemplifies the fundamental right to language, speech, and argument by those considered incapable of using language properly—by "the part of those who have no part," of those never given access to the realm of speech and meaning making.

In the opening line, the oak tells us: "They did not use to be so demanding. They never hurried us into anything more than a gallop, and that was rare; most of the time it was just a jigjog foot-pace. And when one of them was on his own feet, it was a real pleasure to approach him. There was time to accomplish the entire act with style."[32] In this simple reversal of perspective, Le Guin sets up the rich aesthetic framework of the story—an aesthetics based on a paradoxical coupling of nonmovement with a kind of sedentary movement that begins with a desire to connect across species lines. Such a conception of movement is meaningless to the human and entirely beyond the realm of human perception. The oak obviously never moves, yet in and through a desire for connection, the oak enacts its being by "approaching" humans "with style" as they come near. This is the oak's form of "communicating," which occurs in an embodied and progressive series of spatiotemporal movements. This is also to say that for the oak, communication is made possible in and through the living act of relation. The tree "greets" humans by looming larger and larger as they approach, then gradually shrinking as they walk away: "I'd approach him steadily but quite slowly, growing larger all the time, synchronizing the rate of approach and the rate of growth perfectly, so that at the very moment that I'd finished enlarging from a tiny speck to my full size—sixty feet in those days—I was abreast of him and hung above him, loomed, towered, overshadowed him. Yet he would show no fear" (267). This activity of greeting is what the oak takes to be its work. In other words, the oak takes connection and relation to others as an ethical imperative. This work ethic constitutes its raison d'être. The "style" of this sedentary movement is designed to show solidarity and build rapport: in the presence of the immensity of the oak, the human shows "no fear" and is invited to further potential connection. The communicative act is one of patience, of an unhurried buildup of trust. It bespeaks a relationship of safety, of care, interest, and even protection: "Sometimes on a hot afternoon one of the adults would stop me right there at our meeting-place, and lie down with his back against mine for an hour or more" (267). The oak makes possible the act of dwelling, in the full Heideggerian sense of the term. It opens a relationship grounded in "gathering" and "safeguarding."[33] The milieu of this safeguarding event is made possible by the oak's ethical commitment to relation. A space grounded in the freedom to relate without violation comes into existence because of the oak, which functions as a bridge between worlds.

We quickly come to understand that the oak is telling this story retrospectively. The reference to being "hurried" in the opening line refers to the mode of existence that comes to take dominion after the introduction of the motorcar. When the motorcar first makes its appearance on the road, the oak assumes it to be a new kind of "creature" but quickly understands it to be a "making" like the carts hitched to horses (268). The motorcar arrives every day at four in the afternoon and returns at five to go in the opposite direction. In this moment, the oak, standing at the side of the road, is forced to "grow" and "diminish" on a "regular schedule" (269). The imposition of a regular schedule brings a new sense of responsibility different from the oak's former responsibility, which was grounded in the creation of a nonpressured, open milieu devoted to gathering and safeguarding. The motorcar does not seek shelter or interest of any kind in the tree. It does not seek or make an open space of gathering possible. In fact, gathering is a concept utterly alien to its being. This is made apparent in the perspective of the driver of the car, who does not even register the tree in his vision. His vision is instead focused on the narrow confines of the road—it is focused, to invoke the title of the story, on the direction of the road.

As the motorcar begins to take dominion, the set of relations established by the oak between human and nonhuman beings starts to subside. The car's noise "over[rides] all voices, even the voice of the song-sparrow" the oak gives a home to (269). Gradually, more cars appear on the road—cars that move faster and faster. The oak has "scarcely time to loom" (270). The cars become more and more common, quickly establishing themselves, as if an invasive species, as "a major feature of the local Order of Things" (270). This invasion brings with it a concurrent transformation in the ecosystem itself: increased traffic demands road "improvements." The road itself becomes the new primary (technologicoanthropocentric) ecosystem, requiring that it be expanded and widened. The growth of the road, brought about by the growth of traffic, subsequently affects the biodiversity of species that formerly crossed the road with little trouble: "grasshoppers, ants, toads, mice, foxes" (270). Unsurprisingly, the cars bring death to many of these creatures.

Soon there are so many cars traveling in opposite directions that the oak must "develop a new level of skill": "I had to go two directions at once" (271). The oak's attempt to maintain relation forces it into a schizophrenic form of mobility, having to grow and diminish at the same time in order to continue its relation to each and every motor vehicle. The oak asks us to fully face this exhausting existence:

> have you ever considered the feat accomplished, the skill involved, when a tree enlarges, simultaneously yet at slightly different rates and in slightly different manners, for each one of the forty motorcar drivers facing two opposite directions, while at the same time diminishing for forty more who have got their backs to it, meanwhile remembering to loom over each single one at the right moment: and to do this minute after minute, hour after hour, daybreak till nightfall or long after? (271)

The aesthetics crafted here by Le Guin reveal a hyperactive modernity, delinked from its former spatiotemporal relations. The escalating appearance of so many motorcars signals the rise of an automatic, self-organizing commitment to growth. This growth is by no means comparable to any notion of growth before, for it demands a leveling of the sensible to the point at which only the direction of the apolitical road is perceptible. In this fixation on the road, which is an asphyxiation on a certain form of progress, we see the grounds being laid for a post-political reality.

The oak makes this diminishment of visual perception and intelligibility starkly clear: "Very few of the drivers bothered to look at me, not even a seeing glance. They seemed, indeed, not to see anymore" (271). This is more than a simple narrowing of focus. The oak here tells us that the very essence of seeing has changed. "Seeing" formerly named the act of taking the diversity of things in, of an exploratory survey of one's environment, with the goal of establishing relations. Seeing was an event of gathering, of establishing a network of connections between the human and a heterogeneous world of other elements and entities. The opening of the story exemplifies this ontological dimension of seeing. The oak describes the connection, curiosity, and safeguarding enabled by a human form of seeing that recognizes the inherently relational nature of its being. In this new order, however, the oak as a compassionate relational being disappears from human perception. In fact, perception itself changes dramatically. In Rancière's terms, the distribution of the sensible has shifted, which in turn has reduced the capacities of human existence. The act of seeing is no longer the event that gives rise to relation; it has become a derivative requirement—a necessary compulsion for the primary task of driving. Put differently, seeing itself is secondary to driving—to the new growth of the motorcar industry. The eyes are entrained on the road and thus all else is thrown into oblivion. The oak understands this to be a static existence, a "delusion of progress": "They seemed to believe they were 'going somewhere'" (271). A relation to ecosystem complexity is erased in favor of a monotonous fixation.

This unidirectional, hyperactive growth continues for another half century, until an event occurs that fiercely delinks the oak from its capacity to take on its responsibilities. One of the drivers whose "need to 'go somewhere' was exceptionally urgent" crashes into the oak and dies (271). Le Guin maintains the aesthetic frame, which requires that we reverse all intention and agency toward the oak: "the urgent car totally violated the Direction of the Road, swinging it round to North–South in its own terms, and so forcing me to leap directly at it. I had no choice. I had to move, and move fast—eighty-five miles an hour. I leapt: I loomed enormous, larger than I have ever loomed before. And then I hit the car. . . . The driver had no time to say anything; I killed him instantly" (273). This reversal, made possible by Le Guin's politicoaesthetic, should not be dismissed as clever storytelling. We have seen from the beginning of the story that in giving the tree intention and agency, the realm of the perceptible changes its coordinates, bringing into vision what humans cannot see. As such, Le Guin's aesthetic constitutes a political act, in the full sense that Rancière uses that term: as the naming of a wrong by the part of those given no part. But of greater importance is the fact that the withdrawal of agency from the human points to an even more troubling change in the ontological character of human existence.

The widespread adoption of the automobile demonstrates more than a simple reduction of the human field of vision. It transforms the human sensory act of vision entirely, and consequently the forms of intelligibility made accessible to human awareness and thought. The sorely contracted field of vision required by constantly looking at the road ahead constitutes a new form of sensory rationality, one not only unidirectional but also antirelational. This antirelational unidirectionality generates in turn a new reality for human existence. Le Guin stages this ontological transformation in the death scene that brings the story to a conclusion. The importance of this moment is emphasized in the telling manner in which the oak expresses an ethical anger greater than that of the killing of the driver:

> It is not [the killing] that I protest. I had to kill him. I had no choice, and therefore have no regret. What I protest, what I cannot endure, is this: as I leapt at him, he saw me. He looked up at last. He saw me as I have never been seen before, not even by a child, not even in the days when people looked at things. He saw me whole, and saw nothing else—then, or ever.
>
> He saw me under the aspect of eternity. He confused me with eternity. And because he died in that moment of false vision, because it can never change, I am caught in it, eternally.

> This is unendurable. I cannot uphold such an illusion. If the human creatures will not understand Relativity, very well; but they must understand Relatedness.
>
> If it is necessary to the Order of Things, I will kill drivers of cars, though killing is not a duty usually required of oaks. But it is unjust to require me to play the part, not of the killer only, but of death. For I am not death. I am life: I am mortal.
>
> If they wish to see death visibly in the world, that is their business, not mine. I will not act Eternity for them. Let them not turn to the trees for death. If that is what they want to see, let them look into one another's eyes and see it there. (273–74)

Let me emphasize what the oak tells us in this moment. It is not the killing that the oak finds an outrage; it is the new structure of the (human) realm of the sensible. This new structure transforms the entire horizon of what makes sense to humans. Sense and sensing are reduced to the demand of identification. Whereas seeing was formerly an act that enabled relationality, invitation, and connection, it has now become a form of policing, an act in which entities are forced to testify, to show their credentials to the new necessities of human reality, so that one may establish them as a potential threat to this new order of existence. The oak is no longer a being that enables extensive relation to all beings in existence; the oak is now a threat to a single species—a species that now claims dominion over the heterogeneity of the world. The oak takes on a peerless identity that separates it from all other entities in existence. Human language, which has changed from an embodied act of creating and associating, is now a tool for mechanistic and militaristic representation. The oak has been transformed into a fundamental threat to human existence, such as that circumscribed human existence has become.

The oak, in identifying this new human perception as a "false vision," makes both a political and ethical claim. It is ethical in the sense that it names the wrong imposed by the new human order that destroys relation. It is political in the sense that it identifies the erasure of the oak as a rich and complex being that offers shelter and the space for humans to expand their field of knowledge and reality. It is ethical, more specifically, in the resistance to the humans' branding of the oak's very being in their reidentification of the oak as the immorality of a death that destroys all human potentiality. It is political, more pointedly, in its confrontation with the new human—the being, that is, that deflects its own insanity onto other beings, whereas it might better be served by seeing that insanity as generated from their new world order: "Let them not turn to the trees for death. If that is what they want to see, let them look into one another's eyes and see it there." The transformation of the identity of the tree into a threat to human existence is a fantasy entirely generated by the new human perceptual problematic. The environment is recast not as the source of life but as a threat to human development and the new human existence. The environment has become the cause of death.

Lest we think this engagement with Le Guin's four-decade-old story is little more than a charming act of literary criticism, we have only to direct our attention to the current realities of ecological degradation proceeding apace after years of legislative efforts to turn the tide. If the oak of this story were alive today, it would be telling us that the United States loses thirty-six million trees annually as a result of urbanization and road development and expansion.[34] The idea that trees must be eliminated for highway construction and billboard advertisement dominates road development.[35] Of more concern, the construction of roads in forested areas causes extensive damage to local wildlife, often leading to extirpation. Animals suddenly change their behavior patterns in response to traffic noise, putting them at risk of moving into predator habitats.[36] Roads also facilitate the spread of invasive species, cause death to animals in vehicle strikes, and become sources for chemical runoff that affects water quality. Ultimately, roads lead to more roads, and subsequently to more deforestation. As we have learned through satellite Landsat data accumulated over the course of decades by NASA, roads have introduced significant deforestation throughout the Amazonian rain forest, making formerly isolated regions more accessible to poaching, mining, and illegal logging.[37]

Le Guin's symbolic break with the human as narrator and as tragic hero allows us to see what humans cannot see and cannot think: the ontology of other species, and the destruction of their lifeworlds. The radical nature of this symbolic break enables us to see in an unconventional manner the rise of the postpolitical and its disavowal of the forms of recognition that would enable humans to comprehend the nature of the ontological transformation they are undergoing. That transformation occurs with the rise of a rigid and contracted technological orientation, one that constructs a new human subjectivity delinked from political concerns. This peculiar type of human—the human of individualism, industrialization, and capitalism—will ultimately reach its completion in the Anthropocene human, who is the being who acts as a geological force, changing biogeochemical forces across the planet for centuries to come. Democracy and equality are not a part of this new human distribution of the sensible. Le Guin's politicoaesthetic act of shifting language and meaning making to the oak, however, brings literature back into the realm of democracy and the struggle for an equal right to existence. As Rancière argues, democracy names a break with the order of sovereign representation. The joining of literature and democracy makes democracy a politics for "anyone at all, no one in particular, no social authority guaranteeing the power of discourse."[38] In this sense, Le Guin extends democracy to the far reaches of the nonhuman world. It would be a mistake to quickly dismiss the narrating oak as mere personification, and a fatal error to identify it as anthropomorphism. By making the oak the narrator of the story, Le Guin shifts the realm of representation and speech to the part of those no longer or never given a part. The oak reveals the incremental overturning of an entire world order. We see the gradual replacement of whole ways of being, ways of relating, ways of seeing, and ways of thinking. Le Guin's story signals the ontological shift from a human civilization that holds a rich set of relations of curiosity and care with an environment to one in which the human loses those relations in the process of being increasingly overwhelmed by a more aggressive disposition. Growth takes dominion as an essential necessity of human existence, and in that postpolitical development, proleptic of the rise of neoliberalism, the oak speaks to us from beyond the horizon of our knowledge, offering us a polemical warning: we have left behind our former human aesthetic, political, and democratic capacities, and we have only one another to blame.

Notes

1. Jacques Rancière, *On the Shores of Politics,* trans. Liz Heron (London: Verso, 1995), 4–5.
2. Rancière, 6.
3. Todd May, *The Political Thought of Jacques Rancière: Creating Equality* (Edinburgh: Edinburgh University Press, 2008), 1.
4. May, 3.
5. May, 45.
6. Rancière, *On the Shores,* 6.
7. Rancière, 8.
8. Rancière, 10.
9. Rancière, 8.
10. Rancière, 8. Rancière is specifically referring here to the French election of 1988 between François Mitterrand and Jacques Chirac, in which Mitterrand was on the verge of losing to Chirac before invoking the antipromise of civil war.
11. Rancière, 11.
12. Rancière, 11.
13. Rancière, 31.
14. Jacques Rancière, *Disagreement: Politics and Philosophy,* trans. Julie Rose (Minneapolis: University of Minnesota Press, 1999), 9, 8.
15. Jacques Rancière, *The Politics of Aesthetics,* trans. Gabriel Rockhill (London: Continuum, 2004), 12.
16. Yves Citton, "Political Agency and the Ambivalence of the Sensible," in *Jacques Rancière: History, Politics, Aesthetics,* ed. Gabriel Rockhill and Philip Watts (Durham, N.C.: Duke University Press, 2009), 122.
17. Citton, 122.
18. Citton, 123.
19. Rancière, *Politics of Aesthetics,* 12.
20. Rancière, *Disagreement,* 32.
21. Rancière, 9.
22. Rancière, *Politics of Aesthetics,* 13.
23. Rancière, 13.
24. Rancière, 15.
25. Davide Panagia, *Rancière's Sentiments* (Durham, N.C.: Duke University Press, 2018), xii.
26. Rancière, *Disagreement,* 11.
27. Rancière, 14.
28. Rancière, *Politics of Literature,* 7.
29. See Louis Althusser, *Reading Capital,* trans. Ben Brewster (London: Verso, 1979), 25–26.
30. Peter Hallward, "Staging Equality," in Rockhill and Watts, *Jacques Rancière,* 143.

31. Hallward, 144.

32. Ursula K. Le Guin, "Direction of the Road," in *The Wind's Twelve Quarters* (New York: HarperCollins, 1975), 267.

33. Martin Heidegger, "Building, Dwelling, Thinking," in *Basic Writings,* ed. David Farrell Krell (New York: HarperCollins, 1977), 352, 355.

34. David J. Nowak and Eric J. Greenfield, "Declining Urban and Community Tree Cover in the United States," *Urban Forestry and Urban Greening* 32 (2018): 32–55.

35. See Nathan Bowe, "Tree-Cutting Plans on Scenic Highway 34 Have Locals Up in Arms," *Detroit Lakes Tribune,* January 11, 2022, www.dl-online.com/tree-cutting-plans-on-scenic-highway-34-have-locals-up-in-arms; David Baron, "In Florida, Billboards Trump Trees," *All Things Considered,* NPR, September 2, 2008, www.npr.org/2008/09/02/94023551/in-florida-billboards-trump-trees; and Laura Williamson McCafferty, "Beauty and the Beast: How the Billboard Industry Makes Money by Chopping Down the Public's Trees," Scenic America, 2007, www.scenic.org/wp-content/uploads/2019/09/beauty_and_the_beast1.pdf.

36. See Kevin Boston, "The Potential Effects of Forest Roads on the Environment and Mitigating Their Impacts," *Current Forestry Reports* 2 (2016): 215–22; and Edelin Jean Milien et al., "Roads, Deforestation, and the Mitigating Effect of the Chico Mendes Extractive Reserve in the Southwestern Amazon," *Trees, Forests, and People* 3 (2021): 1–7.

37. Kasha Patel, "Building Roads in the Congo Rainforest," Earth Matters (blog), NASA Earth Observatory, November 27, 2019, www.earthobservatory.nasa.gov/blogs/earthmatters/2019/11/27/building-roads-in-the-congo-rainforest-photo-story.

38. Rancière, *Politics of Literature,* 12.

CHAPTER 5

Wayward Possibilities

Errant Black Women and the Intimacies of Freedom

MATTHEW SCULLY

> "Power" in the general sense is therefore not only a name, but a catachresis. Like all names it is a misfit. To use this name to describe a generality inaccessible to intended description is necessarily to work with the risk that the work "is wrested from its *proper* meaning," that it is being applied "to a thing which it does not *properly* denote" *(OED)*. We cannot find a proper place—it must be effaced as it is disclosed.
>
> —Gayatri Spivak, "More on Power/Knowledge"

> Being black and female licensed every brutal act. In the face of all of this what could one do, but refuse the categories?
>
> —Saidiya Hartman, *Wayward Lives, Beautiful Experiments: Intimate Histories of Riotous Black Girls, Troublesome Women, and Queer Radicals*

The plantation, Jim Crow, incarceration, policing—these systems of gendered racial capitalism in the United States have consistently worked to guarantee that narratives of progress conceal the fact that there has been no progress at all. In *Scenes of Subjection,* Saidiya Hartman famously refers to emancipation as a "nonevent."[1] More recently, Rinaldo Walcott develops a notion of the "long emancipation" to account for the fact that "emancipation is a legal process and term that . . . marks continued unfreedom, *not* the freedom it supposedly ushered in."[2] Black studies therefore teaches that emancipation, as it is named by the Emancipation Proclamation (1862) and then by the Thirteenth Amendment (1865), ought to be read as a postpolitical operation that empties politics of its force and substance. Postpolitics refers to the specific form of depoliticization through which the political—in this instance a contestation over equality and freedom for Black subjects—is replaced by a consensual mode of governance that maintains the inequality and unfreedom consigning Black life to a space of abjection.[3] Such logic is there on the surface, as when the Thirteenth Amendment bans slavery and involuntary servitude, "except as a punishment for crime." Since "black personhood remains legible primarily as criminality" in the United States,[4] this emancipation can only be read as a fantasy, one that works to appease the political demands for an equality and a freedom that would overthrow the white supremacist superstate of the United States. Both Hartman and Walcott thus eviscerate the "as if" structure of abstract equality under liberalism: "The fragile 'as if equal' of liberal discourse inadequately contends with the history of racial subjection and enslavement, since the texture of freedom is laden with the vestiges of slavery, and abstract equality is utterly enmeshed in the narrative of black subjection, given that slavery undergirded the rhetoric of the republic and equality."[5] Because postpolitics names a logic by which the political becomes occluded through processes of repression, disavowal, and/or foreclosure, the "nonevent" of emancipation seems to be an exemplary instance of postpolitics in the Americas. Because slavery functions as one foundation for, and ongoing condition of, modernity, we might say that we have always been living within a postpolitical age.[6] However asymmetrical and uneven, however inadequate as "a form of *suture*," those gathered by this "we" live under the consensus of unfreedom, albeit in radically different ways.[7] Postpolitics ensures the perpetuation of forms of consensus that undermine, in advance, acts of political dissensus that might threaten the order of things.[8] Yet the discourses of postpolitics and those of Black studies have, for the most part, remained separate.

There are numerous reasons for this separation, but Calvin Warren's strong critique of politics offers one explanation for this missed conversation. Focusing on the metaphysical anxiety introduced by the figure of the free Black in the nineteenth-century United States, Warren insists that "neither progressive legislation nor political movements have been able to transform black ~~being~~ into human being, from fleshless bodies to recognized ontologies."[9] Politics, in Warren's analysis, which ought to be renamed policy, appears merely as "the symptom of this tense metaphysical structure" such that "we must look elsewhere for the essence of politics, law, and culture."[10] Warren continues, "One cannot think the free black within an antiblack world without resorting to the fantastical and the absurd."[11] Anti-Blackness forecloses the subjectification introduced by the signifier "free Black" such that to occupy this catachrestic position means to experience psychosis. Whiteness offers the only position of freedom in an anti-Black structure by disavowing its own catachrestic status to posit itself as an ontologically stable position.

In this turn to psychoanalytic language, I am not merely suggesting an analogy between the structure of the psyche and that of society; nor am I suggesting that one can psychoanalyze social phenomena. I reference psychosis because of its dependence, especially in Lacanian theory, on processes of foreclosure that precisely explain the problem of anti-Blackness, thereby revealing the mutual imbrication of the political and the psychical. Black Lives Matter protests must keep occurring because, according to the hegemonic order, Black lives do not matter to the United States except as material to be used (up). Black Lives Matter aims to resist the commodification and fungibility of Blackness that appear structurally pervasive because there is no signifier of Blackness in the symbolic order that can account for anything other than anti-Black formulations. In other words, Black lives are literally and symbolically "expelled" from civil society through a process of foreclosure:[12] there is no signifier for Black life from the point of view of anti-Blackness.[13] The lack of such a signifier means that "black ~~being~~ incarnates metaphysical nothing, the terror of metaphysics, in an antiblack world."[14] For Warren, the free Black figures racial psychosis because it names a delusional subjectivity: the free Black cannot have being in an anti-Black world. Black people are reduced to a "function," that of guaranteeing, via their incarnation of nonbeing, the being of whiteness.[15] Or, to take Walcott's example, the (false) narrative of abstract equality promised by the legal fiction of emancipation disavows equality and freedom. More fundamentally, as Warren makes clear, it forecloses the Black subject. This emphasis on psychosis and foreclosure changes the grammar of W. E. B. Du Bois's infamous question,

"How does it feel to be a problem?"[16] Turning this question back on the objective structure of the anti-Black world, Warren might be said to be asking of the social order, via the figure of the free Black, "How does it feel to produce the problem?" For the anti-Black world, in its construction of whiteness through the negating foreclosure of Blackness, produces the metaphysical crisis of the human.

I foreground Warren's critique because it offers perhaps the strongest challenge to politics as policy in the context of Black studies, and this challenge makes explicit the notion that politics as usual actually functions as what Jacques Rancière renames "the police."[17] Given the political problem of subjectification in Rancière, of a nominalization that calls forth something new and impossible into being within the order of things, Warren's critique of politics suggests the need for another operation to challenge postpolitical foreclosure. Rather than recuperate liberal politics, we need, following Warren's critique, an alternative form of politics. One such alternative appears in Rancière's theory of politics as dissensus. Rancière renames what often goes by the name of politics as the police, and in opposition to this police order, Rancière theorizes political subjectification as "the production through a series of actions of a body and a capacity for enunciation not previously identifiable within a given field of experience, whose identification is thus part of the reconfiguration of the field of experience."[18] Black Lives Matter protestors taking to the streets or Black women given voice and sensation in Saidiya Hartman's *Wayward Lives, Beautiful Experiments* refuse, in their dissensually embodied practices of appearing, the logic by which white supremacy expels and suppresses Black life.[19] Rather than a conflict between identitarian positions, which would return to postpolitical occlusion, as outlined by Warren, such a reconfiguration of politics as dissensus introduces "the anxiety of antagonism" that "precipitates" a "narrative crisis."[20] Frank B. Wilderson III controversially insists on a fundamental difference between *"legible conflicts"* of positions and "*illegible antagonisms* of Blacks" that in fact subtend such conflictual positions.[21] These antagonisms are illegible because the (whitened) symbolic order has expelled the signifier that would make them legible. The foreclosed element that has been expelled from the symbolic order—for Warren, the free Black—reappears in the real. The

Black political subject thus appears as antagonistic because the dominant order cannot bear its presence. Wilderson helpfully glosses such an unbearable encounter when he argues that the condition of Black suffering offers a problem with "no imaginable strategy for redress—no narrative of social, political, or national redemption."[22] Liberal reforms, in other words, offer no solution to the problem of anti-Black violence. Wilderson's turn to narrative reveals that the appearance of antagonism ruptures the representational and aesthetic norms of the police order. If the police order insists on consensual narrative practices that work to foreclose the threat of dissensus, what specific aesthetic practices enable or inaugurate the unbearable political procedures that might embody such a threat? What styles of narrative stage the unimaginable?

This question subtends Hartman's *Wayward Lives, Beautiful Experiments: Intimate Histories of Riotous Black Girls, Troublesome Women, and Queer Radicals,* the very title of which links the anarchic practices of waywardness with the aesthetic of the beautiful. Hartman's title thus announces a conjunction of wayward living and an aesthetic in a gesture toward that which escapes the consensual impositions of a police order that cannot bear the intimacies and excesses characteristic of style.[23] Style is precisely that which cannot be fixed, and as such, style figures and keeps open a potentially anarchic impulse threatening to a post-political order that presents itself as totalizing and stable. Throughout her text, Hartman focuses on catachrestic subjects, whose Blackness, queerness, and errancy marks them as unrepresentable within the dominant order. Lee Edelman defines catachresis as "the trope which coins a name for a still unnamed entity, which gives face to the faceless."[24] Catachresis "names what is otherwise nameless."[25] In an anti-Black order, Black freedoms—of movement, existence, or sexuality—can only appear as catachreses, for such freedoms appear unnamable the moment they become decoupled from whiteness. Where Edelman foregrounds the role of catachresis in queer theory, R. A. Judy recognizes its centrality within Black studies. The African-Arabic slave narrative, Judy argues, exposes "the catachresis at work in the biological misnomer of race," such that "Negro" reads as "a misapplied metaphor."[26] Yet precisely because catachresis punctures the matrix of the symbolic and imaginary orders, it offers a potential way to disturb the racial regimes of representation. "A catachresis ruptures the field of representation, given that it lacks a literal referent," argues Warren, and because of this rupturing force, "catachresis provides a way out of" the impasse of representation, "since it *creates a fantastical place* for representation to situate the unrepresentable."[27]

Catachresis functions as an organizing figure for Hartman's political aesthetic precisely because the political project of Hartman's *Wayward Lives* lies with its rupture of the representational field. Rather than offer either a narratively or a representationally "integrationist" framework, as one finds in liberal narratives of progress, Hartman develops a catachrestic series of scenes that disturb any normative framework readers might hope to impose.[28] That is, the Black women of *Wayward Lives* continually exceed the frame, and this excess figures a freedom that appears by severing the cohering efforts of the symbolic and imaginary orders to suture dissensus. Hartman's political project manifests not only in the content of her narration but also at the level of her style. For Rancière, where politics "works on the whole" to construct "new collectives"—the proletarian, the free Black—literary dissensus "consists in creating new forms of individuality that dismantle the correspondences established between states of bodies and meanings."[29] To trace the appearance of this dissensus, I focus not on the archival work of *Wayward Lives,* its practices of citation, or its inclusion of photographs and visual culture, but on the rhetorical and figurative movements of the text that invent and imagine new modes of freedom, especially the "beautiful experiments" included in the third and final section of the book.[30] The Black women who appear in this section—including Esther Brown and Mabel Hampton—exemplify Hartman's broader project in their intimate revolts against the anti-Black order that seeks to govern their errant and anarchic lives.

So how does Hartman's work speak to questions of postpolitics? To some extent, this chapter produces the very kind of *mésentente* it describes by putting Hartman and Black studies into the same frame as Rancière and postpolitics.[31] By doing so, I do not aim to align the two or resolve their tensions; instead, I hope, following the logic of *mésentente,* to construct a dissensual aesthesis that reconfigures each of them.

The postpolitical, or what Rancière names postdemocracy, designates a tautological construction that systematically prevents in advance the possibility of surprise: only certain political actors are allowed to appear; only certain affects, sensations, and bodies can be accounted for. Hartman develops what she terms in a prefatory "Note on Method" a "close mode of narration" to describe and figure dissensual voices and experiences of "errant" Black women that rearrange hegemonic narratives that exclude them (xiii). Hartman's "close mode of narration" works "by describing the world through their eyes" and thus offers an account of figures deemed unaccountable by dominant narratives (xiii). In her concluding response to the *Journal of African American History* book forum on *Wayward Lives,* Hartman describes this narrative style as "the entanglement of narrator and character" that

> made palpable what was shared, the dreams and aspirations that bridged a century of wayward practice, the long history of gender trouble and sexual variance, aesthetical Negroes inventing possibility and trying to make art of life. It was also an attempt to collapse the subject-object divide, topple the hierarchy of reason, and enact other ways of knowing and doing. I strived for the language of *just us,* the brilliance of the circle.[32]

Hartman insists on an affective, embodied engagement and intimacy in this description of her close mode of narration. *Wayward Lives* thus experiments with form to construct narratives of anarchic Black women whose politics appear in their intimate acts of errancy and waywardness that disturb what the police order claims to be possible or acceptable. Hartman's narrative itself appears as a wayward series of vignettes following the everyday experiences, sensations, and imaginative acts of a variety of characters—frequently those "minor figures" excluded from accounts of history—who antagonize the tautological enumerations of inequality in their stylized efforts "to make art of life."[33] Against the vicious circles of postpolitical inequality, Hartman imagines new subjects and affects and locates the return of the political in the intimacies of equality and freedom shared within the triangulated relation of narrator, narratee, and reader.

NARRATIVE INTIMACY

As a narrative that seeks to locate the anarchic practices "of the multitude, the dispossessed, the subaltern, and the enslaved," *Wayward Lives* dissensually places readers in a series of scenes that frame the book's many minor figures (xiii). Hartman thus privileges a narrative style that constructs an intimate portrait of her characters, which positions narrator/narration and character in close proximity and which takes seriously the possibility of "minor revolutions" that can nonetheless disturb the postpolitical order to create a more livable life. Esther Brown, one of Hartman's minor figures in *Wayward Lives,* appears to readers via a series of negative formulations: she "did not write a political tract on the refusal to be governed"; "she didn't pen any song lines"; "she didn't commit to paper her ruminations on freedom" (229). She does not appear in any of the grand narratives of the 1910s and 1920s. While she and Emma Goldman (1869–1940), the Russian-born American anarchist, "crossed paths" on the streets of New York City, they "failed to recognize each other" (229). The conditional then appears in Hartman's characterization of what might have been had Esther Brown's actions been recognized, legible, or visible: "The cardboard placards for the tumult and upheaval she incited might have said: 'Don't mess with me. I am not afraid to smash things up'" (229). "But," Hartman insists, "hers was a struggle without formal declarations of policy, slogan, or credo" (229). Hartman's critical voice here intervenes in the description of Esther Brown, though at times the two registers—scholarly intervention and redescription of the archival traces—become indistinct. Esther Brown is neither Lucy Parsons nor Ida B. Wells, but she nevertheless offers a theory of freedom—enacted through an embodied politics—every bit as rigorous in Hartman's political narration, for Brown "knew first-hand that the offense most punished by the state was trying to live free" (230). In her free movements—the very freedom of which she is routinely denied by the white supremacist, heteropatriarchal state—Brown was "ungovernable," and "her way of living was nothing short of anarchy" (230).

In the intimate portrait of Esther Brown that follows, Hartman immerses her readers in Brown's milieu. We are given rich descriptions of her life, movements, and desires. We follow her on the streets of Harlem, in the routines of work, and in her embrace of social life. Here, Hartman's "close mode of narration" bespeaks the narrative voice's intimate proximity to Brown. This voice appears to be enunciated from a position spatially and temporally close to Brown, in which Hartman reaches back to the atmosphere of New York City in the early twentieth century. At other times, however, this voice appears to operate in the mode of free indirect style. When Hartman writes, "Why should she toil in a kitchen or laundry in order to survive? Why should she work herself to the bone?," it is unclear whether the voice is Hartman's or Brown's, or some harmonization of the two (234).

While Hartman's "close mode of narration" sometimes appears as free indirect style, her methodological insistence on this close mode of narration avows an intimacy that, paradoxically, the impossibly close free indirect style disavows. D. A. Miller describes the strange logic of free indirect style as performing "the stark opposition between character and narration . . . *at ostentatiously close quarters.*"[34] In free indirect style, "narration comes as near to a character's psychic and linguistic reality as it can get without collapsing into it, and the character does as much of the work of the narration as she may without acquiring its authority."[35] Free indirect style maintains the difference between narration and character even as they approach each other asymptotically. Free indirect style therefore depends on a precarious dialectic of distanced proximity and a proximate distance. As Miller insists, "free indirect style gives a virtuoso performance, against all odds, of the narration's persistence in detachment from character, no matter how intimate the one becomes with the other."[36] In its capacity to place Hartman's narrative voice alongside and even within her narrated voices, free indirect style serves as one strategy of Hartman's close mode of narration.

Yet the two forms of Hartman's narration—free indirect style and close mode of narration—are also importantly distinct in the kinds of embodied intimacy and proximity they encourage. In Esther Brown's mise-en-scène, Hartman's narration embraces attachment rather than detachment, and it also often appears as description. She takes the time and space to frame Brown and her world, an act of care that responds to the violence of the archive and police records, which primarily register Brown's "criminality." Hartman's intimate narration emphasizes that the law criminalized "the forms of life created by young black women in the city," such that Brown's shifts "from job to job and lover to lover" made her legible to the police and the police order only as "immoral and likely to become a threat" (236). Hartman's own narrative circle, with its "just us" conjunction (24), disrupts the tautologies of anti-Blackness that police Brown and relegate her to a minor role, a role that renders her Blackness and womanhood legible only in terms of criminality. Throughout this description, Hartman appears alongside Brown in her day-to-day desires and activities. Where free indirect style in Miller's definition foregrounds psychic proximity, the close mode of narration in *Wayward Lives* also emphasizes physical proximity.

With Hartman's investment in minor figures, she seems to offer two different approaches to politics. On the one hand, there is a politics of making appear those figures who would otherwise appear discounted—that is, those who would not count in the police accounting of the world. In this sense, *Wayward Lives* offers a new collective in its chorus of voices and figures, of which Esther Brown is one part. On the other hand, and at the same time, this politics of appearing takes appearing itself as an issue. *Wayward Lives* cannot be reduced, that is, to a liberal politics of inclusion. Yet readers might ask, what is political about a close mode of narration? What political work does *Wayward Lives* perform, and for whom?

For the most part, her minor figures left no writing to be read; instead, Hartman must read their lives and embodied movements against the grain of what has been detailed and accounted for by the archives of the state (including birth certificates, police reports, and legal documents).[37] Reflecting on some of these minor figures, Hartman writes, "In Gladys and Mabel and Mattie and Edna, I saw all of those I loved. In the fierceness of their want and the collective desire to break every structure that confined them to the bottom, I saw a blueprint for another set of arrangements."[38] The affective desires and actions of these women generate Hartman's own affective attachment to them, which harmonizes into a collective practice of Black living. In its proximity to the narratees, Hartman's narration exceeds mere representation and expresses both new subjectivities—such as Esther Brown—and new collectivities. The text's narrative intimacy generates a choral effect: Hartman's narrative voice and Esther Brown's voice harmonize to speak as if from within the same chorus, part of the same choreography of freedom.

The Anarchy of Freedom

Before elaborating on these figures of the chorus and choreography, I want to linger with the anarchic expressions of the text, especially in the case of Esther Brown. As Hartman writes, "Esther Brown longed for another world. She was hungry for more, for otherwise, for better. She was hungry for beauty" (235). Brown, according to Hartman, wanted "to make an art of subsistence. She did not try to create a poem or song or painting. What she created was Esther Brown" (235). Brown's very "manner of walking" in the Harlem streets "threatened to undo the city, steal back the body, break all the windows" (234). The anti-Black social order responds to such a threat—and curtails its own anxieties—with the tautology of the law, specifically vagrancy laws (241–42). For a Black woman like Brown, "to be charged was to be sentenced," which emphasizes the police order's proleptic capacities of foreclosure: "What mattered was not what you had done, but the prophetic power of the police to predict the future, and anticipate the mug shot in the bright eyes and intelligent face of Esther Brown" (242). The police order and its laws "suture blackness and criminality" (250). This suture maintains and perpetuates "an encirclement of unfreedom" that is the postpolitical status quo.[39]

Hartman concludes this portion of her narrative with the recognition that "the afterlife of slavery unfolded in a tenement hallway and held Esther Brown in its grasp" (256). In other words, the police order's structuring anti-Blackness manifested itself in Brown's everyday existence. With her narrative proximity, Hartman claims that Brown both understood the anti-Blackness of the law and "refused *to live in its clauses and parentheses*" (256; emphasis in the original). Instead, Brown created a new grammar in her movements, as when she decides to stay with a friend in Harlem to enjoy "drinking and carousing," a mode of living that Hartman reads as part of a "wild experiment in black freedom" (256). Brown's errancy, her willingness to follow her own anarchic desires, positions her as an embodiment of Black life and freedom. The convergent proximity between Hartman's voice and Brown's interiority here approaches collapse, for it remains ambiguous whether this refusal ought to be read as Hartman's critical description or as Brown's critical praxis. As a result of this narrative style, the politics of *Wayward Lives* cannot be easily located, such that the dissensual acts may appear with the characters, the narration, or their choral alignment. According to Hartman, Brown's refusal marked her desire "to destroy" the world defined by the state; she was "the sort of girl who would not hesitate to smash things up" (256). The conditional appears as a privileged mode of Hartman's narrative. Brown's resistance occurred in her everyday existence and its disregard for the police order, yet Hartman reads in this "minor revolt" an expansive potential of disturbing the anti-Black order that attempts to foreclose Black life. Walcott argues, "Emancipation was and is a compromise meant to retain control over Black bodies, Black life-forms, and our movement while appearing to offer significantly changed conditions from those of enslavement and colonization."[40] In Hartman's narrative mode, readers come to recognize, alongside Hartman herself, that Esther Brown saw through this facade of emancipation. She refused to wait for freedom to appear; instead, she created, in her anarchic movements, a form of life radically constituted by freedom instead of its deferral and continued evisceration. "What she created," in other words, "was Esther Brown," and the "beautiful life" she makes for herself is a life denied to her. Brown makes possible what the anti-Black order deems to be impossible. She lives her life as if not in subjection, and she thereby converts the as if of freedom to an actual experience. Her figurative and bodily enactments of freedom produce a new mode of being.

In her foreword to William C. Anderson's *The Nation on No Map: Black Anarchism and Abolition,* Hartman writes that "'anarchism' gathers and names the practices of mutual aid and the programs for survival that have sustained us in the face [of] unimaginable violence."[41] Elaborating on "the anarchism of Blackness" means "dreaming and rehearsing how we might live otherwise in the present and break with the fatal terms of the given, the brutal imposed order of things" (xiii). Esther Brown's ungovernability, her refusal to abide by the state's demands, marks a mode of waywardness, which is, according to Hartman, "a practice of possibility at a time when all roads, except the ones created by *smashing out*, are foreclosed" (228; emphasis in the original). Brown follows her desires and prefers "strolling along Harlem's wide avenues" to working in confinement all day (234). In following her anarchic and "ungovernable" desires (230), Brown participates in the "everyday choreography of the possible" of Harlem's streets, which Hartman describes as "a long poem of black hunger and striving" (234). Anti-Blackness forecloses Black life, yet Black life appears nevertheless. Because Hartman writes, via her close mode of narration, "from inside the circle" (xiv), the place of psychosis in fact seems to be reversed: it is the free white, rather than the free Black, who appears to be psychotic and pathological. In other words, shifting from the world of anti-Blackness to the world of Black life enacts a figural annihilation of the former. *Wayward Lives* therefore seems less interested in a negative critique than in a positive (political) articulation.[42]

This articulation depends on the failure of postpolitics to eviscerate politics and the spaces of the political through processes of foreclosure. *Wayward Lives,* in its close mode of narration, demonstrates that the police order's attempts to foreclose the possibilities of Black life and freedom can only succeed in repressing such possibilities. In contrast to the foreclosed element, the repressed keeps returning, and that which is disavowed must be managed. The postpolitical order absorbs Esther Brown's movements and actions into a logic of criminality, thereby disavowing what Hartman rereads as her dissensual politics of freedom. Hartman's focus on the social practices and interiority of Esther Brown, through her close mode of narration, offers a way of interrupting this process of postpolitical absorption. Because of the structures of foreclosure and repression, the political aesthetic must take place on the intimate register. The real political implications of narrative style appear in its ability to catachrestically name that which remains unnameable as such in the language of the police order: Black freedom, embodied in Esther Brown's anarchic movements that refuse to follow the given, anti-Black plotting of Black life that produces forms of social death. By catachrestically expressing modes of Black freedom, Hartman reveals that whiteness disavows its own catachrestic status. *Wayward Lives* thus offers a change of scene: readers are placed within the intimate circle of these errant figures, an anarchic location that disrupts the objectifying gaze of postpolitics.

From Inside the Chorus

While I have focused on Esther Brown, *Wayward Lives* seeks not to reify the individual but to recognize the individual as part of a collective. This collective becomes figured as the poetic and erotically charged arrangement of the chorus. To be placed in the circle of the chorus of figures in *Wayward Lives* paradoxically interrupts the encircling powers of the police. Dance, the chorus, and choreography come to figure in different ways a mode of being free within a space of unfreedom, all of which become most explicit in the penultimate chapter, "The Beauty of the Chorus":

> Like the flight from the plantation, the escape from slavery, the migration from the south, the rush into the city, or the stroll down Lenox Avenue, choreography was an art, a practice of moving even when there was nowhere else to go, no place left to run. It was an arrangement of the body to elude capture, an effort to make the uninhabitable livable, to escape the confinement of a four-cornered world, a tight, airless room. Tumult, upheaval, flight—it was the articulation of living free, or at the very least trying to, it was the way to insist *I am unavailable for servitude. I refuse it.* (299; emphasis in the original)

This quotation again blurs Hartman's voice and the women's voices recounted in *Wayward Lives,* in this case Mabel Hampton, a "chorine, lesbian, working-class intellectual, and aspiring concert singer" (xxi). Mabel Hampton appears as "one among the chorus," in which "she knew that she was slipping into another arrangement of the possible, the costume of another existence" (301, 302). Dancing in the music hall, Hampton experiences the collectivization—the becoming communal—of the chorus, through which "a line of separate dancers" becomes transformed "into a shared body finding a common rhythm" (303). In such a process, the collective depends on each individual, and yet each individual must become "something other than" themselves (303). The chorus constructs its unity out of a harmony, a dialectic of parts and whole. Hartman narrates Hampton's difficulty with this deindividualizing process, a process that, like jazz, poses a challenge: "to improvise within the space of constraint, bending and breaking the rules without breaking the form" (303).

Hartman's repetition of a key phrase, "different set of arrangements," joins Hampton's experiences in the chorus and those in "the private parties hosted by friends in Harlem" (304). Such spaces provide "a loophole of retreat" within the police order.[43] Hampton comes to desire Gladys, an older woman in another chorus line, and the beautiful experiments of the chorus and private gatherings shape Hampton's "sensual education," first through Gladys and then through Ruth (323):

> The public sex and collective lovemaking, like the environment, were beautiful, worldly-wise, and testimony to a distinctly modern life. In the elegant flat, the sharp edge of pleasure, the moans, whispers, and laughter blanketing the room, the choked breath of orgasm shattered the boundaries of the self, effaced the lines of social division, unmade men and women. The utter dissolution of the bounded, discrete self was the gift. The gay rebels and the gender queers savored the lush refuge; welcomed the opportunity to jettison propriety. Guests mingled across the divide of class and race, strangers became intimates, an English aristocrat fell in love with a Negro actress. (323–24)

Nothing "unsettles the fantasy of sovereignty" and insists on the subject's nonsovereignty like sex.[44] Against oppressive regimes of "capture," Hampton's sexual and eroticized liberation from the patterns of surveilled life constructs a new time and space.[45] The apartment becomes significant for these figures not as a private space but as an alternative public with new possibilities. The men and women collectively build a dissensual common space, thereby subversively redeploying the otherwise private space of the apartment. "Eros" is made "into a communal luxury" (325). Hampton's story blurs those divisions organizing existence, especially public and private, which ostensibly separate the choreography of the chorus line from that of the bedroom. Mabel Hampton's experiments in freedom make her into an exemplary political figure whose very activity "institutes a place, a singular theatre of operations."[46] Hampton does not merely practice the art of dance; she, like Esther Brown, also reveals that life itself can be made into an art, which allows her to claim "space in a world that granted you none" (337). Hampton's narrative also reveals that the art of the chorus has an erotic dimension that constitutes a being-in-common not dependent on stable ontology or sovereignty. Choreography and the chorus "rupture" the whole representational regime that works to fix Black women in a particular place.[47] In its insistence on collective harmony and improvisation, dance maintains the anarchic impurity of rupture by taking place within the form of enclosure, and dance as practiced by Hampton immanently refuses to be bound by the hierarchies and divisions organizing existence.[48] Dancers in a chorus line together must find "a common rhythm" not determined in advance (303).

Because the chorus dissolves individual distinctions, any figure within the line can stand in for another—hence Hampton's difficulty with its de-individuating procedures. This metonymy also generates a synecdoche, for any figure in the chorus can also stand in for the whole, precisely because of the becoming-communal of the chorus. The nonsovereign form of the chorus therefore offers a double logic of metonymy and synecdoche that works against police logic, in which synecdoche in particular works as a master trope of violently subjugating parts for whole, as is the case in the U.S. Constitution's governing synecdoche, "we the people." Being one of the women on the chorus is inimical to such forms of interpellation because the chorus emphasizes an iterative activity that seeks to maintain, rather than foreclose, surprising possibilities of freedom and equality, much like Hartman's own stylistic performance. Hartman's close mode of narration locates her and her readers within this chorus, itself a "dance within an enclosure" (347). In "The Race for Theory," Barbara Christian writes that for her, literature—as well as reading and writing—"is an affirmation that sensuality is intelligence, that sensual language is language that makes sense."[49] Christian thereby refuses the separation of sensuality and intelligence that operates as yet another mode of policing; indeed, sense etymologically and definitionally includes both feeling and thought. Hartman's focus on intimate narration similarly works to show readers the sense of thought and thought of sense in the everyday lives, activities, and desires of its minor characters. In this manner, Mabel Hampton's—and, through the magic of close narration, Saidiya Hartman's—constructions of freedom within the chorus offer new forms of life and living despite the anti-Black order's insistence on anti-Black violence.[50] The anarchic practices of Hartman's wayward figures, whose Blackness, sexuality, embodiment, and movement all appear "too much" in the gaze of the anti-Black state, develop new styles of sensing and thinking a world against forms of anti-Black foreclosure.

Because *Wayward Lives* shows the manifestations of the postpolitical's constitutive and structural anti-Blackness in the everyday lives of its characters, it also foregrounds resistance at this level by narrating the anarchic thoughts and feelings of its minor figures who work to build new forms of Black life. In her attention to these characters, Hartman insists that to think and to feel are mutually constitutive. Kwame Holmes writes, "Thanks to a recent wave of Black feminist urban histories, we can know something of Black women's experience in these years, but Hartman asks a more challenging question: Have we felt these histories?"[51] Hartman rejects the "clinical detachment" of "traditional social historical methods," which often exclude that which does not "make sense" according to their own frameworks.[52] Hartman claims these Black women and men made "an art of life," and Hartman follows their lead by making her own scholarly project an art.[53] There is a poiesis or poetics of *Wayward Lives* that, in its very expression, creates a new mode and style of Black life. Hartman therefore follows Audre Lorde's claim: "The white fathers told us: I think, therefore I am. The Black mother within each of us—the poet—whispers in our dreams: I feel, therefore I can be free. Poetry coins the language to express and charter this revolutionary demand, the implementation of that freedom."[54] Freedom is an embodied practice, one with its own fabric of intelligibility and sensibility. This fabric reconfigures the white supremacist order founded on the unfreedom of Black subjects.

In keeping with her dissensual practices, Hartman develops a poetic narrative style to construct the political aesthetic of *Wayward Lives*. By poetry I refer to the strict sense of poiesis as an activity of making or bringing into existence, of illuminating things such that their very sensibility changes. Poetry operates "as illumination," according to Lorde, because "it is through poetry that we give name to those ideas which are—until the poem—nameless and formless, about to be birthed, but already felt."[55] Poetry is "a revelatory distillation of experience"; it offers a strategy to name the nameless.[56] Hartman's catachrestic strategy in *Wayward Lives* is to recognize the "errant path" and "unregulated movement" taken by a range of anarchic Black figures as a "social poesis that sustains the dispossessed" (227). Her close mode of narration enables a set of new scenes within which the intimate revolutions of Black life become perceivable and thinkable.

"The chorus," Hartman writes, "is the vehicle for another kind of story . . . one in which all modalities play a part," and her close mode of narration mimetically reflects this alternative practice (348). The chorus as a "resource for collective action" models the kind of revolutionary transformation that could make possible those modes of being free rendered impossible by the police order. *Wayward Lives* itself embodies this new possibility by refusing to offer a protagonist; instead, the book stages a chorus of voices, figures, acts, and feelings that answer the question of how to live free. "This choreography is 'headless,'" writes Marquis Bey, because it is "without ruler . . . and it spills out."[57] This "Black feminist anarchism cannot be contained by inclusion into any organization; it has to be a modality."[58] Style—of a close mode of narration, of the body, of being—figures this modality without reifying it into another hierarchical organization. With this claim I do not mean to suggest a nonpolitical or extrapolitical excess, a kind of "pure form" that cannot be reabsorbed by the police order; instead, I emphasize the figurality of Hartman's style to stress that the collective movements followed in *Wayward Lives* insistently work to short-circuit postpolitical processes of reabsorption, even if this resistance cannot be guaranteed in advance. Hartman inverts the order of things by demonstrating that the position of psychosis is in fact occupied by those subjects who can only imagine freedom through the subjugation of others, through the perpetuation of circles of unfreedom. The politics of *Wayward Lives* appears in its invention of new modes of writing and being, which express the new modes of living freely practiced by the many minor figures who appear throughout its pages.

Hartman's intervention into Black studies, with its stress on the revolutionary practices contained within the intimate and embodied actions of anarchic Black women, offers scholars of postpolitics a generative mode of conceptualizing political dissensus in the context of everyday life and minor figures. Mass collective movements, such as general strikes or protests, offer one possible form of rupturing postpolitical consensus, but the errant movements and desires of subjectivities offer another way of disrupting its tautologies of inequality and unfreedom. These intimate acts recognize that postpolitical structures operate on both macro and micro levels of existence. To combat such structures, political agents therefore need to imagine new forms of collectivity as well as new styles of being, feeling, and thinking. *Wayward Lives* stands as one such account of a stylized expression of freedom—one that refuses to be fixed in its insistence on the permanent revolution of errant desires and potentialities.

Notes

1. Saidiya V. Hartman, *Scenes of Subjection: Terror, Slavery, and Self-Making in Nineteenth-Century America* (Oxford: Oxford University Press, 1997), 116.

2. Rinaldo Walcott, *The Long Emancipation: Moving toward Black Freedom* (Durham, N.C.: Duke University Press, 2021), 1; emphasis in the original.

3. For more on this logic, see Japhy Wilson and Erik Swyngedouw, "Seeds of Dystopia: Post-politics and the Return of the Political," in *The Post-political and Its Discontents: Spaces of Depoliticisation, Spectres of Radical Politics,* ed. Japhy Wilson and Erik Swyngedouw (Edinburgh: Edinburgh University Press, 2014): 1–22.

4. Jeannine Marie DeLombard, "Dehumanizing Slave Personhood," *American Literature* 91, no. 3 (2019): 495.

5. Hartman, *Scenes,* 116.

6. For one discussion of this constitutive relationship between slavery and modernity, see Paul Gilroy, *The Black Atlantic: Modernity and Double Consciousness* (London: Verso, 1993), especially chapter 2, "Masters, Mistresses, Slaves, and the Antinomies of Modernity."

7. Frank B. Wilderson III, *Red, White, and Black: Cinema and the Structure of U.S. Antagonisms* (Durham, N.C.: Duke University Press, 2010), 249; emphasis in the original.

8. For a discussion of postpolitics and consensus, see Juan Meneses, *Resisting Dialogue: Modern Fiction and the Future of Dissent* (Minneapolis: University of Minnesota Press, 2019), vii–viii.

9. Calvin Warren, *Ontological Terror: Blackness, Nihilism, and Emancipation* (Durham, N.C.: Duke University Press, 2018), 48.

10. Warren, 50.

11. Warren, 51.

12. Jacques Lacan, "Response to Jean Hyppolite's Commentary on Freud's 'Verneinung,'" in *Écrits,* trans. Bruce Fink (New York: Norton, 2006), 323. As Lacan suggests, foreclosure *(Verwerfung)* "cut[s] short any manifestation of the symbolic order" (323).

13. Seshadri-Crooks argues that whiteness functions as a master signifier whose function is to guarantee meaning in the symbolic order. Kalpana Seshadri-Crooks, *Desiring Whiteness: A Lacanian Analysis of Race* (London: Routledge, 2000).

14. Warren, *Ontological Terror,* 5.

15. Warren, 5.

16. W. E. B. Du Bois, *The Souls of Black Folk* (New York: Dover, 1994), 1.

17. Jacques Rancière, *Disagreement: Politics and Philosophy,* trans. Julie Rose (Minneapolis: University of Minnesota Press, 1999), 28.

18. Rancière, 35.

19. Saidiya Hartman, *Wayward Lives, Beautiful Experiments: Intimate Histories of Riotous Black Girls, Troublesome Women, and Queer Radicals* (New York: W. W. Norton, 2019).

20. Jared Sexton, "Afro-pessimism: The Unclear Word," *Rhizomes: Cultural Studies in Emerging Knowledge* 29 (2016), ¶ 11.

21. Frank B. Wilderson III, *Afropessimism* (New York: Liveright, 2020), 223; emphasis in the original.

22. Wilderson, 15.

23. Such notions of style appear in Roland Barthes, *Writing Degree Zero,* trans. Annette Lavers and Colin Smith (New York: Hill and Wang, 1977), 10–13.

24. Lee Edelman, "Imagining the Homosexual: *Laura* and the Other Face of Gender," in *Homographesis: Essays in Gay Literary and Cultural Theory* (New York: Routledge, 1994), 231.

25. Edelman, 232.

26. Ronald A. T. Judy, *(Dis)forming the American Canon: African-Arabic Slave Narratives and the Vernacular* (Minneapolis: University of Minnesota Press, 1993), 94.

27. Warren, *Ontological Terror,* 144, 145; emphasis in the original.

28. Saidiya V. Hartman, "The Position of the Unthought," interview by Frank B. Wilderson III, *Qui Parle* 13, no. 2 (2003): 184–86.

29. Jacques Rancière, *The Politics of Literature,* trans. Julie Rose (Malden, Mass.: Polity, 2011), 41–42.

30. Examples of such interventions can be found in "Book Forum: Saidiya Hartman, *Wayward Lives, Beautiful Experiments: Intimate Histories of Social Upheaval.*" *Journal of African American History* 106, no. 1 (2021): 103–35. For a recent intervention into debates on methodology in Black studies, especially regarding archival work and historicism, see Stephen Best, *None Like Us: Blackness, Belonging, Aesthetic Life* (Durham, N.C.: Duke University Press, 2018).

31. I leave *mésentente* untranslated to emphasize its resonances in French. As Panagia notes, its frequent translation as "disagreement" rather than "misunderstanding" misleadingly "implies a relation of opposition in the vein of a contradiction"; "a disagreement is something you can (typically) resolve (with empirical evidence, for instance) or disregard." Davide Panagia, "Rancière's Style," *Novel: A Forum on Fiction* 47, no. 2 (2014): 290. "Misunderstanding" or "missed listening" "is not a concept for the understanding: it is, rather, a practice of politics that disarticulates the conditions of sensibility (i.e., the frictionless turbine of equivalence) for understanding" (290).

32. Saidiya Hartman, "Intimate History, Radical Narrative," *Journal of African American History* 106, no. 1 (2021): 129; emphasis in the original.

33. Hartman uses the term "minor figure" to refer to her cast of characters: "They have been credited with nothing: they remain surplus women of no significance, girls deemed unfit for history and destined to be minor figures" (xv). Hartman instead "recognizes the revolutionary ideals that animated ordinary lives" (xv). When known figures do appear in Hartman's narrative, such as W. E. B. Du Bois, they are defamiliarized, and the emphasis remains on the everyday.

34. D. A. Miller, *Jane Austen, or The Secret of Style* (Princeton, N.J.: Princeton University Press, 2003), 59; emphasis in the original.

35. Miller, 59.

36. Miller, 59.

37. Hartman describes her creative reconfiguration of the archive and its omissions in "Venus in Two Acts" as "critical fabulation." Saidiya Hartman, "Venus in Two Acts," *Small Axe* 12, no. 2 (2008): 11–12.

38. Hartman, "Intimate History," 128.

39. Walcott, *Long Emancipation,* 107.

40. Walcott, 44.

41. Saidiya Hartman, "Black in Anarchy," foreword to William C. Anderson, *The Nation on No Map: Black Anarchism and Abolition* (Chico, Calif.: AK Press, 2021), xiii.

42. As Bey says of *Wayward Lives,* "Hartman does not wish to dwell in negation ('the passion for destruction') but emphasizes how that negation is exceeded in what we ultimately hope for—to create something new." Marquis Bey, *Anarcho-Blackness: Notes toward a Black Anarchism* (Chico, Calif.: AK Press, 2020), 65.

43. With this phrase, Hartman alludes to the well-known expression used by Harriet Jacobs in *Incidents in the Life of a Slave Girl* (Mineola, N.Y.: Dover, 2001), in which Jacobs (as Linda Brent) conceals herself in a garret for nearly seven years before escaping to the North.

44. Lauren Berlant and Lee Edelman, *Sex, or The Unbearable* (Durham, N.C.: Duke University Press, 2014), 2.

45. Hortense J. Spillers, "Mama's Baby, Papa's Maybe: An American Grammar Book," *Diacritics* 17, no. 2 (1987): 67.

46. Jacques Rancière, *Aisthesis: Scenes from the Aesthetic Regime of Art,* trans. Zakir Paul (New York: Verso, 2013), 99.

47. Rancière, 104. In this section, Rancière discusses the aesthetic practice of Loïe Fuller.

48. Reading Hartman's "everyday choreography of the possible," Bey writes, "A coalitional, collective quotidian choreography of possibility. . . . It is anarchism that is choreographed through the way we move and think about our bodies. Anarchic subjectivity in that we come into being through an *anarchy of becoming,* a way to exist in the world where our existence is predicated on how we aid each other mutually, refuse the violence of the State, dismantle hierarchies, concede to a non-coerced ethic . . . of opacity" (68; emphasis in the original).

49. Barbara Christian, "The Race for Theory," in "The Nature and Context of Minority Discourse," ed. Abdul JanMohamed and David Lloyd, special issue, *Cultural Critique* 6 (1987): 61. Quashie discusses Christian's essay in relation to Hartman's *Wayward Lives:* Kevin Quashie, "A Flash of Life and Light," *Journal of African American History* 106, no. 1 (2021): 122–26.

50. The constructions of freedom in and of *Wayward Lives* align with Quashie's project to imagine a world of Black aliveness "so as to surpass the everywhere and everyway of black death, of blackness that is understood only through such a vocabulary." Kevin Quashie, *Black Aliveness, or A Poetics of Being* (Durham, N.C.: Duke University Press, 2021), 1.

51. Kwame Holmes, "Engaging Wayward Methods," *Journal of African American History* 106, no. 1 (2021): 115.

52. Holmes, 115.

53. Hartman, "Intimate History," 129.

54. Audre Lorde, "Poetry Is Not a Luxury," in *Sister Outsider: Essays and Speeches* (Berkeley, Calif.: Crossing, 2007), 38.

55. Lorde, 36. Hartman cites this essay in "Intimate History," the closing response in the book forum devoted to *Wayward Lives.*

56. Lorde, "Poetry Is Not a Luxury," 37.

57. Bey, *Anarcho-Blackness,* 68.

58. Bey, 68.

CHAPTER 6

False Specters of the Political

Revisitation, Digital Documentary Vernacular, and the Postpolitical after January 6

STEPHEN CHARBONNEAU

In his opening salvo against the risk of a "January exception" to congressional impeachment powers, House manager Jamie Raskin (D-Maryland) implored his audience to revisit the events of January 6, 2021, by viewing a compilation video.[1] This moment launched the second impeachment proceedings of President Donald J. Trump over his incitement of supporters at a January 6 rally to disrupt the ratification of the 2020 presidential election. Trump's perpetuation of what is now called the big lie that the election was stolen as a result of voter fraud prompted thousands of followers to storm the Capitol. The attack forced congressional members and their staff to flee, temporarily delaying ratification of the 2020 election until Congress was reconvened later that evening. President-elect Joe Biden's win was eventually confirmed at 3:24 a.m. on January 7.

The footage Raskin introduced compelled a look back on the violence of January 6, but it also proffered a vision of future hazards should the logic of a January exception be upheld. The video, compiled by law firm Debevoise & Plimpton, drew on a wide array of footage from smartphones, body cameras, surveillance systems, cable news, and social media accounts. The imagery presented wove a coherent picture of insurrection from a deluge of digital recordings and live coverage, balancing the establishment of a narrative with a distinct sense of chaos, trauma, and democratic precarity. Of course, this was not the first time that recorded media had been used as evidence of executive transgressions and potential crimes. The existence of "highly incriminating audiotapes" contributed to the resignation of Richard Nixon in 1974, and "taped depositions from key figures" played a role in the impeachment proceedings of Bill Clinton in 1999.[2] Debevoise & Plimpton also assisted with the use of audiovisual material during the first Trump impeachment.[3] Nevertheless, the video compilation used during the second impeachment of Trump functioned in a different way. Rather than serving as a record of illicit solicitations, confessions of wrongdoing, or untrustworthy testimony, the video presentation offered less of a revelation and more of a revisitation. The insurrection was a thoroughly public event that not only occurred in broad daylight but also threatened the safety of the same Congress members who were now serving as jurors. The scene of the crime and the scene of adjudication (which are one and the same) both converge on a third scene: the televisual broadcast of the proceedings. This third scene is less participatory, given the passivity of viewership, even as it is undoubtedly constitutive of the whole affair because the proceedings are designed for the populace in hopes of reasserting democratic norms.

The notion of revisiting is understood here as an attempt at political restoration after the turmoil of January 6. The rationale is clear: the need to revisit is motivated by the desire to ensure that such an event does not happen again. I want to tread lightly, however, when I speak of a restoration, which resonates here with healing and implies in this instance a return to a more stable status quo. To some extent, the restoration sought by the second impeachment of Trump and the later hearings of the House Select Committee on January 6[4] is different from the principles of transitional justice that inform truth and reconciliation efforts around the globe, with South Africa being one of the most prominent examples of this. The latter instance implies a restorative reckoning with past crimes, often state sponsored, in order to gesture at justice while officially recognizing victims' pain.[5] An accounting for historic injustices and human rights violations are at the heart of transitional justice processes. Reconciliation is thus sought through an acknowledgment of past harms that promises a different path ahead.

It is hard to deny that there is a degree of pertinence between the principles of transitional justice and efforts to shed light on and redress the storming of the Capitol that took place on January 6, 2021. In the latter case, attempts to hold Trump as well as his enablers and followers to account are to some extent coextensive with the shoring up of our democratic institutions in the face of antidemocratic forces mobilized by the big lie. Yet our impeachment procedures and the hearings in the U.S. House of Representatives (along with the Justice Department's investigation into Trump and the wider effort to overturn the results of the 2020 presidential election) were not directed at anything akin to the legacy of apartheid or state-sponsored acts of genocide. Rather, these congressional efforts were committed to an ideal of a return to a presumably more comfortable, proximate past rather than a more radical redress of deep historical wrongs.[6] To this extent, restoration has a more limited connotation, and an implied validation of the way things are in spite of the temporary uptick in antidemocratic fervor represented by Trump and his America First movement. The assumption here is that reasonable order will prevail once we acknowledge and move past the autocratic glitch of January 6. Therefore, I use the term restoration ironically to describe the intent of these proceedings and their use of documentary recordings, as well as a critique that helps us see how impeachment, House hearings, and Justice Department investigations are both necessary and delimiting, glossing over entrenched historical problems with our electoral system.

I seize on this historic moment as an opportunity to consider the significance of the insurrectionist act and its documentary representations within the philosophical framework of postpolitics. I am thus most interested in representations of the insurrection featured in the February 2021 impeachment proceedings, their intended use, and the ways they trouble this overarching restorative project. To that end, my approach draws together concepts developed within a specifically documentary tradition (including its digital transformations) with philosophical critiques of the postpolitical. We will see how the postfoundational bases of postpolitical thinking is transparently rendered in a digital documentary vernacular whose sense emanates from a visceral arrangement of diverse sights and sounds (from smartphones, surveillance cameras, cable news, etc.) that overwhelm as much as, if not more than, they orient. I aim to show not only how this is part of a longer history binding the documentary tradition to democratic governance but also how the specific moment of the second Trump impeachment presents a theatricalized opportunity for considering the themes of postpolitical precarity and their aesthetic manifestations. I first set the stage for this argument about the postpolitical, January 6, and what I'm calling a digital documentary vernacular. The next section grounds these ideas in a close analysis of the compilation video highlighted above, featuring its unique status as an evidentiary object, its embrace of an aesthetics of disorder and precarity, and its differential display through competing modes of perception. Fundamentally, I find the work of remembrance and revisitation through digital documentary means a precarious project, but one that nevertheless helps us articulate our postpolitical predicament while falling short as a restorative gesture.

Postpolitics and Digital Documentary

Chantal Mouffe, Jacques Rancière, Slavoj Žižek, and Erik Swyngedouw, among others, have articulated the dilemmas associated with the postpolitical as an historical condition, albeit from varied perspectives. Japhy Wilson and Swyngedouw specifically recognize a core precarity in our postpolitical landscape in the mid-2010s.[7] They find that emergent acts of resistance are profound, meaningful, and numerous, rattling a decades-long postpolitical entrenchment of "reasonable" governance. However, they also suggest that the postpolitical persists despite these disruptions, even if its status is more akin to an automaton's lurch than a confident and spirited stride. Clearly this precarity–persistence antinomy still characterizes the postpolitical landscape of the 2020s, but how does it help us understand the current iteration of white nationalism and the autocratic, conspiratorial American right? Such a development represents a reactionary movement that appears to upset our already stifling postpolitical balance, but it simply meets this with white nationalist dreams of voting-rights curtailment and blatant disregard of legal and judicial procedures. Nevertheless, as far as the United States is concerned, does this reactionary movement—of which the January 6 insurrection is a tangible expression—leave scratches or open wounds? Does the radical right leave our postpolitical condition agitated but essentially intact? Is it simply another instance of the zombification of our democratic system, or does it represent something more—or less? How might documentary representations of this movement offer us critical perspective into this moment and the aesthetic character of our postpolitical predicament?

In answering these questions, we might be tempted to consider the insurrection to be a distinct act, a term defined by Žižek in a particular way.[8] For him, a true political act entails "the art of the *impossible*—it changes the very parameters of what is considered 'possible' in the existing constellation."[9] Certainly the attack on the Capitol was shocking and traumatic for the country, but it seems to fall short of this definition. Rather than disturbing our postpolitical order in any fundamental way, it is perhaps more accurately read as a symptom of such a condition, a tangible expression of our inability to visualize and recognize the roots of our social and economic ills. In his characterization of a genuine political act, Žižek clarifies for us what it is not. Writing over twenty years ago, he underscores its borderlines through a discussion of late twentieth-century conservatism: "The obvious counter-argument here is that today it is the (political) Right that is accomplishing the acts, boldly changing the very rules of what is considered acceptable-admissible in the sphere of public discourse: from the way Reaganism and Thatcherism legitimized the debate about curtailing workers' rights and social benefits, up to the gradual legitimization of the 'open debate' about Nazism in revisionist historiography."[10] Nevertheless, Žižek reminds us that an authentic political act "does not only retroactively change the rules of the symbolic space; it also disturbs the underlying fantasy—and here, concerning *this* crucial dimension, Fascism emphatically does *not* pass the criterion of the act." Such movements yield "pseudo-events" in which radical change is resisted in order to sustain the "fantasy that underlies our capitalist social edifice" while also surfacing its "implicit" biases and inequities.[11] The sustenance featured here reinforces the view that the very boldness of Trumpism is a symptom of our postpolitical condition—a feature, perhaps, and not a flaw. It is likely evident of a further entrenchment of our postpolitical arena, one that Wilson and Swyngedouw suggest "staggers blindly forward in the absence of its once-inspiring master discourses," leaving us with a "perverted form of a 'zombie neoliberalism.'"[12] If "staggering" accurately describes the postpolitical condition, then perhaps this has aesthetic reverberations. The theatricalized impeachment arena in February 2021, relying as it does on digital documentary evidence, offers us an opportunity to consider the status of the aesthetic in the postpolitical and what this says about a broader relationship between democracy and the documentary form. If the postpolitical lurches along, then an aesthetics of disorder might be expected as a corollary, or as an index of the precarity–persistence dynamic that constitutes our era.

Given the prominence of evidentiary media in these proceedings, we have an opportunity to consider how this footage contributes to these processes and what this case study might tell us about the documentary tradition and its relationship to the postpolitical landscape. Indeed, as I have already noted, the proceedings opened with a carefully edited compilation film of the events of January 6. Multiple scenes converge as the recordings from that fateful day are played within the Senate chambers and broadcast to audiences around the world. The legacy of the classical, expository documentary persists (with its associated values of rationality, centrality of evidence, and persuasion), but here it is also rearticulated and updated within a digital documentary vernacular in which a kaleidoscopic juxtaposition of views and formats (including body cameras, smartphones, surveillance footage, tweets, and cable news clips) narrates and memorializes the day's disturbance. In what follows, I specifically highlight the deployment of an emergent digital documentary vernacular within a broader theatricalization of the postpolitical in hopes of illustrating how the former gives expression to the latter.

By digital documentary vernacular, I refer to the everyday and digitally specific practices that people engage in to represent the world and their place in it. This extends the concept of vernacular video as discussed by Jean Burgess and Joshua Green and further defined by Mandy Rose and Jon Dovey while placing greater emphasis on the uniqueness of digital expressivity and its documentary dimensions.[13] For starters, a parallel can be drawn between the troubled bases for both digital documentary and the lurching postpolitical condition. As Wilson and Swyngedouw note, "key thinkers of the postpolitical share a postfoundational ontology, according to which there is no essential ground to any social order. . . .

[They] begin from the position that all social orders are profoundly contingent, and structured to conceal their own absent ground."[14] Any and all social configurations (understood in this context as politics) are necessarily overshadowed by fault lines, gaps, and absences, which energize intrusions and acts of resistance (understood as political). Such contingency and frailty have unique resonance when considered alongside documentary filmmaking. Consider, for instance, the way Rancière routes his reflection on documentary film through the gateway of memory. He insists that memory is "not the store of recollections of a particular consciousness."[15] Rather, it is "an orderly collection, a certain arrangement of signs, traces, and monuments."[16] Memory is something that "must be created against the overabundance of information as well as against its absence."[17] For Rancière, the work of remembering is closely related to the historiographic project of documentary filmmaking because both entail arrangement in the face of a constitutive abundance. Such abundance can be taken to refer to the broader reservoir of footage available to filmmakers (as opposed to the footage that winds up in the resulting film), as well as the abundance of historical world itself, out of which the documentary emerges.

Placing abundance at the heart of the documentary enterprise necessarily renders it fungible and shaky. To create in the face of such abundance is to engage in a profoundly contingent practice, and our awareness of the fact that documentaries can be made in a multitude of different ways from different perspectives always forges a shifting field of possibility that undermines the authority of what we see on screen. In this sense, there is a distinctly postfoundational character to documentary in a manner that rhymes with Wilson and Swyngedouw's summation. However, this aspect of documentary filmmaking reverberates most clearly in digital ecologies where abundance is even more profoundly and transparently felt. Film scholar Thomas Elsaesser's description of his tumble through a series of YouTube videos likens this digital abundance to a "boiling sea of magma" where one encounters "strange organisms, pulsing, moving and mutating, depending on the tags one enters or encounters, as YouTube sorts, filters and aggregates the choices I am not even aware of making."[18] Abundance overwhelms in digital ecologies. The intervention of digital documentary forms often entails more than the generation of original footage; it also involves the appropriation, arrangement, and representation of the "signs, traces, and monuments" one encounters in digital searches. The labor of revisitation and memorialization is even more apparent in evidentiary videos such as the one shown during Trump's second impeachment proceedings. The abundance from which these sights and sounds are drawn is affectively felt, fueling their metonymic power in relation to the events of January 6. The unsteady social basis for the postpolitical is the mirror image of the cascading digital abundance from which the evidentiary video's sights and sounds are drawn. The necessary theater of impeachment thus showcases a unique correspondence between a digital documentary vernacular and democratic governance in this postpolitical moment. Both reach for reason in the face of a vast unsteadiness. In this way, the heavily contingent nature of digital documentary evidence—and our knowledge of this—is closely aligned with the foundational precarity of the postpolitical and even offers us a kind of affective map for the latter.

An entanglement between documentary form and Western democracy can be traced back to the first half of the twentieth century. A full accounting of this aspect of the documentary tradition falls outside my scope here, but suffice it to say that the development of documentary film as mass communication is closely wedded to twentieth-century modernity and urbanization. John Grierson famously followed Walter Lippmann's line of thinking in *Public Opinion* (1922) when he endorsed the documentary film's appropriateness for the pace and advances of modern life.[19] Moving images could more succinctly and powerfully dramatize the events of the day in a manner that accommodated the speed of everyday existence in the late industrial era. In doing so, cinema would engage citizens who would otherwise feel overwhelmed by the transformations of modernity, enriching democracy as a result. Ian Aitken further elaborates on Grierson's famously dichotomous definition of documentary (the creative treatment of actuality) by clarifying Grierson's differentiation between "actual" and "the real."[20] The former refers to the "phenomenal" reality encountered by the camera, whereas the latter gravitates toward the "abstract and general . . . [and is] of greater significance than the empirical and particular." This "aesthetic of symbolic expression" empowers documentarians to convey the "underlying determining forces" that shape images of reality recorded by the camera.[21] Grierson's vision for documentary thus fuses idealism and aestheticism, structured communication and the uncanny moving image. Grierson's ambitions for documentary are realized through a contradiction in which the purposefulness of exposition and utility are always wedded to the surplus of aesthetic experience generated by cinema.[22] From this point of view, the documentary film sits precisely at the intersection of rationalism and modernism; it may be read as either a possible solution to the challenges posed to democracy by modernity, or their symptom.

With this history in mind, it is no surprise that we should read democracy and documentary in relation to one another in this particular moment. Each informs the other in light of twenty-first century media ecologies and our postpolitical condition. A digital documentary vernacular prioritizes an aesthetics of disorder that serves as both a map and symptom of our times. As we will see, the use of evidentiary video at the outset of the second Trump impeachment circumscribes the overall rehabilitative power of these proceedings. They simultaneously offer us a record of our precarity and a stilted reassurance that our system will continue to lurch forward permanently, but always perilously.

A Jumbled, Orderly Collection: Evidentiary Footage at the Second Trump Impeachment

The last half of this chapter will focus specifically on the Debevoise & Plimpton compilation video discussed at the outset. Much more work needs to be done on the use of evidentiary video throughout these proceedings, but a focused analysis of this particular object of study will help illustrate the correspondences discussed thus far. In doing so, we will focus on the relationship between an aesthetics of disorder and revisitation to underscore the mutual interiorization of a digital documentary vernacular and the postpolitical condition. This argument parallels a line of thinking outlined by Steven Shaviro in a different context: his work on postcinema. Shaviro notes that the relationship between the emergence of a cinema that is no longer bound to clear and coherent spatiotemporal coordinates is more than simply a reflection of underlying neoliberal and post-Fordist economic forces (in a manner following that of base/superstructure). Rather, he argues that the aesthetic characteristics of contemporary films and even music videos are "expressive" but "both *symptomatic* and *productive*."[23] "These works are symptomatic, in that they provide indices of complex social processes. . . . But they are also productive, in the sense that they do not *represent* social processes, so much as they participate actively in these processes, and help to constitute them."[24] I am attempting a similar argument here: the aesthetic character of these evidentiary documentary objects is expressive in this way in that it participates in and extends the processes that perpetuate the postpolitical, all while, through this excess, offering us illustrations of our dilemma.

The second impeachment of Trump opened on February 9, 2021, with Representative Raskin's introduction of the Debevoise & Plimpton video: "What will the January exception mean to future generations if you grant it? I'll show you." After this brief statement from the Senate dais, Raskin places his mask on (in accordance with Covid-19 protocols) and pivots to the monitor in the Senate chamber while the news broadcast shares the screen for the live audience at home. With no commentary, the video opens with the simple presentation of a date—January 6, 2021—over a black screen before cutting to repurposed broadcast footage of Trump addressing his supporters at the "Save America" rally gathered in the Ellipse on the National Mall in Washington, D.C. "We will stop the steal," he pronounces to the offscreen cheers of the attendees. Brief excerpts of the speech ring out, concluding with Trump's exhortation to the crowd to march to the Capitol ("We're going to walk down, and I'll be there with you. . . . We're going to walk down to the Capitol."). This opening salvo quickly cuts to smartphone footage on the ground, initially incorporating views of rallygoers in the crowd during the speech before shifting to the march itself. The chant "let's take the Capitol" is heard among those assembled, and one marcher, seen at the center of the frame, is elevated while exclaiming, "We are going to the Capitol where our problems are. It's that direction" as he gestures down Pennsylvania Avenue. The video is once again punctuated by a black screen with white text stating, "As

President Trump continues his speech, a wave of supporters begins marching to the Capitol." We return to smartphone footage and see a protestor kick down a barricade with a sign that reads "Area Closed." As the march proceeds, the video briefly toggles between past and present by reinserting a moment from Trump's speech (seen from the perspective of the crowd) in which he can be heard proclaiming, "They gave tens of thousands of votes. They came in in duffle bags. Where the hell did they come from?" Returning to the swarm of protestors descending on the Capitol, we hear a voice echo the same false refrain concerning illegitimate ballots: "Where the hell did they come from?"

At this point in the video—approximately ninety seconds in—we are on the cusp of revisiting the insurrectionists' breach of the Capitol's perimeter. However, this opening offers us an opportunity to reflect on the unique status of this evidentiary video within the impeachment process as well as within the broader history of the use of media as evidence in the courts. In his book, *Mechanical Witness: A History of Motion Picture Evidence in U.S. Courts,* Louis-Georges Schwartz traces the history of the use of film and video as evidentiary media, noting that for much of the twentieth century "the courts came to consider film and video as the most reliable form of evidence."[25] There is more to the story, however, as he points out. Before the emergence of video in the 1960s and 1970s, films were "construed . . . either as physical proof (Gulf Life v. Stossel) . . . or as pictorial communication of witness testimony (International Union v. Paul S. Russell)." Thus, "two theories of truth, one based on seeing evidence and the other on hearing testimony, came into conflict." In the case of the former, "witnesses had to attest to [the film's] veracity with testimony about its making and projection." In the latter instance, "the medium was not supposed to make it better proof than what could have been said on the stand." However, these curtailments of film's evidentiary status were less prominent in the case of video. The medium of video was, in fact, "more readily integrated into trials" in part because it was "less disruptive," "easier to authenticate," and "less expensive" than celluloid.[26] In fact, before 1992, video was understood as "a purveyor of fact (United States of America v. Guerrero)" and was elevated to the status of a "window onto events."[27]

Nevertheless, according to Schwartz, the 1992 Rodney King case "precipitated a shift in the value of motion picture evidence."[28] The video footage of King's beating at the hands of Los Angeles police officers was read differently in the courts than it was on television, and for Schwartz, this is a reminder that seeing is always shaped by an "institutional frame." Schwartz notes that some criticisms of the officers' acquittal on April 29, 1992—especially the statement issued at the time by the Society for Cinema Studies (today the Society for Cinema and Media Studies)—assumed that "images function the same way on television and in court."[29] Such an assumption obscures the existence of a specific "juridical mode of interpretation" where "èvidentiary videos do not terminate in . . . the subject of common sense."[30] While the sharing of footage showing police brutality "on television was a direct, incontrovertible recording of indefensible violence by the State's repressive apparatus," the display of the same footage on a "video monitor in the courtroom appeared to be ambiguous."[31] In actuality, the introduction of the King footage into a judicial setting effaced the "very marks of historical trauma on the tape" which would otherwise "imply a subject embedded in the situation in which the tape was shot." As Schwartz notes, the "materiality of vision disappears in the process of translating the image into a set of facts."[32] To sum up, different institutional viewing contexts yield distinct modes of perception.

The case of Trump's second impeachment and the use of evidentiary video by the House managers allows us to both extend and augment Schwartz's historical insights while leaning into its postpolitical implications. The live broadcast of the proceedings already troubles Schwartz's competing frames of vision, respectively aligned with the judicial and the televisual. To some extent, the impeachment proceedings were as much televisual event as political process. As such, the registration of historical trauma as well as the presentation of evidence are simultaneously present in the compilation video offered by House manager Raskin, although perhaps divergently received depending on whether one's viewing situation is in the Senate chamber or watching online elsewhere. From this vantage point, the footage shown would be more likely recognized as a shocking insurrection outside of the Senate chamber, whereas the semijuried role of senators would align their perspective with that of fact-checking and evidentiary verification. However, specific aspects of this case turn this bifurcation on its head, considering the coinciding of the scene of the crime with the scene of adjudication. This strange alignment between the "situation in which the tape was shot" and the space of semijudicial review keeps the "markers of historical trauma" proximate, tactile, and accessible. The first ninety seconds of the evidentiary video described above takes the viewers—whether they are present in the Senate chamber or online—to the brink of the Capitol perimeter's breach and the crowd's violent clash with Capitol police. In this revisitation, the barbaric intrusion of the insurrectionists into the Senate chamber is placed on display for judgment in that very same space, thereby potentially reinscribing the vision's materiality. From this point of view, the tendency of some Republican senators to look away from footage of the insurrection on display suggests that markers of the event are still close and tangible.[33]

While the intersection of the scene of the crime and the impeachment inquiry intensifies the historical trauma depicted in the video footage, other facets of the Debevoise & Plimpton video turn the example of 1992 on its head. Whereas the King video documents the state's barbaric racism as Los Angeles police officers brutalize Rodney King, the evidentiary video presented by House manager Raskin depicts violence of a different sort. In this case, insurgents direct their anger and fury at the democratic process itself; the theater of the state is breached as clashes unfold with the Capitol police.[34] In fact, the first ninety seconds of the video are weighed down with anticipation of the breach itself. The opening segment's pivot from broadcast footage of Trump's rants to a compilation of smartphone footage from a distant crowd of enthusiastic supporters inscribes a deep sense of dread and anticipation for the inevitable violation of the space of electoral certification. An unmistakable edit in this segment teases out the link between Trump's appeal and the mob's inevitable actions when we hear his earlier refrain—"Where the hell did they come from?"—repeated verbatim by an angry protestor among the crowd descending on the Capitol. The state turns on itself as a sitting executive steers an impassioned crowd toward the legislative branch in hopes of changing the election's outcome. In place of police officers beating an African American man in an all-too-familiar act of anti-Black racism,

Capitol police are placed in the position of holding the line against an angry assemblage of conspiracists. Impeachment, then, becomes the ultimate theater for finding redress when a president eggs on a multitude of followers to move against democratic proceedings, placing police officers in harm's way as they protect against this unimaginable breach. The dramatic structure of the video entails an arrangement of sights and sounds from the insurrection that showcase the vulnerability of our democratic processes in hopes of shoring them up, to avoid their return in some future January exception. Precarity and persistence are rendered aesthetic values for those within the Senate chamber and for those without.

The video proceeds in its documentation of the day's events with additional text announcing that the "crowd [has breached] the protective barricades of the Capitol as Congress meets to count and affirm the votes of the Electoral College." The violence that has loomed over the first minute and a half of the video is more proximate than ever, setting up the dramatic use of parallel editing to presage the convergence of democratic certification and insurrection, of politics (institutional status quo), and the political (rebellion, disruption, intrusion). At this point, we are plunged into the violence of the front line: insurrectionists clash with Capitol police as they weaponize security barriers. Metal barricades and chain link fences are toppled; the outnumbered, overwhelmed police officers fail to prevent hordes of protestors from breaking through the perimeter and racing toward the Capitol, seen in the distance. The view of this scene comes from a smartphone; it firmly locates us on the side of those pushing and pressing forward. This view from within the throng of protestors is soon displaced by a televisual one of the House chamber, where the joint session of the Senate and the House of Representatives is commencing at 1 p.m. Eastern Standard Time. The edit is briefly preceded by the sound of two gavel strikes, smoothly transitioning from outside to inside while also spotlighting the clash between the two scenes given to us: the institutional and the insurrectional. The outside cacophony yields to political ritual as the sergeant at arms of the House proclaims, "Madam speaker! The vice president and the United States Senate!" The vice president's entrance into the chamber is shown courtesy of C-SPAN, the audiovisual medium of record (as indicated by an on-screen watermark logo).

Parallel editing is a classic cinematic means of communicating continuity and temporal simultaneity. By cutting from outside to inside the Capitol, the compilation video demonstrates that these two scenes—toppling the barricade and initiating ballot certification—are temporally proximate, if not simultaneous. But more than this, we know that these scenes are also spatially contiguous and on a collision course, thanks to an external view of the Capitol, toward which the insurrectionists are headed. The temporal and spatial alignment of the footage is reinforced as the video then toggles outside, showcasing additional smartphone footage of confrontations between protestors and police officers, including one insurrectionist who warns an officer, "We outnumber you a million to one out here," as well as a mob shouting, "Let us in!" Furthermore, the use of expository text announces that "President Trump continues his speech as Members take their seats," then cutting to news footage of Trump insisting that the "Constitution says you have to protect our country . . . and you can't vote on fraud. And fraud breaks up everything, doesn't it? When you catch somebody in a fraud, you're allowed to go by very different rules." Our view of Trump immediately shifts after his delivery of this line back to C-SPAN's coverage of certification, but this time, our focus is directly on Vice President Pence in front of the American flag on the dais in the House chamber. Nevertheless, aurally, we remain with Trump. His ominous words ring out over an image of Pence in the House: "So I hope Mike [Pence] has the courage to do what he has to do." In this case, Trump is pinning his hopes of overturning the 2020 presidential election onto Pence's role in the certification process. In the weeks leading up to January 6, Trump had been pressuring Pence to reject the results of the Electoral College rather than follow the parliamentarian and the conventions of congressional authority.[35]

The nimble way this sequence presents competing but contiguous views requires viewers to shuffle multiple modes of reception. Parallel editing techniques ensure that the spatiotemporal relationships between the events shown (protestors overwhelming police; commencement of certification; Trump's speech) are clear and closely aligned; the sequence is nevertheless energized by a clash of viewing modes in which the embedded and handheld visions of insurrection are juxtaposed with static, mainstream, and professional visions of certification. Perspectives from above and below are entangled; this in turn aesthetically forewarns us of the intersection of procedural pageantry with the visceral nature of insurrection, disruption, and uprising. This early fusion of perspectives fulfills the needs of the multiple modes of interpretation at work here, following Schwartz's assessment above. Specifically, the use of continuity techniques to maximize temporal proximity and topographic orientation secures an evidentiary view of the video footage and appeals to a mode of interpretation in accordance with the impeachment viewing context. Above all, however, this arrangement of sights and sounds aligns with judicial values of rationality, judgment, and the determination of guilt, offering a manifestly rhetorical intervention via the grammar of film. Such a logic addresses both audiences—the one in the Senate chamber and the one online—as worthy of persuasion; audiences are treated as a community of viewers whose assessment of guilt is both politically and constitutionally desirable. In other words, even if the constitutional threshold of the two-thirds supermajority necessary to convict is not reached in the Senate, then at least the case for conviction (of which this compilation video is a component) would at least have been convincingly made for the public at large.

This appeal to a quasijudicial mode of interpretation is not sufficient, however. The video's reliance on an arrangement of footage according to rationality, clarity, and spatiotemporal orientation is not the whole story. Rather, the compilation video also aims to "terminate in . . . the subject of common sense." The shock that accompanies the logic animating the video is conveyed as much by the contrasting scenes as by specific depictions of violence and confrontation. Up to this point in the video, the biggest surprise is the ease with which the protestors overcame the barricades and the relative dearth of police presence on the Capitol steps. We have yet to encounter the most famous scenes of fierce engagement within the halls of the Capitol itself and the crushing bottleneck of the Capitol entrance. Yet the rotation of views from within the surge of protestors and the ceremonial proceedings of electoral certification from the House chamber—with clips of Trump's bombastic encouragement mixed in—clearly evoke a sense of dramatic, if not emotional, overwhelm as this series of events unfolds. In this sense, the reliance on parallel editing reminds us that such a staple of continuity editing often does more than simply communicate the fact that distinct actions are occurring close in time or simultaneously. Instead, the conveyance of simultaneity often implies a comparison between two or more differentiated lines of action, thereby accentuating anticipation for resolution through dramatic collision. The alternation between each set of events is not merely evidentiary; it is also emotional and climactic. Rather than efface the "very marks of historical trauma," this use of parallel editing undoubtedly enhances and restages these marks for the audience by prioritizing dramatic collision and a sense of elemental shock. If Schwartz is correct that the "materiality of vision disappears in translating the image into a set of facts" within a judicial mode of interpretation, then something else is going on here. The dueling viewing contexts yield multiple modes of interpretation—juridical and affective—in which the rational and the visceral, the cognitive and the shocking, are fully entangled.

Such convergences are only intensified by the inevitable breach into the halls of Congress—a breach that has been anticipated all along. The pattern I have described of alternating interior and exterior views continues until the 5:34 time mark, when smartphone footage captures the scene from within the Capitol at a high angle as insurrectionists incessantly pound on a glass pane until it shatters. The scenes next featured in the video conjoin unfettered chaos with the spatial confines of doorways, corridors, lobbies, hallways, and the Senate and House chambers. Chance encounters, confrontations (some deadly), and desperate retreats play out as the debates are halted, Congress is placed under lockdown, and Congress members evacuate. The shooting of Ashli Babbitt, the intervention of officer Eugene Goodman to "divert [the] mob away from Senators and the Vice President," and the pinning of officer Daniel Hodges in a Capitol doorway are some of the most harrowing and traumatic moments featured in the video.

In fact, the narrativization of all these disparate moments, condensed and sequenced, continues to serve both evidentiary and affective ends. In her February 10, 2021, column for the *Washington Post,* Margaret Sullivan observes that her familiarity with some of the compilation video's footage has not blunted its emotional impact.[36] In fact, she insists that one would be justified in thinking that the "impact of those horrible sounds and images would have faded through sheer repetition." Instead, she asks her readers why this was not the case when the compilation video was screened by the House managers: "What is it about the Jan. 6 footage that defies the thermodynamic law of the Internet age, that makes it grow *more* compelling with time?" Her answer speaks to the video's narrativization, as it was "not until Tuesday's presentation . . . [that] anyone [had] a chance to process what the clips showed. . . . Now, we could finally see context. We could see cause and effect." The compilation video takes what had been a "jumble of disaggregated clips, dumped onto social media" and renders it as "an orderly collection, a certain arrangement of signs, traces, and monuments," to return to Rancière's discussion of memory.[37] Yet this meaningful sequence, which offers a comforting narrational logic, also unsettles and disturbs. It may make one "ill" and could have a "traumatizing" effect on the viewer.[38]

This compilation video is just an example of the wide range of digital material offered as evidence during the 2021 impeachment proceedings. There is much more to say about the incorporation of police body camera footage and photography as a means of narrativizing and revisiting the traumatic events of January 6. Impeachment's status as a televisual spectacle would also need to be acknowledged to fully assess its mitigation of the damage done to our democratic traditions by the insurrection and the conspiratorial cultures from which the latter sprang. Nevertheless, this discussion of the Debevoise & Plimpton compilation video can serve as an entry point into how an emergent digital documentary vernacular is a discursive as well as practical extension of postpolitical crises and conditions. In this sense, we are presented with an affective map of our postpolitical state through a staging of Wilson and Swyngedouw's precarity–persistence dilemma. The impeachment process more generally may seek to revisit, resolve, and ultimately return to a stable democratic order, but these efforts are constrained by an inescapably fragile future tense (reinforced by Raskin's introductory comments) as well as by an aesthetic precarity constituting the documentary record that opened these proceedings. Such precarity coincides with the digital documentary vernacular, which includes visuals drawn from security cameras, cable channels, and smartphone footage taken from multiple sources, which are then animated via an appropriative editing style that establishes dramatic spatiotemporal connections. The postfoundational ontology of postpolitical thought, then, finds expression in the video's motley remix of digital imagery and audio, reproducing Elsaesser's descent into the digital swirl of YouTube.

If a postpolitical perspective is insistent on the fallibility and contingency of our social order, then a digital documentary vernacular similarly reminds us that signification depends on arrangement as an orderly but always tentative collection and memorialization. The latter endorses an aesthetics of frailty in which overwhelm and insecurity are not flaws but instead features of our digital aesthetic experience, echoing the postpolitical view of Trumpism as expressive of rather than antagonistic toward our postpolitical circumstances. In this sense, digital documentary encapsulates our dilemma in aesthetic form by mapping our postpolitical condition, but it also leaves us bereft of a clear pathway toward a deeper and more profound acknowledgment of historic wrongs and their present-day implications. The restorative project of impeachment is thus left hollow and incomplete. To return to Rancière's comment on documentary film, remembrance "must be created against the overabundance of information as well as against its absence." The traces of that very creation are palpable throughout this evidentiary video, ensuring that its own contingency remains at the surface, toggling between exposition and affect while thwarting any sense of closure.

Notes

1. The phrase "January exception" was used by Representative Raskin to demonstrate the dangerous implications of Senator Rand Paul's point of order that it would be unconstitutional to pursue an impeachment trial of former president Donald Trump, considering the latter is no longer in office. This claim—if affirmed—implies that presidents can engage in unconstitutional behavior in their final weeks in office with impunity. See Emily Czachor, "What Is a January Exception? Impeachment Manager Says Failure to Convict Could Set Dangerous Precedent," *Newsweek,* February 9, 2021, www.newsweek.com/what-january

-exception-impeachment-manager-says-failure-convict-could-set-dangerous-precedent-1568065.

2. Justin Hendrix, "Social Media Video Evidence in Impeachment Trial: Lessons from International Tribunals," Just Security, February 5, 2021, www.justsecurity.org/74565/social-media-video-evidence-in-impeachment-trial-lessons-from-international-tribunals.

3. Mike DeBonis, Tom Hamburger, Karoun Demirjian, and Amy Gardner, "House Democrats Building Elaborate, Emotionally Charged Case against Trump," *Washington Post,* January 29, 2021, www.washingtonpost.com/politics/house-democrats-building-elaborate-emotionally-charged-case-against-trump/2021/01/29/d35170fe-626c-11eb-9061-07abcc1f9229_story.html.

4. The full name of the committee is the Select Committee to Investigate the January 6th Attack on the United States Capitol, but it is often shortened to the House Select Committee or the January 6th Committee. The committee was terminated in 2023 and their website archived (https://www.loc.gov/item/lcwaN0036971/).

5. See Paul Gready, *The Era of Transitional Justice: The Aftermath of the Truth and Reconciliation Commission in South Africa and Beyond* (New York: Routledge, 2011).

6. The constraints of such a process reflects the limitations of a politics of consensus, the history of which has been written about by historians; Wall, for instance, notes how this dream of consensus persists in the present and often betrays a certain "nostalgia for an earlier age." Wendy L. Wall, *Inventing the American Way: The Politics of Consensus from the New Deal to the Civil Rights Movement* (Oxford: Oxford University Press, 2008), 290.

7. Japhy Wilson and Erik Swyngedouw, "Seeds of Dystopia: Post-politics and the Return of the Political," in *The Post-political and Its Discontents: Spaces of Depoliticisation, Spectres of Radical Politics,* ed. Japhy Wilson and Erik Swyngedouw (Edinburgh: Edinburgh University Press, 2014), 10.

8. Slavoj Žižek, *The Ticklish Subject: The Absent Centre of Political Ontology* (London: Verso, 2000), 199.

9. Žižek, 199.

10. Žižek, 200.

11. Žižek, 200; emphasis in the original.

12. Wilson and Swyngedouw, "Seeds of Dystopia," 4.

13. See Jonathan Dovey and Mandy Rose, "This Great Mapping of Ourselves: New Documentary Forms Online," in *The Documentary Film Book,* ed. Brian Winston (London: Palgrave Macmillan, 2013), 366–67; and Jean Burgess and Joshua Green, *YouTube* (Cambridge: Polity, 2009), 25.

14. Wilson and Swyngedouw, "Seeds of Dystopia," 10–11.

15. Jacques Rancière, *Film Fables,* trans. Emiliano Battista (New York: Bloomsbury, 2016), 157.

16. Rancière, 157.

17. Rancière, 158.

18. Qtd. in Dovey and Rose, "This Great Mapping," 368. Also see Thomas Elsaesser, "Tales of Epiphany and Entropy: Around the World in Eighty Clicks," in *The YouTube Reader,* ed. Pelle Snickars and Patrick Vonderau (Stockholm: National Library of Sweden, 2009), 181, 183.

19. See Zoë Druick and Deane Williams, eds., *The Grierson Effect: Tracing Documentary's International Movement* (London: British Film Institute Press, 2014).

20. Ian Aitken, *Film and Reform: John Grierson and the Documentary Film Movement* (London: Routledge, 1990), 7.

21. Aitken, 7.

22. Also see Brian Winston, *Claiming the Real: Documentary: Grierson and Beyond* (London: British Film Institute, 2009).

23. Steven Shaviro, *Post-cinematic Affect* (Winchester, Eng.: Zero/Collective Ink, 2010), 3; emphasis in the original.

24. Shaviro, 3; emphasis in original.

25. Louis-Georges Schwartz, *Mechanical Witness: A History of Motion Picture Evidence in U.S. Courts* (Oxford: Oxford University Press, 2009), 6.

26. Schwartz, 5.

27. Schwartz, 6.

28. Schwartz, 6.

29. Schwartz, 7.

30. Schwartz, 8. In this context, Schwartz's use of "common sense" refers critically to an idealist perspective "unconditioned by any institutional frame" or an assumed perspective "that comes naturally to everyone, everywhere" (7).

31. Schwartz, 8.

32. Schwartz, 10.

33. See Karoun Demirjian, "As Video of the Capitol Riot Played, Some GOP Senators Turned Away," *Washington Post,* February 9, 2021, www.washington post.com/politics/2021/02/09/trump-impeachment-live-updates/#link-NBU4 S74MBJGVTEM36CWW5Z7VKY.

34. See Tom Dreisbach, "Nearly 1 in 5 Defendants in Capitol Riot Cases Served in the Military," *All Things Considered,* NPR, January 21, 2021, www.npr .org/2021/01/21/958915267/nearly-one-in-five-defendants-in-capitol-riot-cases -served-in-the-military.

35. See Michael S. Schmidt, "Trump Says Pence Can Overturn His Loss in Congress. That's Not How It Works," *New York Times,* January 5, 2021, www .nytimes.com/2021/01/05/us/politics/pence-trump-election.html.

36. Margaret Sullivan, "The Jan. 6 Images Were Already Disturbing. The Impeachment-Trial Video Makes Them Terrifying," *Washington Post,* February 10, 2021, www.washingtonpost.com/lifestyle/media/impeachment-insurrection-vid eo/2021/02/09/85463eb0-6b1f-11eb-ba56-d7e2c8defa31_story.html.

37. Sullivan. See also Rancière, *Film Fables,* 157.

38. Sullivan, "Jan. 6 Images."

CHAPTER 7

Dissensus, Refusal, Participatory Music

Negation and Rupture in Crowd in C

ERIC LEMMON

Participatory music poses significant creative, social, and political dilemmas for audiences, performers, and authors alike. These dilemmas—questions of authorship, the usurpation of traditional concert relationships, or the displacement of productive labor onto audiences—have not dissuaded composers working in the Western concert art music tradition as they have sought to break down social and political barriers between themselves, the performers, and the audience. Well-known composers in the genre, including Pauline Oliveros, Christian Wolff, and Huang Ruo, have written pieces that explicitly explore their own role as composers in relation to the other primary constituent parties of the concert music experience.[1] Indeed, in the case of Wolff and Oliveros, the composers explore these relations specifically for their political natures.[2] Other composers who center their practice around electronic and electroacoustic music have also become interested in handing control of the musical production of such works over to the audience, often with the intent of emphasizing the social dimensions of this participatory paradigm, and have done so through the mobilization of digital and network technologies. For example, Luke Dahl, Jorge Herrera, and Carr Wilkerson describe their participatory computer music system *TweetDreams* as a "collaborative musical experience" and intend it to be "a way to bring people who are co-located and spread across the globe into a real-time, communal and public music-making experience."[3] Another work by Jason Freeman, entitled *Glimmer,* uses cameras and light-detection software to track light sticks as they are waved by audience members in order to generate notation live for a small chamber orchestra of string musicians.[4] Commenting on the motivation for composing and designing *Glimmer,* Freeman posited that "drawing listeners into active creative roles" is a way to give them "a new reason to listen closely, since they have a personal stake in the sounds they hear."[5]

In the normative, social, and institutional configurations of Western concert art music, composers create musical works, which are then interpreted by performers, while the audience staidly listens in the proscenium setting. The act of a composer handing a portion of the creative control of the artistic work to the audience or, more commonly, to performers, can thus be seen as a political act within this context. This dimension has been covered recently in scholarship about democracy in music, such as in Emily Payne and Philip Thomas's essay on Christian Wolff's *Exercises,* a set of musical works that offers "skeletal, indeterminate notation" that requires "players [to] negotiate a way of working with the score and with each other, making decisions prior to, and during, the moment of performance."[6] Georgina Born also gives careful consideration to audience roles for emergent, political collectives in various musical settings and the relationships between composers, performers, and audiences. The essay comes with especially astute observations on the "audiencing" enacted by the Clapton Ultras, a group of soccer fans with leftist politics, which—through musical cheers and spectacle, along with the group's practice of engaging as an audience, which reshaped the norms of the sporting event—"portends an audience . . . consciously forming itself, becoming conscious of themselves as actors, subjects of the performance event."[7] Politics informed by the French philosopher Jacques Rancière in improvised settings, jazz music most specifically, has also been explored by Dan DiPiero and Chris Stover.[8]

However, what is commonly only given cursory mention in these discussions is how individual or groups of audience members are situated in relation to one another within a participatory music space, how they negotiate power within the context of these settings, and how the specific form of this space typically reflects what is assumed to be a consensus-based political paradigm. Indeed, the aesthetic dimensions of this space are negotiated among the members of the audience during the constitution of the musical work while the audience also—often at the same time—plays the role of apprehenders or spectators. The frame of these works, whether they are set up by composer, performer, or presenter, or even if they are just concertgoing norms, constrain the power that participants can wield. In other words, the participatory space features norms and protocols that govern what the actuated audience may do.

I analyze this micropolitical space, and contestations of and within it, to illustrate how far it offers commentary for our broader postpolitical moment. In mobilizing the term micropolitical to describe this space of participatory music, I mean to use it to characterize a politics that is hyperlocal, perceptible, and present.[9] This contrasts with the monumentality and abstractness of the postpolitical, as the participatory music event's configurations are tangible to attendees, and its principal temporality is in the now; poiesis and esthesis are occurring simultaneously. Indeed, many critiques of the postpolitical paradigm are largely directed toward the macropolitical structures that govern national and supranational institutions. Grand metapolitical analyses of the hyperphenomenal postpolitical structure such as Mouffe's or Žižek's typically insist on a radical usurpation of the order (somehow) based on the ethical rendering that the structure is nefarious.[10] However, exhortations to move against postpolitical structures often run up against the scope of the stated task, as well as the macrostructure's inertia, its nebulousness, and its Shoggoth-like resistance to blows. This is where micropolitical spaces such as a participatory music event may serve as an illuminating subject of analysis and as a cogent metaphor that offers concrete means to deconstruct and resist hyperphenomenal objects like the postpolitical amoeba. Indeed, the participatory music event's normative configurations mirror the shape and form of the postpolitical wherein contestation over what parts actually "have a part" is forbidden by a range of sociotechnical and musical devices. Yet it is exactly in the combination of its hyperlocal, tangible, and normatively foreclosed nature that this political space can serve as a blueprint for how all political spaces can be reconfigured.

Here I will largely engage with Rancière's concepts that are set up in contrast to a normative understanding of politics: a "set of procedures whereby the aggregation and consent of collectivities is achieved, the organization of powers, the distribution of places and roles, and the systems for legitimizing this distribution," among constituent parties (so key for a postpolitical order).[11] This normative understanding of politics is what Rancière instead terms "the police."[12] For Rancière, politics, instead of being a divvying up of resources and/or a struggle for power, is a "determined activity" that ruptures the "tangible configuration" at hand and reconfigures it, or the "parties, parts, or lack of parts" that it contains.[13] Politics puts on display the contingent nature of the police order, and in truly political moments, equality and recognition are demanded by those whom the police order does not recognize as even deserving of recognition. In Rancière's view, dissensus—the "conflict between a sensory presentation and a way of making sense of it, or between several sensory regimes and/or 'bodies'"—is at the heart of this demand for both recognition and equality because it "redraws the frame within which common objects are determined."[14]

Because both sensory presentation and the ways of making sense of said sensory presentation are central to truly political acts, aesthetics plays a role in maintaining the police order as well as in any attempts to agitate for the expansion of equality. In the case of a participatory music experience, vast musical aesthetic choices abound. What instruments do the participants play? What musical notation system is deployed (e.g., Chinese *Guqin* tablature or the Western system of neumes), if one is deployed at all? What pitch system is used, if it is used at all? Is timbre structured? Do the participants activate sound without a fixed or extant musical system, or are they merely granted a space to make sound? Who makes all the above choices and who does not? The choices that must be made for sensory presentation are boundless, and each choice politically inflects the participatory space.

Similarly, the ways of making sense of these sensory presentations are as numerous as there are subjects to attend to them; personal history and neurodiversity are individual, as is affect chimerically lurking between audible perception and cognition. The unique physical structures of the pinnae of our ears filter sound into distinctly sized ear canals, while participants are (I hope) not so compressed into one another's space that they collapse into the undifferentiable space of a black hole. As such, the acoustic experience differs from person to person and from spot to spot within the performance area. The sense making therefore affects participants' comprehension of the musical symbol, and by extension their aesthetic preferences and choices as they return musical utterances into the participatory space.

Rancière's philosophy is largely concerned with universal notions of politics and equality, although he does draw on different examples across time and space to illustrate his theoretical assertions. However, it does raise interesting questions for the participatory music space and how agents that normatively have no part in the part are able to rupture any tangible configurations therein. How does the form of the police order and the political filter down to the local level of a concertgoing audience? Given the centrality of aesthetics to the dissensual moment, in what way does the space of a participatory work of music take on the formal figure of the police order, and in what ways can participants manifest a political moment? What consequences does this political moment then have for the aesthetic experience of the work? Through an analysis of Sang Won Lee's participatory computer music work *Crowd in C,* I will address some of these pertinent questions by examining the functioning of the work alongside an analysis of documentation from a live performance. This analysis will highlight how the postpolitical space and structure of a participatory musical work can be tugged and torn until it collapses or is reframed in unexpected ways, ultimately revealing the contingent nature of political spaces.

Participatory Music as Consensus-Based Police Order

Participation in music as a genre or as a means of musical production is often analyzed for its relevance for practitioners and scholars working within and on music improvisation, therapy, ethnography, and education.[15] That the field of music theory, or discussion centered on the Western concert art music tradition, has far less to say on participation points to the long-standing colonialist, gendered, and white racial frames within the practice (e.g., the expectation that a white male composer writes masterpieces for idolatrous audiences, or the fact that most music theory frameworks have been constructed for the purpose of analyzing European art music). Recently, however, a range of critical observations that discuss participation as well as musical works that deploy technology in the service of participation has emerged within the field of generative computer music.[16] The literature is principally focused on using new interfaces for musical expression to activate the audience, with a focus on sociality and engagement via the integration of wireless technology and personal consumer devices. An add-on effect, however, is that the technological interfaces and musical modes of engagement in these works also more readily reveal how power over the aesthetics of a participatory work is negotiated within a consensus-based space during its course.[17] That these works are consensus based and operate as a simulacrum of a political public (in the Habermasian sense) reveal how the normative participatory space formally operates as a police order.[18]

First, participatory music is most colloquially understood in contrast to the traditional experience of musical works where the audience principally listens. In participatory music, instead of attending to performers or sound sources (in the case of traditional spectatorship), the audience is mobilized to take part in the productive process. However, the act of spectatorship (or in music's case, listening) can itself be seen as a participatory act, a point made by Rancière in *The Emancipated Spectator* and then expanded on by Claire Bishop in her critique of participatory art in *Artificial Hells*.[19] After all, it is the act of listening that constitutes the musical symbol itself for the audience member. However, I use participation here to mean that audience members are producing the physical and musical trace at the same time as they are also apprehending it (whether that be electronic or analog contributions to the productive environment). In the case that the number of members in the audience is greater than one, participants are able to apprehend others' musical ideas and can use those ideas as an impetus to imitate, manipulate, or respond to other individuals' musical ideas.[20] These circulating musical ideas, generated by interlocuting participants, thus serve as a form of sonic discourse. By combining the potential for participatory dialogue as music is being produced with the idea that smaller, discursive subunits congeal into larger musical structures, members of a participatory musical setting negotiate the direction of the work during the work's performance. This is an informal political process that occurs within a space akin to a Habermasian public.[21]

That this consensus-based space is like a public should not be surprising; audience members already self-organize by choosing to attend the concert. The audience's gestures act as an expressive form that reflects a personal preference for performing an action that produces a particular sound, whether that be to create an individualistic expression or to join an ongoing musical texture. Meanwhile, the resultant sound is emitted not usually for another particular individual in the audience but for the entirety of the audience as part of the broader musical texture. The participatory musical setting thus has a social dimension wherein the audience members as interlocutors contribute to the internal musical discourse of the work via referents that are both intrinsically and extrinsically significant. Finally, for the participating audience, the musical discourse is embedded within social, political, and linguistic conventions that demarcate the space of the public. For example, *Crowd in C* is out of the Western concert art music tradition. This tradition has its own set of social and political norms, some innocuous and others problematic. For example, in this tradition, it is considered rude to leave before the end of the performance, and the normative figure of the composer is white and male. Similarly, in participatory music, the framing of the work as such encourages its own protocols and markers. Participants are usually expected to make music using the instrument and instructions provided. Nevertheless, it is within this space, with all its codes, discourses, and markers, that the audience's participatory gestures and musical elements accrete into larger structures, and that the participants' responses to one another in time within this constituted space qua public result in a politics of aesthetic preference.

In part, a focus on analyzing participatory computer music works and their systems is motivated by the clarity with which one can track the circulation of musical ideas within these cybernetic systems, where the concrete protocols, code, and the digitization of individuals' inputs serve to illustrate the political public constituted by the audience within participatory music. One can watch and hear—through digital sound synthesis of audience inputs and system outputs—musically significant ideas propagating through the audience and follow how consenting participants take up these ideas and play with them. Similar to being able to scrutinize the act of pulling the lever at the voting box and then counting the ballots, the preferences of audience members (or at least their closest preference) can be specifically examined.[22] However, any promise to completely transfer the struggle over the piece's aesthetic direction to the audience is dubious; the very protocols and codes that enable audience onboarding and accessibility and that make analysis easier also constrain and mediate the audience's aesthetic choices. It also forecloses possibilities for musical-political agitation against deeper structural and institutional systems in the concert music setting in favor of a simulation, wherein the political or active engagement with musical materials necessarily results in a work whose aesthetics are minimally changed from performance to performance despite the changes in audience membership, times, and places. Still, it is within these protocols and codes, as well as the social and political norms of concertgoing, that Rancièrian political action is reified, as the participants who have no part of the part that enables and constrains them can seize power in unexpected ways. A brief overview of how *Crowd in C* operates will prepare a discussion of participatory musical works in relation to Rancière's conceptual police, dissensus, and politics, as well as elicit questions on what exactly participatory music can poetically offer to the current political moment.

Sang Won Lee's *Crowd in C*

Crowd in C is a computer music system as well as a work of participatory music developed by Sang Won Lee, a computer scientist with an interest in musical human–computer interfaces. The work was first presented in 2015 at a Michigan Mobile Phone Ensemble concert at the University of Michigan, Ann Arbor.[23] Taking its moniker from Terry Riley's well-known minimalist work *In C,* the web-based instrument Lee developed encourages social interaction by offering audience members the option to create and modify their own melodies through a simple graphical user interface (GUI). Users are additionally given the option to browse, like, and copy others' melodies by bringing them up on their own device.[24] Participants generate sound via the Web Audio API, a JavaScript-based application programming interface (API) that allows for "processing and synthesizing audio in web applications" on their personal devices.[25] Sound is played directly from the device's built-in outputs for the participant and those around them to hear. By using the Web Audio API, Lee created a work that would be immediately accessible to those using their mobile phones, or any other device that could be transported into the concert hall and that runs a modern web browser. In performances of this work, the colocated audience members manipulate the GUI while sound plays from their devices, creating a lush musical texture in aggregate. For the purposes of this description, a participant is a member of the audience taking part in the musical experience, while the performer takes on a quasitechnical role, and whose choices loom over the aesthetic direction of the work. The performer manages the formal structure of the work: when the piece starts and stops, when key changes occur, or when new options for social interaction are introduced to the audience interface. The performer often sits on a stage or at the focal point of the hall alongside a screen that displays a social scoreboard. The role of the performer does not necessarily have to be taken on by the creator of the work and system, but Lee has tended to fill that role in the past.

The core music generation feature of *Crowd in C* is the web GUI, which has five "note-dots." These are linked in a chain superposed on seven horizontal and alternating light gray and gray bars that indicate scalar degrees (similar to the keys on a piano). The scale degrees in this context refer to the numerical distance, in consecutive steps, that a note is from a tonic within the Western system of neumes. For example, in C major, C would be scale degree 1, D–2, E–3, and so on. The note-dots can be moved by dragging them around the interface's two-dimensional plane with a mouse, or alternatively fingers in the case of a capacitive touch screen (like those on many modern mobile devices and tablets). Controlling the temporal placement of sonic events is a "play-dot," which traverses the chain of note-dots at a fairly constant rate. Participants have a modicum of control over the rate of traversal according to the distance they place the note-dots apart from one another. When the play-dot arrives at a note-dot as it travels along the chain, it plays back the scale degree on which the note-dot rests, which is inferred by users through the aforementioned alternating bars that traverse the GUI. The play-dot loops. So long as a participant has a browser open and the sound of their device on, sound will be generated continuously (Figure 7.1).

With the system providing the audience the ability to like, compare, and copy others' melodies, Lee describes it as a "temporary social network," with the "short tune . . . used as a musical profile," much like the dating app Tinder.[26] More specifically, he sees the purpose of facilitating these types of social interactions through the application as allowing a user to "express oneself, to attract more people and to find a (musical) match among the participants."[27] Further, Lee believes that an audience member being able to both see and hear another member's melody inspires the participants to discover new means of playing the instrument.[28] When a participant likes another's tune, the other is notified with a message "[NAME] likes your tune!" If the other likes the original participant's tune as well, it displays to the original participant, "It's a match!

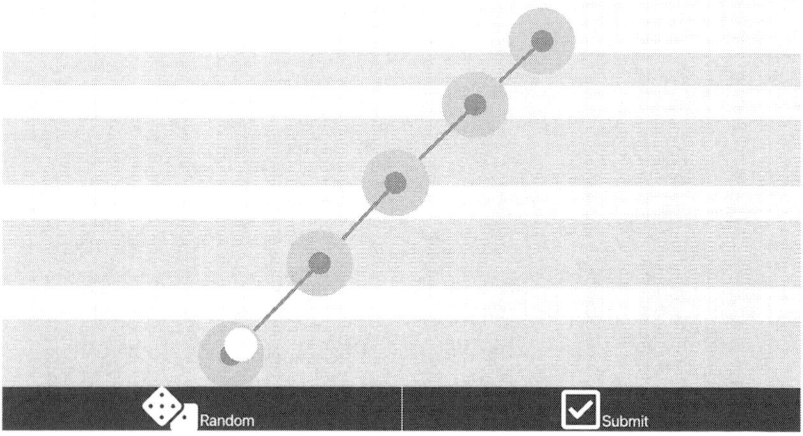

FIGURE 7.1. Example of the user interface in Sang Won Lee's *Crowd in C.* Sang Won Lee and Aaron Willette, *Crowd in C,* in *Proceedings of the 2019 Conference on Creativity and Cognition,* 428.

[NAME] liked you back!"[29] Dating app familiarity aside, Lee's system forms a distributed network of social relations via this particular subunit of the system, as only those who have been liked—or liked back—are notified of who liked their tune. At the same time, mutual likes generate sonic events different from those made by the play-dots toward the end of the musical experience, when the software is formally advanced by the performer of the work.

A centralized performer interface within the computer music system also influences the social and political relations.[30] On this performer interface, all current participants who have logged into the system via their browser are listed. It also displays separately the participant whose melody is the most liked and the participant whose melody is the most copied. Further, this interface allows the performer to control the harmonic content of the work as it progresses (Figure 7.2).[31]

An example of this would be the performer changing the scale in use from the initial key of C major to another collection of pitches via a live-coding interface in JavaScript that propagates the new harmonic language to participant devices. It also allows the performer to send messages to all the currently logged-in participants, an act that Lee et al. describe as an intervention. During performances of the work, this messaging system is

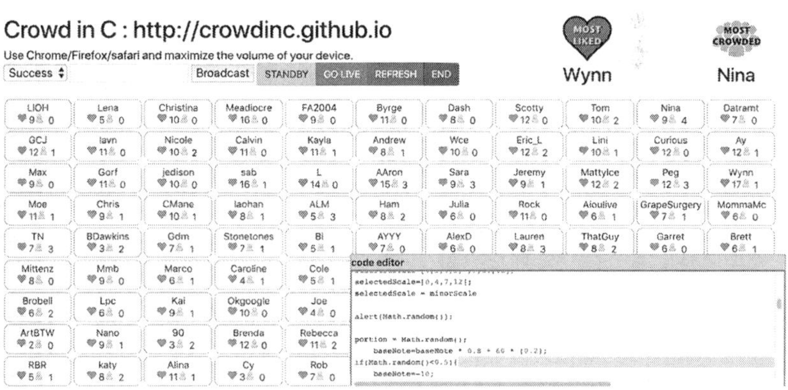

FIGURE 7.2. Example of the performer's GUI in Sang Won Lee's *Crowd in C.* Sang Won Lee and Aaron Willette, *Crowd in C,* in *Proceedings of the 2019 Conference on Creativity and Cognition,* 429.

used both to guide the audience through the application's functions and to remind users of its features. In analyses of user interactions after these performer interventions, Lee et al. report that the audience responded immediately to these prompts, which subsequently affected the aesthetic experience of the work.[32] In performances of *Crowd in C,* this interface is projected onto a large screen so that the audience can see the list of current participants, as well as the most liked and most copied melodies. Indeed, it is with the capture of data on the most liked and most copied melodies that Lee's piece explicitly allows us to examine how the expression of aesthetic (and/or social) preference for a particular melody impacts the mimetic circulation of these melodic subunits. Lee's system provides an effective sociotechnical means to demonstrate the work's space as functioning like a consensus-based political public.

Beyond the coding that controls sound generation and helps to construct the musical and social space of the piece, Lee and his collaborators also developed an interaction trace logger. This system records the kinds of interactions and data on the participants involved in the interaction on a relational basis. For example, the interaction trace logger will track who likes which melody and from whom the respective melody came. It will also log if a user performs any actions subsequent to this initial action—if users like a melody and then subsequently revise their own, for example, then these actions will be coupled and logged for future analysis.[33] The logger does not display this information to the audience in real time and it is not available publicly. The developers' goal in building this logger was to be able to "understand if audience members' intentions in interacting with the instrument are purely musical or social (e.g., a participant decided to revisit and revise a melody after seeing someone else's melody)."[34]

Many of the functions and protocols described here pose significant questions, as they relate to common cultural, social, and political critiques of the mobilization of new technology in the service of artistic practices. Lee himself notes that epistemological problems in electronic music and its virtuality can lead to moments of confusion for members of the audience.[35] For example, it may not initially be clear to users how their participation is part of the broader texture of *Crowd in C.* Further, the capability for individual sense making of the aesthetic object and participatory setting is made all the more unstable when the performer, unseen by the audience, changes the musical mode and automatically pushes it to all the users' devices. The interface has not changed but the pitches have, with no apparent warning or reason. The user's sense of sound and sense making of self in relation to the participatory setting is immediately cast into disarray, and the virtuality of the computer music setting and the performer/author's real control cracks through the confines of the police order. The participant may then reasonably ask, "Am I a part with no part?"

Indeed, the creator/programmer and the performer retain much of the musical control over the work. The audience, meanwhile, is nudged to behave in certain ways. For example, the performer's GUI, which is projected for all to see and which includes what is akin to a social scoreboard with the most liked and most copied melodies displayed prominently, is tinged with the disciplinary control of the panopticon.[36] The projected GUI displays whether audience members are logged in at all, thus effectively publicizing whether a member is engaging in the norm of the participatory setting. As a result, the participant has been induced into a "state of conscious and permanent visibility that assures" the sustenance of the participatory aesthetic rendering.[37] Further, the audience participant is explicitly encouraged to continuously engage with the work through the scoreboard and to discipline their expressive utterances to effect what they perceive to be high-scoring melodies according to the current audience's taste or tastes. These social goals are in direct competition with a user's desire to experiment with the interface to produce results more in line with personal aesthetic preferences. On top of this, the norms of the participatory space itself disciplines audience members to participate. Sitting alone in the context of a hall without participating, where one is meant to be actively engaging in poiesis while all others around you are, is something one would be cogently aware of thanks to the social context of the space and one that participants would feel pressure to conform to. Still, given this consensus-based space, where audience member control over their aesthetic experience is limited for practical purposes related to audience onboarding, accessibility, and aesthetic vision, there is also the potential for political moments to occur that affect the aesthetic and disciplinary experience from a Rancièrian perspective, which can be seen from a nuanced consideration of the data logged and video documentation from live performances of *Crowd in C*.

Dissensus and Refusal in *Crowd in C*

Because aesthetic preference is so central to the means by which participatory works constitute themselves as musical symbols (in the semiotic sense), politics from a Rancièrian perspective can offer a new mode with which to consider how audiences themselves are able to decenter power from the grip of the performer-author and usurp the consensus-based model I have argued to exist earlier. While power over the musical texture writ large is being negotiated in real time by the audience via the inputs of participants according to their aesthetic apprehension, the music is ever mediated by Lee's generative algorithms for sound production. Clearly, political and musical choice over the aesthetic direction of the work is largely foreclosed by the strictures that the software places on the musical range and the social space, and the possibilities for musical expressivity are narrowed by normative modes of interaction with the participatory artwork. It would seem, then, that within these normative features of the participatory music setting and its police order, Lee has the most influential voice in the aesthetic rendering of negotiated power at play and the audience is confined within a microcosmic, postpolitical space that is utterly contingent on their adherence to these norms—norms that most are happy to acquiesce to. Indeed, Lee plays the role of Mouffe's governing technical "expert," whose choices the audience *should* accept for them to be integrated into the participatory musical experience.[38] These technical choices include questions on musical structure and form as well as broader aesthetic direction: musical mode, pitch structure, rhythmic choices, external discursive references (i.e., Terry Riley's *In C*), aggregate texture, musical interface design, social scoreboards, and more.

Still, it is through some of the sociotechnical devices that Lee instituted in *Crowd in C* (e.g., the interaction trace logger, the social scoreboard) and the documentation of the musical event itself that participants can be seen as engaging in a Rancièrian style of politics within such a musical work. As part of their reflection on and analysis of the social engagement that occurred in *Crowd in C* during a performance at the Virginia Tech School of Performing Arts, Lee et al. describe the kinds of melodies that were arranged by the participants on the GUI during the course of a performance.[39] Surprisingly, the most popular melodies frequently turned out to be visual symbols, including a star, the initials of the school, or the letter W, which the system then dutifully translated into sound (Figure 7.3). Lee describes this result as being entirely astonishing, as he expected the audience members to interact with the GUI and arrange their melodies according to the aesthetics of the music generated; visual referents were not imagined as playing a role.[40] Yet here is the first, although brief, moment of Rancièrian politics within the space of *Crowd in C,* as audience members are no longer participating on the basis of their preference for the particulars of the sonic aesthetics of their melodies. Instead, they have stepped outside sound itself and usurped the intended impetus for social relations and consensus-based politics by complicating these dimensions with visual and more concretely referential—even semantic—symbols. Moreover, before performing this work, Lee delivers brief remarks directing the audience to the requisite web page for participation, as well as instructions on how to use the GUI. Lee's remarks clearly situate the melodies as being *composed* as opposed to *drawn,* which makes the choice of audience members who utilize visual representations all the more opposed to the original police order of *Crowd in C*—at least until the first visual symbol is submitted and the rest of the audience gradually becomes aware of that possibility in creative play.[41]

Perhaps more subtle, but certainly far more consequential to the experience of the work (and participatory works in general), is the figure of the participant who refuses to engage in the poietic process. In a wide-angle shot of the audience from an audiovisual recording of a performance of *Crowd in C* that took place at the 2016 Web Audio Conference, such a figure (whom I will call participant X) can be seen attending to the music. Once the audience has been prepped through Lee's remarks, the audience members around participant X have readied their mobile devices and the performance starts, but participant X makes no motion

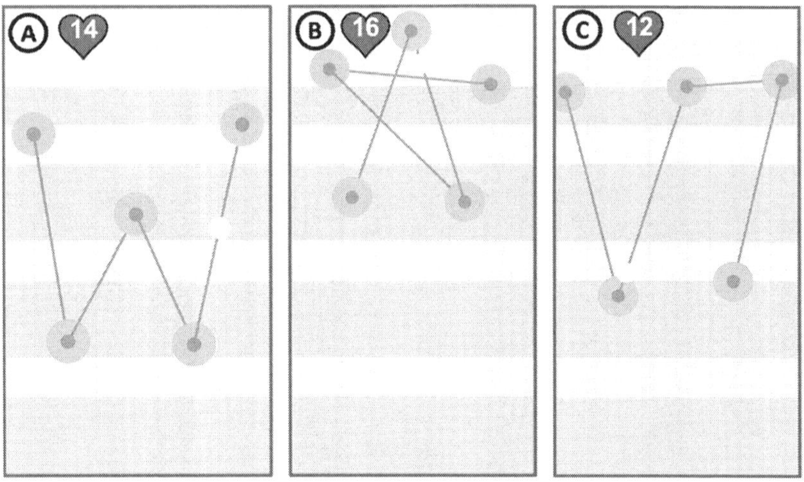

FIGURE 7.3. Visual symbols that altered the distribution of the sensible from graphical renderings of musical ideas to musical renderings of graphic ideas. Sang Won Lee et al., "The Effect of Social Interaction on Facilitating Audience Participation in a Live Music Performance," in *Proceedings of the 2019 Conference on Creativity and Cognition* (San Diego: ACM, 2019), 115.

to take out a phone or engage in the process of music making; nor does participant X do so for the rest of the performance.[42] One or even a few participants engaging in this form of refusal during this particular performance would ultimately only have a modicum of influence on the direction of the musical work; indeed, the audience had dozens of attendees, and throughout the duration of the performance, the musical texture was rich with the idiomatic simple wave forms that give the work its gentle character. Still, participant X's presence points to the potentials of outright collapse in *Crowd in C.* What if the audience was entirely made up of participants like participant X, who would rather only listen, or who simply do not want to submit to the structures of the participatory setting or system?

Though they did not occur en masse in this particular performance, such intentional or unintentional refusals can utterly collapse the consensus-based space and aesthetic experience. Indeed, they have occurred elsewhere, including in my own work. From 2019 to 2022, I coded and composed a computer music system and participatory work of my own, entitled *Politics I,* to explicitly highlight this consensus-based political space and explore how restructuring audience interactions with it mediates the aesthetic outcome. In *Politics I,* audience members are given agency (much like in *Crowd in C*) to affect the aesthetic direction of the work and are explicitly given information about how their actions impact the direction in return. In a December 2022 performance at the Xenakis Networked Music Performance Marathon, the work began, but absolutely nobody engaged. The system sat silent without input, and there was simply no music for a time until the audience was mobilized.

Viewed from within the neoliberal problematics of participatory art, or in this case participatory music, where the productive labor for musical creation is pushed off onto audiences, participant X subtly usurps the sensible configurations of music production within *Crowd in C* (or *Politics I*). Instead of laboring to perpetuate sound production and variation, participant X engages in an older, more traditional sensibility, whereby participation occurs through the constitution of the musical symbol through individual perceptualizations of sonic vibrations, which is then understood through personal history—an emancipated spectator. Such participants thereby divest themselves of the poietic process. This traditional sensibility of experiencing music may engender a truly political and dissensual moment for the sense making of Lee's (and my own) participatory work. When enough members of this constituted public refused in *Politics I,* for whatever reason, the work ceased completely, or the density of its texture was so sparse as to affect the aesthetic experience significantly. In this moment, the sensible configuration opens like a chasm for the audience: Is the work over? Has something gone wrong? Or, for those participants familiar with and subscribing to a hagiography of Cage, are the sparse sonic protrusions and interruptions of silence the music itself? For both audience and composer, then, the desire to simply listen rather than participate becomes a Rancièrian political act for which the stakes could not be higher in Lee's *Crowd in C* and my *Politics I.* Indeed, these actions demonstrate clearly that audience members maintain their status as musical and political subjects, even as they sit in silence. Further, the fact that solely attending subscribes to the disciplinary norms of etiquette in the concert art music setting is all the more subversive; it turns the institution's norms against itself.

The collapsing participatory artwork (so denied actualization by the audience's resistance to engage) differs from spectacles resistant to "alternative interpretations and/or subversive readings" that permit more clearly delineated frames of interpretation by political communicators.[43] And while the emancipated spectator (who always asserts political agency by interpreting the trace) is ever present, the uncertain state of the participatory artwork does something unexpected to those engaging in the productive process.[44] The teetering of the artwork turns the audience's attention toward the institution itself: the Oz behind the curtain, the concert hall, the other audience members, even themselves. The shambling wreckage of the failed art space reifies audience members' political agency by forcing them to ask: "what *should* I be doing *here?*"—with "should" being both an ethical and technical question. It also exposes the setting's dependence on the choices made by the creator and/or performer that circumscribe the space. Finally, the collapse of participation raises a gray specter for this postpolitical simulacrum: the space only exists so long as everyone experiences and accepts it.

Between the lines of consensual participation and the Rancièrian political exist small refusals and resistances, points where audience members tear and tug at the fabric of the postpolitical form. Each push (operating inputs based on visual rather than aural aesthetics; engaging the work purely by apprehending the trace; or even disrupting the concert with music of their own design) heralds a torrent that can overcome the intended, normative aesthetic rendering of the musical, participatory police order. This police order can, of course, fold back onto these utterances that represent a participant's demand for musical recognition by accepting certain audience behaviors as part of the musical work. For example, Lee could simply claim, ex post facto, that the act of drawing letters or symbols with the play-dot chains is an acceptable and welcome part of the piece. Or the maw of Cageian silence (a figure for the Rancièrian aesthetic regime if there ever was one) could easily be incorporated into the possibilities of *Crowd in C* with the simple gesture of a claim. Yet these events reveal the contingent nature of the participatory work and its production as an aesthetic object. The audience has the power not only to reconfigure (or nullify) the event as it occurs within the confines of its police order but also to force changes to the composition writ large. The audience—the part that has no part—recomposes the bounds of the possible within the work.

Given the low stakes of participatory musical spaces and events, what does a participant's ability to rupture and refuse have for our broader postpolitical moment—a moment that has utterly failed to address the gargantuan stakes of issues like climate change, the ethics of contemporary technologies like AI and widespread, web-based surveillance, or neoliberal capitalism? As a reflection of the postpolitical, participatory spaces offer audiences a chance to realize their political and musical agency within it and expose the police order that is powerless to bind them if they so choose. In this way, the codes that shape the participatory music event are like the foreclosing and controlling "ideological predeterminations" of our postpolitical world.[45] These predeterminations nevertheless must still "reassert themselves, to make themselves effectively ingredient to the event," even as the event "includes dimensions that aren't completely actualized."[46] The realization by participants, then, that these dimensions are multiplicitous, and that these spaces, and spaces like them, can be reconfigured at any moment, reveals the possibilities for ever immanent agitation against any closing off of potential.

Notes

1. Barbara Rose Lange, "The Politics of Collaborative Performance in the Music of Pauline Oliveros," *Perspectives of New Music* 46, no. 1 (2008): 39–60; Stephen Chase and Philip Thomas, eds., *Changing the System: The Music of Christian Wolff* (Burlington, Vt.: Ashgate, 2010); Jutta Toelle and John A. Sloboda, "The Audience as Artist? The Audience's Experience of Participatory Music," *Musicae Scientiae* 25, no. 1 (2019): 67–91; and Huang Ruo, *Resonant Theatre No. 1: The Sonic Great Wall* (London: Ricordi, 2016).

2. Lange, "Politics of Collaborative Performance"; Emily Payne and Philip Thomas, "Ensemble Relations in Christian Wolff's *Exercises*," in *Finding Democracy in Music,* ed. Robert Adlington and Esteban Buch (London: Routledge, 2020), 101–24. Other composers have sought to decenter the composer's role more generally: Robert Adlington, *Composing Dissent: Avant-Garde Music in*

1960s Amsterdam (Oxford: Oxford University Press, 2013); George Lewis, *A Power Stronger than Itself: The AACM and American Experimental Music* (Chicago: University of Chicago Press, 2008); and George Lewis, "What Is a Co-author?," Pew Center for Arts and Heritage, August 14, 2014, www.pewcenterarts.org/post/keynote-essay-george-e-lewis-what-co-author.

3. Luke Dahl, Jorge Herrera, and Carr Wilkerson, "*TweetDreams*: Making Music with the Audience and the World Using Real-time Twitter Data," in *Proceedings of the International Conference on New Interfaces for Musical Expression,* Oslo, Norway, 2011, doi.org/10.5281/zenodo.1177991, 4.

4. Jason Freeman, "*Glimmer*: Creating New Connections," in *Transdisciplinary Digital Art: Sound, Vision, and the New Screen,* ed. Randy Adams, Steve Gibson, and Stefan Müller Arisona (New York: Springer, 2008), 270–83.

5. Jason Alexander Freeman, "*Glimmer* for Chamber Orchestra and Audience" (PhD thesis, Columbia University, 2005), 11.

6. Emily Payne and Philip Thomas, "Getting Exercised: Ensemble Relations in Christian Wolff's *Exercises,*" in Adlington and Buch, *Finding Democracy,* 101.

7. Georgina Born, "Reinventing Audiences: Imagining Radical Musical Democracies," in Adlington and Buch, *Finding Democracy,* 198–99.

8. Dan DiPiero, "Rancière and Improvisation: Reading Contingency in Music and Politics" (207–29); and Chris Stover, "Rancière's Affective Impropriety" (230–61), in *Rancière and Music,* ed. João Pedro Cachopo, Patrick Nickleson, and Chris Stover (Edinburgh: Edinburgh University Press, 2020).

9. Many theorists would recognize spaces such as the participatory music event as micropolitical in the sense I describe here, but their work also examines how local and individual political structures interact with larger ones to better understand their broader subjects of critique. Emily Apter's work on micropolitics draws on the work of Deleuze, Guattari, and Foucault, while Brian Massumi's discussions of affect in politics also draw on Deleuze and Guattari. Emily S. Apter, *Unexceptional Politics: On Obstruction, Impasse, and the Impolitic* (New York: Verso, 2018); Brian Massumi, "Affect in the Key of Politics," *Identities* 8, no. 1 (2011): 37–44; Gilles Deleuze and Félix Guattari, *A Thousand Plateaus: Capitalism and Schizophrenia* (Minneapolis: University of Minnesota Press, 1987), 208–31; and Michel Foucault, *Discipline and Punish: The Birth of the Prison* (New York: Vintage Books, 1995), 149–50.

10. Slavoj Žižek, "Carl Schmitt in the Age of Post-politics," in *The Challenge of Carl Schmitt,* ed. Chantal Mouffe (London: Verso, 1999), 18–37; Chantal Mouffe, *For a Left Populism* (New York: Verso, 2018).

11. Jacques Rancière, *Disagreement: Politics and Philosophy* (Minneapolis: University of Minnesota Press, 1999), 28.

12. Rancière, 28.

13. Rancière, 28–29.

14. Jacques Rancière, *Dissensus: On Politics and Aesthetics,* trans. Steve Corcoran (London: Continuum, 2010), 139.

15. A cursory glance over the literature on these musics highlights their usefulness to their respective fields of study: R. Keith Sawyer, *Group Creativity: Music, Theater, Collaboration* (New York: Routledge, 2014); Brynjulf Stige, "On a Notion of Participation in Music Therapy," *Nordic Journal of Music Therapy* 15, no. 2 (2006): 121–38; Sue Patterson et al., "Implementing Music Therapy on an Adolescent Inpatient Unit: A Mixed-Methods Evaluation of Acceptability, Experience of Participation and Perceived Impact," *Australasian Psychiatry* 23, no. 5 (2015): 556–60; Peter Gouzouasis, Martin Guhn, and Nand Kishor, "The Predictive Relationship between Achievement and Participation in Music and Achievement in Core Grade 12 Academic Subjects," *Music Education Research* 9, no. 1 (2007): 81–92; Margaret S. Barrett and Heather M. Smigiel, "Children's Perspectives of Participation in Music Youth Arts Settings: Meaning, Value and Participation," *Research Studies in Music Education* 28, no. 1 (2007): 39–50; and Jeff Packman, "Singing Together/Meaning Apart: Popular Music, Participation, and Cultural Politics in Salvador, Brazil," *Latin American Music Review* 31, no. 2 (2010): 241–67.

16. See Jason Freeman, "Extreme Sight-Reading, Mediated Expression, and Audience Participation: Real-Time Music Notation in Live Performance," *Computer Music Journal* 32, no. 3 (2008): 25–41; Dahl, Herrera, and Wilkerson, "*TweetDreams*"; and Yongmeng Wu et al., "Open Symphony: Creative Participation for Audiences of Live Music Performances," *IEEE MultiMedia* 24, no. 1 (2017): 48–62.

17. Eric Lemmon, "The Politics of Aesthetic Preference in Participatory Music," *Organised Sound* 28, no. 1 (2023): 53–63.

18. Simply put, a Habermasian public sphere is just the kind of normative political space that Rancière would term the police.

19. Jacques Rancière, *The Emancipated Spectator,* trans. Gregory Elliott (London: Verso, 2009), 22. Claire Bishop, *Artificial Hells: Participatory Art and the Politics of Spectatorship* (London: Verso, 2012), 275.

20. Sawyer, *Group Creativity;* Jane W. Davidson and James M. M. Good, "Social and Musical Co-ordination between Members of a String Quartet: An Exploratory Study," *Psychology of Music* 30, no. 2 (2002): 186–201; and Sang Won Lee et al., "The Effect of Social Interaction on Facilitating Audience Participation in a Live Music Performance," in *Proceedings of the 2019 Conference on Creativity and Cognition* (San Diego: ACM, 2019), 108–20.

21. Jürgen Habermas, *The Structural Transformation of the Public Sphere: An Inquiry into a Category of Bourgeois Society* (Cambridge: Polity, 1989); Nancy Fraser, "Rethinking the Public Sphere: A Contribution to the Critique of Actually Existing Democracy," in *Habermas and the Public Sphere,* ed. Craig J. Calhoun (Cambridge, Mass.: MIT Press, 1992): 109–42; Michael Warner, *Publics and Counterpublics* (Cambridge, Mass.: MIT Press, 2002).

22. Whether audience members' aesthetic preferences are a "product of history reproduced by education" or the result of rational, individualized choices

during the course of a participatory work is irrelevant to the analysis at hand; it is enough that choices exist and are made, thereby shaping the political-aesthetic space. Pierre Bourdieu, *Distinction: A Social Critique of the Judgement of Taste,* trans. Richard Nice (Cambridge, Mass.: Harvard University Press, 1984), 3.

23. Lee's work has been variably called *Crowd in C* and *Crowd in C[loud].* Sang Won Lee and Aaron Willette, *Crowd in C,* in *Proceedings of the 2019 Conference on Creativity and Cognition,* 430.

24. Lee and Willette, *Crowd in C,* 428–29.

25. Lee and Willette, 427, 430; W3C Audio Working Group, Web Audio API, December 2, 2020, www.w3.org/TR/webaudio.

26. Lee and Willette, *Crowd in C,* 428.

27. Lee and Willette, 428.

28. Lee and Willette, 428–29.

29. Lee and Willette, 429–30.

30. Lee and Willette, 430.

31. Lee and Willette, 430.

32. Lee et al., "Effect of Social Interaction," 113.

33. Lee et al., 112.

34. The authors do not clearly define the difference between purely musical and purely social interactions. However, Lee does observe a difference between audience members who steadfastly remain with the note-dot GUI, experimenting with output sounds, without ever viewing another audience member's melody. This contrasts with audience members who might view another melody, then return to their own to edit, or copying the other's melody and then editing from there. Lee et al., "Effect of Social Interaction," 113; and Sang Won Lee, email to author, March 2, 2023.

35. Sang Won Lee, email to author, December 28, 2020.

36. Michel Foucault, *Discipline and Punish: The Birth of the Prison* (New York: Vintage Books, 1995), 200–209.

37. Foucault, 201.

38. Mouffe, *For a Left Populism,* 4.

39. Lee et al., "Effect of Social Interaction," 114–15.

40. Sang Won Lee, email to author, December 28, 2020.

41. Sang Won Lee, *Crowd in C[loud]* at Web Audio Conference 2, Georgia Institute of Technology, Atlanta, 2016.

42. Lee, wide-angle shot of audience in *Crowd in C[loud]* at Web Audio Conference 2, 3:06–15.

43. Çiğdem Çıdam, "Spectacles, Political Education, and Democracy: Rereading Rousseau's *Letter to M. d'Alembert,*" *Polity* 55, no. 3 (2023): 597.

44. Rancière, *Emancipated Spectator,* 22.

45. Massumi, "Affect in the Key of Politics," 42.

46. Massumi, 42.

CHAPTER 8

A Haunted Present

Postpolitics, Nuclear Waste, and the Colonization of the Future

JUAN MENESES

The current postpolitical moment is one of reckoning. This is paramount because the forces behind it are the same ones causing the cancellation of the future.[1] The signs unmistakably show—if one cares to see them—that multiple and ongoing crises closing in on our lives are becoming more and more inescapable. Financial crashes, the assault on gender and sexual identities, food shortages, the crumbling of institutions of governance, disastrous blips in the globalized chains of production, the heating of the planet, unresolved military conflicts, widespread ethnic and racial violence, the monumental concentration of wealth by fewer and fewer individuals and the accompanying increase in inequality, pandemics, the erosion of means to participate in the democratic process, the return of authoritarianism, and so many other predicaments are, sadly, becoming normalized as accepted circumstances under which people must get on with their lives. In fact, the term "crisis" itself no longer describes a temporary break in the present but the epistemic landscape in which we must strive to find possibilities for the practice of politics.[2] This means that living in a world in constant turmoil is compounded by the stealthy erasure of the political; it also poses questions about how our prospects and actions today are connected to a future that looks increasingly bleak.

The response to this reckoning so far has been tragically, if predictably, inadequate. Quality jobs, housing, health care, education, and so many other basic elements necessary for living a good life are being cannibalized by a neoliberal ideology that has put everything up for sale. To see this point clearly, we can also turn to the current planetary environmental crisis (climate change, but so much more), for which the only global course of action has been to double down on a business-as-usual agenda. In the words of Greta Thunberg, the frustrating response by governments has been a constant and unabashed "blah blah blah."[3] Thunberg—one of the most prominent youth activists today, although certainly not the only one[4]—has sought to confront the multiple failures in governance and leadership that are putting the future well-being of her generation and subsequent ones at risk; only time will tell whether any tangible results will have been attained by the platforms she represents.[5]

These preoccupations are concerned with the immediate future. In this sense, the future is where hope lies for a world that will not burst into flames (literally and otherwise), for a lifetime that is not assailed by the threat of rampant insecurity, and for democracy to remain the system that organizes life in common. Yet there is another way to think about the foreclosure of the future that has less discursive traction than this kind of generational angst but is nevertheless important to consider if we aim for a complete assessment of the historical processes connecting the present and the future state of things. I am referring to a future many, many years from now. What will the world look like, politically, not in twenty or fifty years, but in two, five, or thirteen centuries? How about three millennia? Will the planet exist then, and if so, would we even recognize it? These are questions that naturally tend to escape discussions of the current erasure of the political.[6] Conditions at those times are unknown, so it may seem futile to speculate about moments so far away; we can only conjecture what the world will look like. Whatever happens then, another argument might go, must surely be less important than the immediacy of the existing violence and looming threats that are producing a world depleted of political options. I couldn't agree more with the sentiment that these are indeed urgent issues. However, to think about (and imagine) the world on a much larger scale is still a crucial matter because the dynamics that are canceling the near future are often connected to those that, operating on a continuum, reach far into the ultrafar future. Rather than a question of immediacy or distance, I am interested here in exploring the postpolitical underpinnings of the extended "regime of historicity"[7] governed by the material impact of some of the things taking place here and now.

Transepochal Connections

I want to invoke a future-oriented present temporality that allows for an engagement with a political landscape that, although none of us will live to see it, we are nevertheless already determining.[8] Conjuring up such a transepochal connection, which requires an imaginative as well as an ethical involvement on our part, is of course to do nothing new. Established along inverted temporal coordinates, a similar operation can be seen at play in the so-called hunger stones that appeared in several central European rivers during a series of extreme heat waves in summer 2022. Bearing inscriptions such as "If you see me, weep,"[9] these stones were placed in the rivers as far back as four hundred years ago to remind the future that low water levels "had brought a bad harvest, lack of food, high prices and hunger for poor people." Arguably, the emergence of such markers of human strife during a spell of droughts estimated to be "the worst in 500 years" recontextualized the struggles of the poor over the centuries, tying them to the question of the current climate crisis.[10] The past–present transhistorical connection inaugurated by the resurfacing of the stones, then, is akin to the type of present–future connection I seek to explore here. To recall Giorgio Agamben's definition of the contemporary, this is a way to establish "a relationship with time that adheres to it through a disjunction and an anachronism."[11] In other words, this imaginative exercise lets us understand our present via a temporal displacement driven by a projection into inscrutable future times. If the hunger stones coupled European famines to climate change—or, put otherwise, if climate change linked us with fifteenth-century European peasants toiling under feudal law—and if, in doing so, they redefined capitalocenic history as a period we cannot simply call the past,[12] other dimensions of human activity such as the disposal of nuclear waste, as I will discuss later, trigger similar connections between now and a time to come that we cannot just call the future.

My intention, however, is not simply to propose an empathetic reflection on the ramifications of our actions in a far-future era. Instead, I deem it much more urgent to think about the connections between the present and the far future in order to uncover a postpolitical horizon already being produced by an ever-expanding form of occlusion. Discussing the elimination of antagonisms and ideological positions in the post–Cold War era, Slavoj Žižek argues that the central force of postpolitics is not its power to repress but its ability to foreclose the political.[13] For the purpose of my argument, I take Žižek's theorization literally—not just to consider the surreptitious ways in which politics has been evacuated from the inside but also, and primarily, as a cancellation of the political meant to be proleptic and everlasting. For their part, Japhy Wilson and Erik Swyngedouw, who build their theorization of postpolitics on the work of Žižek and others, describe the postpolitical moment through the metaphorical language of "seeds of dystopia" and the reaping of the resulting fruit harvested in a "political desert."[14] Such an environmentally apt metaphor can also be taken as a warning with a particular temporal accent, whereby we will continue to reap the dystopia that we sow as long as the state of affairs remains the same. This is, thus, as much an appraisal of the present as it is a haunting of the future. If, according to Jacques Derrida, "haunting belongs to the structure of every hegemony,"[15] we should then understand postpolitics as a haunting metahegemony because it is predicated on the hegemonic imposition that the idea of hegemony itself is obsolete—as in the Fukuyamian end-of-history paradigm—and has the ability to reach beyond the confines of the conjuncture that gives rise to it. With a discussion of Michael Madsen's 2010 documentary *Into Eternity: A Film for the Future,* I will show via another form of haunting—an aesthetic one—the postpolitical connections between our present (which I will qualify as already postapocalyptic) and the future that we are haunting. First, however, I want to probe a different kind of future-oriented imaginative exercise that fuels the postpolitization of the present and actively conceals how certain political elements are consequently already being foreclosed.

Longtermist Fantasies and the Cancellation of the Present

While the future is currently being canceled for those hoping to live in a better society, the future as the time for economic exploitation is more open than ever. Of course, certain capitalist practices have classically engaged with the future, from speculation to insurance, and from risk management to market prediction.[16] Yet we are at an unprecedented moment where the future is becoming a new terra nullius ripe for exploration, appropriation, and extraction in the latest stage of capitalism's evolution. The future has grown increasingly consequential not just as symbolic of a supposedly better time to come—as the classical narratives of Western modernity would have it—but also as signifier of the post-political present.

In recent years, several ultrawealthy individuals have offered highly public demonstrations of their visions of a technofuturistic society guided by the financial and industrial activities of their own companies. In a telling instantiation of this idea, Elon Musk of Tesla, Richard Branson of Virgin, and Jeff Bezos of Amazon entered what most media outlets celebrated as a "billionaire space race."[17] A spectacle with deep and clear ideological roots in the Cold War, this new space race has been less a technical feat than the (re)mobilization of space travel as a metonym for the resource-guzzling and unstoppable capitalistic enterprises pursued by these men's companies; behind such an extravagant display of technical prowess there is nothing but an exclusionary politics to come that is ultramonetized, inescapable, and inseparable from a certain masculine insecurity.[18] Whereas they have indeed already begun altering the nature of basic pillars of social life such as work, education, health care, and culture, the fanciful and hubristic technoneoliberal fantasies of these "entrepreneurs" also threatens to materialize into a teleological force shaping everybody's future, including the very survival of human life on this planet. As Bezos has said in expressing a goal common to many of these latter-day behemoth companies, "Over centuries, many people will be born in space" and "live on . . . colonies. Then, they'll visit Earth the way you would visit, you know, Yellowstone National Park."[19] Others, like Musk, anticipate that this will happen in a much shorter time, claiming that there is a good chance life on other planets will be possible—via colonization, naturally—during their own lifetimes.[20]

These predictions, however, have not always been expressed in celebratory tones. The mobilization of apocalyptic rhetoric has also been a potent instrument for the postpolitical orientation of the present toward the future as undertaken by Bezos, Musk, and company. As Erik Swyngedouw has shown, this rhetoric "is an integral and vital part of the new cultural politics of capitalism . . . for which the management of fear is a central leitmotif. . . . At the symbolic level, apocalyptic imaginaries are extraordinarily powerful in disavowing or displacing social conflict and antagonisms. As such, apocalyptic imaginations are decidedly populist and foreclose a proper political framing."[21] Swyngedouw's remarks are concerned with governance and the managerialization of representative politics, but apocalyptic rhetoric has also proven useful for the enterprises of these billionaires. In fact, one could easily argue that the deployment of this rhetoric by certain sectors of big business is a natural occurrence in a political culture dominated by the one principle fueling both governance and corporate activity, namely financial profit at the expense of everything else. In that vein, Musk asserted at the unveiling of the new Cybertruck that Tesla's goal is to "be a leader in apocalypse technology," adding that "when the apocalypse comes, you'll be glad [the vehicle is] bulletproof."[22] In a world where these companies' arrogance and lack of oversight are already making public life extremely unsafe,[23] it would not be entirely unwarranted to take Musk's fantastical allusions to the apocalypse (including his smug reference to the need for bulletproof protection) less as a prediction than a threat: be prepared for what's coming; there is nothing you can do anymore. Whether articulated in celebratory or foreboding terms, the dystopic, *Mad Max*–style technoneoliberal "vision" of the billionaire class is ultimately grounded in the imposition of an "ideology of the future *now,* which . . . paralyses all thought about the future" proper.[24] At the same time, their hubristic fantasies are provoking a slippage of the political that amounts to the cancellation of the present.

Nowhere is this as evident as in the effective altruism movement, which has been supported financially by prominent tech billionaires such as Musk, disgraced cryptocurrency investor Sam Bankman-Fried, and PayPal cocreator Peter Thiel. On the face of it, effective altruism's mission to "find the best ways to help others, and put them into practice" might seem an unproblematic premise.[25] However, the movement has been denounced for being driven by a "dangerous ideology."[26] Going beyond the problems intrinsic to the idea of philanthropy, critics have accused its proponents of embracing elitism, Western ethnocentrism, and eugenicist theories; flaunting moral corruption; and exhibiting predatory behavior.[27] Furthermore, effective altruism would be of far less concern if most of its financial backing did not stem from immense fortunes—including those made from cryptocurrency trading—made possible by rampant capitalism, or if it did not espouse the idea that, to help the future, one must make as much money (and as quickly) as possible.[28]

Another crucially problematic component of the effective altruism agenda is what its advocates call longtermism, a school of thought preoccupied with the deep future. While its practitioners claim to be concerned with causing the most positive impact on humanity in the far future, longtermism has in fact a postpolitical agenda at its core. First, it claims to be "fundamentally apolitical" in the way all true capitalists insist their business is free of any ideological leanings.[29] One can look, for instance, to the "value-neutrality thesis" according to which "technology is a morally neutral object,"[30] and which allows its defenders to argue that "a failure to develop technological civilisation would imply that we had fallen victims of an existential disaster."[31] This is nothing more than a concealment, under rhetorical pretenses, of the political dimensions of technology and the destructive outcomes of its deployment. Second, longtermists weaponize the speculative nature of their predictions about the future—which are as indisputable as the movement's financial backing by tech billionaires is unmatchable—to justify morally their "altruistic" operations in the name of humanity. Certainly more than a simple matter of the ends justifying the means, this amounts to an unsubtle sleight of hand that obscures the means with an end that is literally impossible to envision, and because of that helps whitewash the capitalistic operations of its wealthy supporters. Third, longtermists aim their efforts toward fighting what they call existential risks—that is, risks that can bring about humanity's extinction. (One presumes those risks stemming precisely from the activities of their financers are exempted from their calculations.) As the measuring rod for the movement's undertakings, this apocalyptic trope of self-preservation establishes that the survival of humanity (invoked as an objective category)[32] must be guaranteed at any cost. However, longtermists' estimations about who must be helped is based on a utilitarian cost-effective analysis.[33] In other words, for longtermists, the fate of (a part of) humanity is in truth an economic game of winners and losers, whereby do-gooders have the only say about what is worth saving and what is not. Last, as a discourse zealously controlled by its gurus, longtermism exerts a stranglehold on the definitions, stakes, and scope of its own agenda—its problematic, as Louis Althusser would put it—causing the architectonics of its own logic, to cite an emblematic postpolitical motto, to admit no alternative.[34]

Technocapitalists' longtermist version of the future as one only they can fix is as misguided as it is dangerous.[35] Given the totalizing presence of their corporations across industrial, social, and ideological planes, the future—and with it the end of the world as we know it—is currently being charted out by the demiurgic pretensions of the billionaires at their helm. If postpolitics names a lapse of the political, tech capitalists' postpolitical schemes bring the posterior element of the "post" in postpolitics further into a future that is already being predetermined in unfathomable ways. They may portray themselves as the "most fervent supporters" of the future, but they can only offer, at best, an accelerationist approach to tech and industrial capitalism; at worst, technocapitalists are nothing but "the future's enemies."[36] This is why one can call the current moment an already postapocalyptic one.[37] Against such longtermist fantasies, I want now to turn to the fact that the colonization of the future is already underway in less spectacular but still materially consequent ways. In the process, I will argue that an aesthetics of haunting can both uncover the postpolitical underpinnings of that phenomenon and create a different political relationship between the present and the ultrafar future.

Future Politics: Haunting the Postapocalyptic Present

The increasingly obstructive and totalizing presence of tech one-percenters' pipe dreams of the kind I have briefly explored makes it urgent to safeguard ways to imagine the connections between the present and the far future, especially when accidental catastrophe is already baked into the question.[38] We can envision this dimension by articulating a critique, following Marc Augé, that reveals how our society "still care[s] about its immediate future, but [does] no longer need to look further ahead."[39] We must look to both the immediate and the distant future, and not simply as a way to estimate the consequences of our actions; this gesture, emphatically, also needs to incorporate what is to come into a reflection about the very nature of politics and the work of the political—that is, by practicing a "politics of posterity."[40] This is precisely what Michael Madsen's documentary *Into Eternity: A Film for the Future* invites us to do.[41] The film considers not the fantasies of those billionaires who claim they will solve the problems of modern life but something much more tangible and real. It centers on the ethical, historical, material, and philosophical dimensions of the construction of an underground repository in Eurajoki, Finland, named Onkalo (Finnish for "cavity") intended to store nuclear waste for a hundred thousand years. Given that nuclear power has become a staple in energy production, especially in the West, the ecopolitical stakes of this technology warrant a reflection on the aftermath of the hypercapitalist, extractivist activities presently carried out in a world in which energy consumption continues to rise dramatically.[42]

While structured into several thematic sections, *Into Eternity* can be described to work narratively at three levels. The first is a visual and auditory meditation of the ongoing construction of the infrastructure, which began in the early 2000s and is projected to be sealed by 2120. We observe the structure in an orchestrated cinematic collision of construction workers' activity, corporate footage extolling the virtues of the enclosure and featuring robotic technology used to store waste in water tanks, and the exterior of the cave, which is surrounded by pristine woods and visited by elk and other animals. Working primarily to provide context, at this level the film offers an assemblage of disjointed time planes featuring the mundane world of labor in the present, the technologized legacy we are leaving behind for an eternal future, and a romanticized, deep ecological time devoid of human presence.

At a second level, the documentary features interviews with scientists, legal advisors, and technicians working on the Onkalo project. These interactions with the film's director, who often speaks off camera, range from the specificities of nuclear energy to the ethical pitfalls of leaving future generations with the burden of our nuclear waste. Of note are Madsen's dogged questions about how those responsible for the repository are preparing the terrain, literally and figuratively, so that people in the future do not enter the sealed chamber and expose themselves to radiation. Images of historical catastrophes are also interspersed in between some of the interviews, working as counterpoints to the certitude with which many of the interviewees speak about the cogency of the Onkalo project. Responses to Madsen's inquiries vary (some are hopeful, others skeptical), but the overall message that emerges is a deferred uncertainty that hammers home the documentary's point: we continue to produce nuclear energy, and by doing so, we condition the welfare of generations who, living so far in the future, will unlikely think, imagine, and communicate in the same ways as we do.

It is at the third level, however, that the documentary performs an important aesthetic intervention. At this level, Madsen speaks to a future audience from inside the dark cavities of Onkalo under the hypothetical premise that people thousands of years from now have indeed gained access to it and their lives have been, one way or another, affected by the presence of our radioactive waste. Adopting a hauntingly apocalyptic tone, and often responding to the problems and contradictions exposed during the interviews, Madsen establishes a transepochal relationship between the present and the future (in the form of the recorded message that the film becomes) by way of questions such as "What led you to open the sealed cave and find the nuclear material stored away?" These moments are particularly aestheticized by Madsen's inventive choice of lighting. Every time he addresses the future on screen, the director strikes a match, which not only illuminates his face but also emphasizes the ephemerality of his message, as each of these scenes ends when the flame goes out, symbolizing that in a relatively short time, his words will be intelligible to humans in the ultrafar future. Furthermore, burning the matches dramatically underscores by inversion the justification underlying most interviewees' responses that for humans to continue on the path of modernity, vast amounts of energy are needed, so by extension, it is simply unavoidable for us to pass our nuclear waste onto future generations. Sufficiently lit by the otherwise tenuous flame of the match, Madsen asserts: "My civilization depends on energy as no civilization before us. Energy is the main currency for us. Is it the same for you? Does your way of life also depend on unlimited energy?"

Madsen's aestheticized attempt to connect with this future audience might at first glance be taken to encapsulate the need to consider how our nuclear waste will affect both the lives of humans millennia from now and the kind of politics they will be able to practice. Yet I see this ultimately as an aesthetic move with a different aim, especially given the unlikelihood that his work will reach humans such a long time from now. Madsen admits that "one hundred thousand years from now is beyond our understanding and our imagination," even wondering in empathetic terms "how far into the future will your way of life have consequences?" While staging his address as an appeal to future humans we can know little about—at a time "where science and technology [might] not matter in the same ways they matter for us now," as Swedish National Council for Nuclear Waste member Carl Reinhold Bråkenhjelm conjectures in the film—Madsen's message is primarily intended for a contemporary

FIGURE 8.1. Still from *Into Eternity.* Used by permission of director Michael Madsen.

audience. It is us in the present who are haunted by questions about our nuclear behavior that, unable to speak for future generations, we cannot answer yet must contend with. In fact, the documentary spends a considerable amount of time revisiting the familiar though important matter regarding how to inform future generations about the perils of entering a nuclear waste repository in the plausible scenario that we will not share a common form of communication.[43] Read metatextually, this can also be understood as a reflection on the difficulty of finding a critical space in the present to think collectively about the issue of our nuclear legacy. How to engage in a collective assessment when the option of not generating nuclear waste is already foreclosed by the postpolitical order in which unbridled energy production and consumption are embedded? In order to tackle this problem, Madsen brings it to the aesthetic plane via the interpellation of his own contemporaries.

More than simply indirectly addressing fellow contemporaneous humans by affecting a conversation with the future, the director's words are also haunting because they occur in an alternative space-time juncture. As Mary Ann Doane has argued, film as a medium allows us to inhabit "*other* times and spaces."[44] In the case of *Into Eternity,* this phenomenon is exploited to fashion the transepochal connection with which the documentarian challenges both the postpolitical inevitability of our nuclear present and the predestined future it legislates. In speaking to the present via his address to the future, Madsen urges current spectators to identify with an unknown time that is not ours and thus entreats us to defamiliarize ourselves from the consensual nuclear politics that admits no alternative. As a result, we are compelled to consider ourselves actors in the (long) historical moment inaugurated by the advent of nuclear technology—a temporality that, as with the intrusion of tech billionaires' fantasies of the future, is already postapocalyptic insofar as the "eternal" life-span of radioactive waste connects us to the ultrafar future. (I will return to this issue in the concluding section of this chapter.) In Madsen's words, "If you, sometime far in the future, find this, what will it tell you about us?" The film, in other words, calls us to bear witness to our own actions on behalf of those who, having had no agency in the matter, will nonetheless bear their consequences.

At the same time, this metahistorical haunting emphasizes our own haunting of the future. In realizing the prophecy that Onkalo's enclosure will be penetrated, both the brutal reality of radioactivity and the post-political indisputability of our ongoing nuclear activity are temporally displaced by the location of Madsen's musings. From this perspective, Madsen is speaking to us from the future, which is illustrated spatially by the fact that, once filled, the repository will be sealed for thousands of years. In Jacques Rancière's words, the film manages to represent "the unrepresentable" by staging "the absence of a stable relationship between exhibition and signification," which "revoke[s] . . . the representative separation between the rationale of facts and the rationale of fictions" and therefore causes "an identity between meaning and non-meaning . . . to coincide with an identity between presence and absence."[45] Madsen's presence in the cave thus becomes coupled with the absence of future generations' agency regarding the (post)political question of nuclear waste disposal. Furthermore, underpinned by computer-generated renderings of the completed repository and other footage from Posiva Oy, the company building Onkalo, the futurity of Madsen's on-camera presence is reinforced by a strategic voyeurism that teases us to imagine the forbidden future from which Madsen speaks the language of nuclear disaster: "You are now in the tunnel. This place is not a place of honor. No esteemed deeds are commemorated here. You should not have come here. You are heading toward a place where you should never go. What is there is dangerous and repulsive. The danger will still be present in your time as it is in ours. Please turn around and never come back. There is nothing here for you. Go no further. You should not be here. Please turn around."[46] Madsen's warnings about our nuclear activity—and not about a future breach of the tunnels—are unremitting; still, we continue to capitulate to our desires.

Inhabiting the interiors of Onkalo, we witness the postpolitical future conjured up by our nuclear arrogance before the invisible effects of radiation begin to be noticed. Our gaze is enticed into this space the way Western archaeologists and other looters were drawn to the insides of pharaohs' tombs, which are mentioned in the documentary as examples of major structures otherwise designed against intrusion. If we can learn

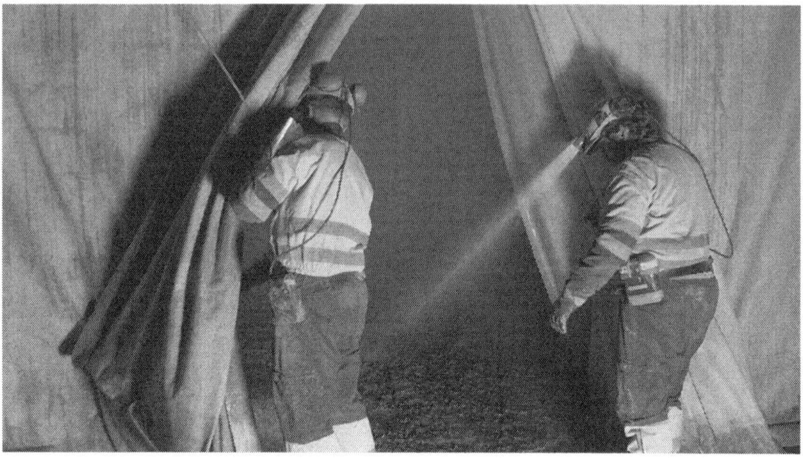

FIGURE 8.2. Still from *Into Eternity*. Used by permission of director Michael Madsen.

anything from the history of intrusion into the Egyptian pyramids—or, more recently, the mission of tech billionaires to permeate everything that exists with their futuristic fantasies—it is that the future may not be such a different time. In the words of radiation safety expert Mikael Jansen, who speaks in the documentary of "hidden treasure" quests and other scenarios "where people even know [nuclear waste] is dangerous but it's also valuable at the same time," the future will be inhabited by "misguided men" who will disregard the warnings "completely." When intrusion is considered to be motivated by reasons other than self-gain, as Madsen ponders, we are still left with a reminder of the hubristic spirit of infallibility that characterizes the historicity of this nuclear postpolitical order from the start: "Maybe you will need to enter if we overlooked something or if repairs are required. Were our calculations and assumptions accurate? Did we make mistakes?" In any case, we can only imagine that exposure to radioactive waste is all but guaranteed. Even if it never happens and Onkalo indeed remains unsealed forever (how long exactly is forever?), that future will nevertheless remain in part predetermined by the threat of radiation for precisely the same period of time. It is in fact with the question of maintaining a politically imaginative relationship with the future that the documentary articulates one of its central themes.

Framed by Madsen's general haunting aesthetics intended to motivate a reflection on the postpoliticization of our nuclear future, a moment in the documentary counterposes two views on the power of the imagination. On the one hand, while entirely bypassing the question whether we are entitled to condition life in the future by putting our waste in the ground, Onkalo's makers entrust the success of their enterprise to human inaction. Commenting on what to do once the repository is sealed, Juhani Vira, Posiva Oy's senior vice president of research, expresses his conviction that the best thing is to leave Onkalo unmarked; for his part, senior communications manager Timo Seppälä is confident the site will simply "be forgotten." Both positions, which stand in contrast with the commonly held idea that future humans should be alerted via markers outside the repository, point in the same direction: humans' curiosity is an obstacle, and it must be deterred to save them from themselves. Just as the agents of postpolitics induce incuriosity in the present to establish a consensual status quo for which an alternative cannot be conceived, the prerequisite that curiosity will bring about catastrophe inevitably spells out a depoliticizing gesture in the future. In the neutral-sounding words of executive vice president of engineering Timo Äikäs, "The safety of disposal shall not be dependent on . . . any acts of human beings to be safe, so it has to be fully passive." Another expert bluntly concurs: "We consider you to be the main threat to the safety of Onkalo." This stance sits squarely against the political substance of our imagination. Curiosity, according to Michel Foucault, "evokes 'care;' it evokes the care of what exists *and might exist;* a sharpened sense of reality . . . ; a readiness to *find what surrounds us strange and odd;* a certain determination to throw off familiar ways of thought and to look at the same things in *a different way* . . . ; a lack of respect for the traditional hierarchies of what is important and fundamental."[47] A call for incuriosity is thus a call for an antihumanist depoliticization of the future. The only option, as Madsen protests, is a commitment that the generations of posterity "remember forever to forget."

In the face of this audacious reliance on incuriosity, the film holds onto the promise of the imagination—even when stretched to its very limits—as the means to codify politically the invisible yet wholly material connection between the two temporalities dictated by the life-span of radioactive waste. Here Madsen hypothesizes whether cultural transmission will enable future generations to imagine us, and therefore understand the dangers of the legacy we are leaving them. The director conjectures: "Maybe our legends will reach you by being told over and over from generation to generation like ancient legends have reached us. Were you warned about Onkalo through legend? Did your parents tell you stories about the fire in the burial chamber in the bowels of the earth?" Implied in Madsen's speculation about the power of storytelling and metaphor is the hope that what might connect us to humans in the ultrafar future is precisely the political element that Onkalo's makers so ardently try to will away: an imaginative kind of curiosity.

Future Conditionals

In commenting on the longtermist fantasies of the tech billionaire class, I argued that we already live in a postapocalyptic moment. Madsen's documentary corroborates this idea, although this must be understood in a different way. If the tech barons seek to cancel the present in favor of a fantastic futurism that obscures their specious capitalist activities, the long life and future impact of nuclear waste that Madsen meditates on prove the extent to which we have already turned the present into a postapocalyptic epoch. As Michel Serres puts it, "Globalized, the present pollution results from the struggle to possess total space."[48] In this sense, the apocalypse is the horizon that demarcates, within the temporal frame of the existence of human life, a break caused by the invention of nuclear technology and the ongoing production of radioactive waste. The emergence of this temporality reveals a colonization of the political possibilities of those in the future (although as non-Western and anticolonial accounts of modernity have shown, this is a form of capture and co-optation with a longer history that includes temporalities other than the future).[49] Put simply, the emergence of nuclear radioactivity inaugurates a temporality that forces us to reassess our understanding of the political and its limits.

In contrast with longtermists' proposition, then, *Into Eternity* insists that we begin imagining a radioactive politics for the future now so as to acknowledge the dystopic state of affairs that we have already put in motion. Deploying a haunting aesthetics with which we can glimpse into a foreclosed future politics, Madsen's film highlights the postpolitical apocalypse that simultaneously will happen and has already happened. This double temporality is key to the film's reflections. If, in Rancière's vocabulary, the political can be materialized (and thus mobilized) once a dissensual "organization of the sensible" is achieved "where there is neither a reality concealed behind appearances nor a single regime of presentation and interpretation of the given,"[50] the question is about how the sensible is distributed over transepochal stretches of time. Much like other environmental issues that are already dictating the terms of life on this planet, the violence caused by our continuous production of radioactive waste is inevitable; whether it can be rendered politically legible is the crux of the matter, and Madsen's cinematic choices do precisely that. Including the ultrafar future in our reflections about politics allows us to attend to the ways politics is turned into postpolitics by way of its curtailment as occasioned by the "paradigmatic capture" that is "the reduction of the range of possibilities inscribed in the present to a pattern that acts as a formatting gestalt."[51] At the same time, however it manifests, the futurity of nuclear waste must not only be the concern of those who come after us but emphatically our own too. In this light, the subtitle of Madsen's film appears particularly relevant: his is not *A Film for the Future* intended as "material witness"[52] for audiences thousands of years from now, but a record of *a* future that becomes, via radioactive imposition, *the* future.

Yet pointing to this postapocalyptic, postpolitical landscape does not mean that the future is entirely predetermined. That is why haunting, which manifests in the liminal space between absence and presence, is a particularly apt aesthetic vehicle. Despite some commentators' dismissals of seriously thinking about this matter,[53] the productive work of *Into Eternity* lies in its emphasis that a critique of the nuclear waste question must incorporate the tensions between predictability and unpredictability; in other words, we must remain in the uncomfortable space between certainty and uncertainty. This opens up the question of decidability. The material reality of radioactive waste will contribute to the foreclosure of the political in the future, but the antagonisms at the center of the struggle to politicize it will still have to be decided. Therefore, reliance on universal categories proves inadequate for the establishment of political relations at such vastly different times.[54] At the end of the day (or, seeing this question from a future perspective, at its beginning), our actions in the present constitute an unstable assemblage of possibilities. There is no way to determine the shape of the future given that the new manifests out of a variety of iterations of "potency," or "the energy that transforms the possibilities into actualities."[55] What is certain, nevertheless, is that the radioactive future begins now.

My reading of *Into Eternity* is ultimately motivated by what has been called the "collectivization of time," whereby our present temporality is not understood as a hegemonic foundation for the future, leaving the latter open-ended as a result.[56] It seeks to animate a futurist conception of the present that refutes an absolutist futurism emblematized these days by the technobillionaire class. Madsen's effort puts in motion an agenda in which undecidability is a question for the future as well as the present in the sense that we must answer the call, at every turn, to take action so the undecidability of what is to come remains as protected as possible. As Max Liboiron reminds us, "industrial pollutants like carbon dioxide or marine plastic are not discreet actors (bad or otherwise) but a set of relations."[57] The same can be said about nuclear waste. Radioactivity gives form to a set of temporal and spatial relations that determine the possibilities of political action. The future cannot be taken simply as an externality, or as a temporal projection of a "generalized catastrophe . . . that expands every time."[58] Despite overeager technofuturistic claims that our prosperity in the present will mean the prosperity of others at a later time, the truth is we are forcing a consensus onto a future world that has not consented to such an operation. Put otherwise, we are defrauding the future. In engaging in a kind of "affirmative speculation" that "*sabotages* the exploitation of potentialities, *produces* the common, and *opens* up innumerable possibilities (unpredictable and, therefore, singular),"[59] Madsen's film is a reminder that, at least as far as our nuclear legacy goes, any attempt at formulating an egalitarian politics must also, by default, contain within itself a postpolitical dimension. The haunting presence of this dimension, however, does not imply a defeat that nullifies the articulation of political struggles. It can instead be taken as a historical marker—like the ones left outside Onkalo to deter future generations from entering, or the fifteenth-century hunger stones—that awakens a sense of responsibility among those willing to construct now a radical politics in and for the future.

Notes

1. Invisible Committee, *The Coming Insurrection* (South Pasadena, Calif.: Semiotext(e), 2009), 23. For an array of discussions on the question of an imperiled future, see Immanuel Wallerstein, Randall Collins, Michael Mann, Georgi Derluguian, and Craig Calhoun, *Does Capitalism Have a Future?* (Oxford: Oxford University Press, 2013); Jaron Lanier, *Who Owns the Future?* (New York: Simon & Schuster, 2013); T. J. Clark, "For a Left with No Future," *New Left Review* 74 (2012): 53–75; Nick Srnicek and Alex Williams, *Inventing the Future: Postcapitalism and a World without Work* (London: Verso, 2016); Mark Fisher, *Ghosts of My Life: Writings on Depression, Hauntology, and Lost Futures* (Winchester, Eng.: Zero/Collective Ink, 2014); and Jamie Susskind, *Future Politics: Living Together in a World Transformed by Tech* (Oxford: Oxford University Press, 2018).

2. Didier Fassin, "Crisis," in *Words and Worlds: A Lexicon for Dark Times,* ed. Veena Das and Didier Fassin (Durham, N.C.: Duke University Press, 2021): 261–76. See also Slavoj Žižek, *Living in the End Times* (London: Verso, 2011); Franco "Bifo" Berardi, *Breathing: Chaos and Poetry* (South Pasadena, Calif.: Semiotext(e), 2018); and Helen Thompson, *Disorder: Hard Times in the 21st Century* (Oxford: Oxford University Press, 2022).

3. Jennifer Hassan, "Greta Thunberg Says World Leaders' Talk on Climate Change Is 'Blah Blah Blah,'" *Washington Post,* September 29, 2021, www.washingtonpost.com/climate-environment/2021/09/29/great-thunberg-leaders-blah-blah-blah.

4. Commentators have noted the privileged position of white activists and have protested the erasure of Black, Indigenous, and global South representation. See, for instance, Aggrey Nyondwa, "The Erasure of Vanessa Nakate Shows Why Africa Needs a Voice in Climate Debates," Firoz Lalji Institute for Africa, November 12, 2021, blogs.lse.ac.uk/africaatlse/2021/11/12/erasure-of-vanessa-nakate-crop-why-africa-needs-voice-in-climate-debates-cop26.

5. I have argued elsewhere that responses of the kind Thunberg's platform has produced to governments' "blah blah blah" are susceptible of becoming engulfed in an illusory dialogue whereby a dialogic engagement over a political

issue is surreptitiously used as a substitute for real political change, thus rendering dissent null. See Juan Meneses, *Resisting Dialogue: Modern Fiction and the Future of Dissent* (Minneapolis: University of Minnesota Press, 2019), especially chapter 5, "Reframing: Visualizing Environmental Violence in the Anthropocene," which deals with this postpolitical phenomenon in relation to environmental destruction.

6. They are, however, not absent in other debates. See, for instance, Daniel Innerarity, *The Future and Its Enemies: In Defense of Political Hope,* trans. Sandra Kingery (Stanford, Calif.: Stanford University Press, 2012).

7. François Hartog, *Regimes of Historicity: Presentism and Experiences of Time,* trans. Saskia Brown (New York: Columbia University Press, 2015).

8. I use the pronoun "we" fully aware of the power disparities between the agents and the victims of forms of planetary violence such as climate change. Following Max Liboiron, I use it to point to "responsibility" as an "obligation . . . to enact good relations" in the second-person plural. Max Liboiron, *Pollution Is Colonialism* (Durham, N.C.: Duke University Press, 2021), 111.

9. Ruairi Casey, "'If You See Me, Weep': Hunger Stones Auguring Drought in Europe," *Al Jazeera,* November 29, 2022, www.aljazeera.com/features/2022/11/29/if-you-see-me-weep-hunger-stones-auguring-drought-in-europe.

10. Jon Henley, "Hunger Stones, Wrecks and Bones: Europe's Drought Brings Past to Surface," *Guardian,* August 19, 2022, www.theguardian.com/world/2022/aug/19/hunger-stones-wrecks-and-bones-europe-drought-brings-past-to-sur face.

11. Giorgio Agamben, *"What Is an Apparatus?" and Other Essays* (Stanford, Calif.: Stanford University Press, 2009), 41.

12. Chakrabarty's work is crucial to understand this planetary history. See Dipesh Chakrabarty, *The Climate of History in a Planetary Age* (Chicago: University of Chicago Press, 2021). On the capitalocene, see Jason W. Moore, *Capitalism in the Web of Life: Ecology and the Accumulation of Capital* (London: Verso, 2015).

13. Slavoj Žižek, *The Ticklish Subject: The Absent Centre of Political Ontology* (London: Verso, 1999), 198.

14. Japhy Wilson and Erik Swyngedouw, "Seeds of Dystopia: Post-politics and the Return of the Political," in *The Post-political and Its Discontents: Spaces of Depoliticisation, Spectres of Radical Politics,* ed. Japhy Wilson and Erik Swyngedouw (Edinburgh: Edinburgh University Press, 2014), 4–5.

15. Jacques Derrida, *Specters of Marx: The State of the Debt, the Work of Mourning, and the New International,* trans. Peggy Kamuf (New York: Routledge, 1994), 37.

16. For an account on this financialized conception of the future, see Jens Beckert, *Imagined Futures: Fictional Expectations and Capitalist Dynamics* (Cambridge, Mass.: Harvard University Press, 2016).

17. Adam Gabbatt, "Billionaire Space Race: Can Bezos's Project Kuiper Catch Up to Musk's Starlink?," *Guardian,* October 15, 2023, www.theguardian.com/sci

ence/2023/oct/15/billionaire-space-race-can-bezoss-project-kuiper-catch-up-to-musks-starlink.

18. For a discussion of an earlier metonymic of a similar kind (GMO technology), see Larry Reynolds and Bronislav Szerszynski, "The Post-political and the End of Nature: The Genetically Modified Organism," in Wilson and Swyngedouw, *Post-political and Its Discontents,* 48–66.

19. Avery Hartmans, "Jeff Bezos Predicts that People Will One Day Be Born in Space and 'Visit Earth the Way You Visit, You Know, Yellowstone National Park,'" *Business Insider,* December 14, 2021, www.businessinsider.com/jeff-bezos-humans-born-in-space-eventually-space-colonies-2021-11.

20. Hamza Shaban, "Elon Musk Says He Will Probably Move to Mars," *Washington Post,* November 26, 2018, www.washingtonpost.com/technology/2018/11/26/elon-musk-says-he-will-probably-move-mars.

21. Erik Swyngedouw, "Apocalypse Forever? Post-political Populism and the Spectre of Climate Change," *Theory, Culture, and Society* 27, no. 2–3 (2010): 218, 219.

22. Victor Tangermann, "Elon Musk: 'We Want to Be a Leader in Apocalypse Technology,'" *Futurism,* May 29, 2020, www.futurism.com/the-byte/elon-musk-leader-apocalypse-technology.

23. Tesla's driverless cars, for instance, continue to be allowed on streets and roads despite the mounting number of accidents and deaths they have provoked. Tesla Deaths offers "an updated record of Tesla fatalities and Tesla accident deaths that have been reported and as much related crash data as possible" (www.tesladeaths.com). For a more general account, see Adam Greenfield, *Radical Technologies: The Design of Everyday Life* (London: Verso, 2017).

24. Marc Augé, *The Future,* trans. John Howe (London: Verso, 2014), 3; emphasis in the original.

25. Center for Effective Altruism, "What Is Effective Altruism?," www.effectivealtruism.org.

26. Émile P. Torres, "Understanding 'Longtermism': Why This Suddenly Influential Philosophy Is So Toxic," *Salon,* August 20, 2022, www.salon.com/2022/08/20/understanding-longtermism-why-this-suddenly-influential-philosophy-is-so.

27. See, for example, Ken Berger and Robert M. Penna, "The Elitist Philanthropy of So-Called Effective Altruism," *Stanford Social Innovation Review,* November 25, 2013, ssir.org/articles/entry/the_elitist_philanthropy_of_so_called_effective_altruism; Joshua Schuster and Derek Woods, *Calamity Theory: Three Critiques of Existential Risk* (Minneapolis: University of Minnesota Press, 2021); Ellen Huet, "Effective Altruism's Problems Go beyond Sam Bankman-Fried," *Bloomberg News,* March 7, 2023, www.bloomberg.com/news/features/2023-03-07/effective-altruism-s-problems-go-beyond-sam-bankman-fried; and Carol J. Adams, Alice Crary, and Lori Gruen, eds., *The Good It Promises, the Harm It Does: Critical Essays on Effective Altruism* (Oxford: Oxford University Press, 2023). For

a critique of philanthropy, see Paul Gomberg, "The Fallacy of Philanthropy," *Canadian Journal of Philosophy* 32, no. 1 (2002): 29–65.

28. See Nicholas Kulish, "FTX's Collapse Casts a Pall on a Philanthropy Movement," *New York Times,* November 13, 2022, www.nytimes.com/2022/11/13/business/ftx-effective-altruism.html; and Phil Torres, "Effective Altruism Says You Can Save the Future by Making Money," *Vice,* June 20, 2017, www.vice.com/en/article/xw83ak/effective-altruism-says-you-can-save-the-future-by-making-money.

29. Adams, Crary, and Gruen, "Coda—Future-Oriented Effective Altruism: What's Wrong with Longtermism?," in *The Good It Promises,* 268.

30. Émile P. Torres, "Against Longtermism," *Aeon,* October 19, 2021, aeon.co/essays/why-longtermism-is-the-worlds-most-dangerous-secular-credo.

31. Nick Bostrom, qtd. in Torres.

32. Crary has shown the clear discriminatory proclivities of the movement. Alice Crary, "The Toxic Ideology of Longtermism," *Radical Philosophy* 2.14 (2023): 49–57.

33. Sigal Samuel, "Effective Altruism's Most Controversial Idea," *Vox,* September 6, 2022, www.vox.com/future-perfect/23298870/effective-altruism-longtermism-will-macaskill-future.

34. Torres, "Understanding 'Longtermism.'" Using Althusser's terms, taken as *"a totality,"* longtermism can be seen as posing "only . . . problems on the terrain and within the horizon of a definite theoretical structure, its problematic, which constitutes its absolute and definite condition of possibility, and hence the absolute determination of *the forms in which all problems must be posed.*" Louis Althusser, "From *Capital* to Marx's Philosophy," in Louis Althusser and Étienne Balibar, *Reading Capital,* trans. Ben Brewster (London: Verso, 2009), 26; emphasis in the original.

35. Morozov calls this solutionism. Evgeny Morozov, *To Save Everything, Click Here* (New York: PublicAffairs, 2014).

36. Innerarity, *Future,* 4. For an account of technocapitalist corporations' pervasiveness, see Jeremy Gilbert and Alex Williams, *Hegemony Now: How Big Tech and Wall Street Won the World (and How We Win It Back)* (London: Verso, 2022). For a critical assessment of accelerationism, see Benjamin Noys, *Malign Velocities: Accelerationism and Capitalism* (Winchester, Eng.: Zero/Collective Ink, 2014).

37. For a full examination of the idea of living in postapocalyptic times, see Srećko Horvat, *After the Apocalypse* (Cambridge: Polity, 2021).

38. For a discussion of the catastrophic accident as immanent dimension of technological advancement, see Paul Virilio, *The Original Accident* (Cambridge: Polity, 2007). For a discussion of how catastrophes have become semiotic units that flatten our comprehension of the violence they unleash, see Jean-Luc Nancy, *After Fukushima: The Equivalence of Catastrophes* (New York: Fordham University Press, 2015).

39. Augé, *Future,* 51.

40. Barbara Adam and Chris Groves, *Future Matters: Action, Knowledge, Ethics* (Leiden, Neth.: Brill, 2007), 115.

41. *Into Eternity: A Film for the Future* (dir. Michael Madsen, 2010).

42. As of this writing, electricity generated by nuclear power constituted 35 percent of all production in Finland, 22 percent in the European Union, and 18 percent in the United States. World Nuclear Association, www.world-nuclear.org/information-library.aspx. At the same time, the rise of so-called artificial intelligence has caused an enormous increase in energy consumption that will have immediate environmental consequences. Dan Milmo, "Google's Emissions Climb Nearly 50% in Five Years Due to AI Energy Demand," *Guardian,* July 2, 2024, www.theguardian.com/technology/article/2024/jul/02/google-ai-emissions.

43. Different options for the kinds of warning messages that might be necessary about the dangers of nuclear waste are discussed in Kathleen M. Trauth, Stephen C. Hora, and Robert V. Guzowski, *Expert Judgment on Markers to Deter Inadvertent Human Intrusion into the Waste Isolation Pilot Plant* (Albuquerque, N.M.: Sandia National Laboratories, 1993).

44. Mary Ann Doane, *The Emergence of Cinematic Time: Modernity, Contingency, the Archive* (Cambridge, Mass.: Harvard University Press, 2002), 3; emphasis in the original.

45. Jacques Rancière, *The Future of the Image,* trans. Gregory Elliott (London: Verso, 2007), 137, 123.

46. Madsen is quoting here language from Trauth, Hora, and Guzowski, *Expert Judgment.*

47. Michel Foucault, "The Masked Philosopher," trans. Alan Sheridan, in *Michel Foucault: Politics, Philosophy, Culture* (New York: Routledge, 1988), 328; emphasis added. See also Perry Zurn, *Curiosity and Power: The Politics of Inquiry* (Minneapolis: University of Minnesota Press, 2021).

48. Michel Serres, *Malfeasance: Appropriation through Pollution?,* trans. Anne-Marie Feenberg-Dibon (Stanford, Calif.: Stanford University Press, 2011), 69.

49. For representative accounts on the history of environmental colonialism exploring the ecological dispossession of indigenous cultures, see Stewart Firth, *Nuclear Playground* (Honolulu: University of Hawai'i Press, 1987); Holly Barker, *Bravo for the Marshallese: Regaining Control in a Post-nuclear, Post-colonial World* (Belmont, Calif.: Wadsworth, 2004); Gabrielle Hecht, *Being Nuclear: Africans and the Global Uranium Trade* (Cambridge, Mass.: MIT Press, 2014); and Traci Brynne Voyles, *Wastelanding: Legacies of Uranium Mining in Navajo Country* (Minneapolis: University of Minnesota Press, 2015).

50. Jacques Rancière, *The Emancipated Spectator,* trans. Gregory Elliott (London: Verso, 2009), 48.

51. Franco "Bifo" Berardi, *Futurability: The Age of Impotence and the Horizon of Possibility* (London: Verso, 2017), 15.

52. Susan Schuppli, *Material Witness: Media, Forensics, Evidence* (Cambridge, Mass.: MIT Press, 2020).

53. Ialenti, who spent two years conducting anthropological research at Onkalo, remarks regarding Madsen's film that "my informants never quoted philosophical works on the sublime or the uncanny. . . . Some explained . . . [that] they simply could not afford to get lost in the existential dread of Madsen's ruminations." Vincent Ialenti, *Deep Time Reckoning: How Future Thinking Can Help Earth Now* (Cambridge, Mass.: MIT Press, 2020), 24.

54. I am thinking here about Oliver Marchart's emphasis on contingency in his theory of postfoundational politics. This may also be of import when considering how to communicate with a society far into the future: what we may deem critical for us now (or, more important, for them then) may not be what they will deem critical to their lives or worth fighting for. Oliver Marchart, *Post-foundational Political Thought: Political Difference in Nancy, Lefort, Badiou, and Laclau* (Edinburgh: Edinburgh University Press, 2007).

55. Berardi, *Futurability,* 1. For a call to "politiciz[e] time" in order to prevent the "defuturing of multitudes," see T. J. Demos, *Radical Futurisms: Ecologies of Collapse, Chronopolitics, and Justice-to-Come* (London: Sternberg, 2023), 11, 12.

56. Innerarity, *Future,* 14; and Jérôme Baschet, *Défaire la tyrannie du present. Temporalités émergentes et futurs inédits* (Paris: La Découverte, 2018).

57. Liboiron, *Pollution Is Colonialism,* 82.

58. Nancy, *After Fukushima,* 7, 34. On the question of the future as externality, see Joan Martinez Alier and Martin O'Connor, "Ecological and Economic Distribution Conflicts," in *Getting Down to Earth: Practical Applications of Ecological Economics,* ed. Robert Costanza, Olman Segura, and Joan Martinez Alier (Washington, D.C.: Island Press, 1996), 153–83.

59. Uncertain Commons, *Speculate This!* (Durham, N.C.: Duke University Press, 2013), 72; emphasis in the original.

AFTERWORD

Between Two Endings, or Prolegomena for Another End

ERIK SWYNGEDOUW

The world will surely end but it will not be the end of our troubles.
—Alenka Zupančič, "The End"

Coming to the end of this phenomenal collection of chapters that surgically tease out the intimate articulation between the process of postpoliticization and aesthetic theory and practice, this afterword attempts to think through the contours of moving beyond the hegemonic dynamics of current postpolitical constellations. The contributions in this book reach out to a diverse set of aesthetic domains, cultural practices, and insights drawn from across the humanities and cognate perspectives. In its stock taking of the current (post)political atmospheres as expressed by and nurtured through a range of cultural and aesthetic registers, the book moves the beacons of critical political theory in ways that account for the privileged role of the senses and sensible perceptions for coconstituting the political predicament much of the contemporary "liberal" world finds itself in. The diagnoses presented throughout the book highlight the variegated configurations of the present postpolitical moment, its antinomies and inconsistencies, and how aesthetic sense affirms or disrupts the very modalities of postpoliticizing governance. I shall focus in this afterword on three interrelated arguments that foreground some of the key issues that echo throughout the book, with an eye toward suggesting ways of thinking through "the end" (of the book, postpoliticization, capitalism, humanity, the world?).

First, postpolitics as a condition and postpoliticization as a process—somewhat awkward terms suggesting a situation "after," as indicated by the prefix "post"—seem to imply that something has ended, but what? Does it not also point at the impossibility of something ending? Or does it, in contrast, operate within a horizon of an end to come? Second, if postpoliticization is a process that "evacuates the political" from the public sphere and inaugurates a certain end to politics, what is this vacated terrain of the political, and how can we think about processes of and possibilities for repoliticization? Finally, if we wish to escape from this paradoxical location between two ends, is another end (of the world) beyond the postpolitical possible? Is there a future beyond the end?

Postpoliticization between Two Endings

Postpoliticization is broadly understood as a specific and contemporary form of depoliticization that is characterized by a declining trust in the functioning of democracy and an erosion of the public sphere. It takes the form of a largely consensual mode of governance whereby agonistic political disagreement has been replaced by technomanagerial governance of the givens of the situation. It operates within an unquestionable framework of market economics, representative democracy, and cosmopolitical liberalism. Symptoms of endemic economic conflict, political contradiction, and socioecological decline are viewed as policy problems that can be managed through technocratic expertise whereby the range of possible "solutions" is strictly defined and circumscribed in advance.[1] The notion of the population as a sociological category has replaced the people as a potentially disruptive political collective. The population forms the aggregated object of opinion polls, surveillance, and biopolitical optimization.[2] Citizens have become consumers; elections are framed as just another choice, with individuals privately selecting their preferred managers of the conditions of economic necessity.[3] This presumed governance idyll is nonetheless cut through by the rise of a populist ultrapolitics of ethnicized and violent rejection, on the one hand, and the exclusion and containment of those who pursue a different politicoeconomic model, on the other. Within this postdemocratic configuration, the space of the political as the arena for the egalitarian encounter and expression of dissenting or opposing views and practices is severely truncated.

Postpoliticization inaugurates both something new, encapsulated by the "post" prefix, and thus the transcendence of an assumedly political past. Something seems to have come to an end. The postpolitical terrain, in ideological terms, became most famously symbolized by Francis Fukuyama's now thirty-year-old proclamation of the end of history.[4] In the aftermath of the historical ideological battle with actually existing socialism, capitalism and liberal democracy proved victorious and would from now on rule supreme. The end of history was also declared to announce "the end of ideology" and even "the end of politics," "whereby both senses of 'end,' as a telos fulfilling itself and as an eliminating gesture, come to coincide exactly."[5] The imagined and practiced possibility of radical transformation of a now consensual socioeconomic order was a thing of the past. There would no longer be intense ideological struggle over the kind of world to be made. In such content, it is easier, as Fredric Jameson insisted, to imagine the end of the world than the end of capitalism. As Alenka Zupančič has repeatedly argued, the end has indeed become an extremely potent signifier.[6]

The fantasy of the end of history, of course, implies not the end of everything but rather that something cannot any longer end. It suggests that some things, conditions, beliefs, modes of doing and acting, and forms of political organization will endure, thereby reinforcing the view that a fantasy about something new and different to come cannot or should not any longer be imagined, let alone struggled for. Capitalism cum liberal democracy is here to stay forever. At the end of history, there is no possible ending for the present status quo. There are no constitutive tensions, conflicts, and associated dynamics that might push the capitalist-liberal caboodle over the edge into a new, let alone better, more egalitarian and emancipatory social, ecological, and political configuration. The end of the present as we know it is foreclosed, forever relegated to the phantasmagorical musings of deluded past generations. Because the fantasy of living in the End Times does not allow for the presence of any internal generative contradictions that propel society forward—those that produce historical time rather than just pass time—change, catastrophic as it may be, can only take place in the face of external shock (a pandemic, a comet hitting earth, etc.). In fact, such an externally induced event becomes something to long for; it might shock us out of our enforced homeostasis.

It is ironic, of course, that radical and epochal technological or organizational changes are announced daily. Consider, for example, the allegedly revolutionary advent of artificial intelligence, mRNA vaccines, or alternative energy technologies that promise important social, cultural, or economic transformations, but always such that the parameters of the overall political configuration remain intact. In other words, some forms of change keep altering the coordinates of everyday life, but they nonetheless remain fully anchored and integrated in the existing postpolitical ordering of things and people.

Nonetheless, over the past few years, and as the postpoliticizing consensual promise of more of the same intensifies, the world at all scales becomes increasingly riddled with all manner of unmanageable conflicts and tensions such as the climate breakdown, geopolitical unrest, new nuclear threats, financial-economic crises, and the like, which seemingly threaten the stability of the postpoliticizing consensus. Alluring images of catastrophic change and the promise of another end to come have become increasingly powerful and prevalent. A stream of apocalyptic films—including Lars von Trier's *Melancholia,* Roland Emmerich's *Moonfall,* and Adam McKay's *Don't Look Up*—as well as an endless array of doomsday novels testify to the widely held fascination of the fantasy of the end to come. Popular science adds to this symbolic universe with the sixth extinction hypothesis and other ecological disaster stories that also regularly fantasize about the end of humans themselves, occasionally even presenting this as the solution to all our problems.

An intersectional knot of all manner of crises has indeed begun to shatter the idyll of living in the end, promising a fantasy of a real, coming end. Financial crisis, migration crisis, Covid-19 crisis, climate crisis, health crisis, energy crisis, employment crisis, social crisis, geopolitical crisis, crisis of democracy, planetary crisis—the list is endless and keeps expanding. They fuse together in a never-ending maelstrom of interlocking doomsday scenarios.[7] As Lauren Berlant argues, the ordinariness of persistent intersecting crises nurtures a sense of the present that is drab and that stifles the search for different political futures.[8]

The eschatological message of an increasingly likely dystopian end to come forms the matrix for the continuous staging of a bewildering collage of endlessly repeated promises of future environmental disasters and socioeconomic or political crises hurling toward us. The doomsday clock keeps ticking and reached ninety seconds to midnight in January 2023.[9] The light at the end of the tunnel relentlessly proclaimed by those who hold on to the status quo seems to be the headlights of a high-speed train thundering in our direction. The climate emergency is the telltale example. Disintegrating ice sheets, scorching heat waves, decimated biodiversity, blazing wildfires, or devastating floods are among the most iconic imaginaries mobilized to foretell a universal future ending that no one really wants but that fascinates many. The potential catastrophic unraveling of the climate parameters has installed itself as the master narrative that undergirds the consensus around the urgency to tackle climate breakdown and the ecological crisis. All this is paralleled by promises of new energy sources, ecotechnical interventions, just transitions, and an arsenal of new policy and managerial interventions that will—so the belief goes—act as an immunological prophylactic against deteriorating environments and its accompanying environmental injustices, and deflect or at least postpone the earth's projected end game for somewhat longer. A forced adaptation to changing and deteriorating conditions seems to be the only possible, desirable, and necessary response.

Nonetheless, these technomanagerial interventions sound increasingly hollow and impotent; they are certainly not equipped to deal with the urgency of the situation as the climate parameters keep speeding southward. We live in an era that stumbles, almost blindly, from one crisis to the next, gradually losing track of which crisis trumps others. Instead of thinking of crisis as a temporal state of rupture that promises a possible catastrophic end if not attended to and thus might open a terrain for exploring new possibilities (as socialist revolutionaries once insisted), it seems that in the present world, crises are what sustain and grease the postpolitical configuration. Endemic crises are turned into problems to be managed and are invariably welcomed by the economic elites as opening new avenues for accumulation and surplus value production and by enlightened political leaders as challenges that announce new possibilities.[10] The Covid-19 pandemic and its management, for example, indeed proved to be a cornucopia of accumulation for many shrewd investors. Nonetheless, most political interventions, economic recipes, technomanagerial innovations, and social changes more generally have been pursued as tentative, but ineffective, responses to crises. Rather than paving the way for new possible tomorrows, crises have become the unrelenting bedrock of our social existence. Life without endemic and recurrent crises is indeed difficult to imagine.

In sum, after the end of history, the metaphor and fantasy of an end to come has been repeatedly and insistently declared. As Alenka Zupančič suggests, catastrophic imaginaries abound, structured around a series of different themes such as war and potential nuclear confrontation, refugee crises, pandemics, authoritarianism, corruption, moral decay, economic insecurity, the dangers of artificial intelligence, and so on, which all seem to converge and point to the same catastrophic horizon without a beyond.[11] The inauguration of the Anthropocene—which itself announces another end—synthetizes the various imaginaries of the end to come that permeate the present. Indeed, the naming of our geophysical epoch as the age of man [*sic!*] announces the end of a nonhuman earth whose geophysical history unfolded at arm's length of humans' dabbling with the earth's lithosphere and troposphere. Humans are now envisaged as the coauthors of the earth's geophysical future, and the script does not point to a happy ending. Here the fantasy of the end of history meets the fantasy of an eschatological end game. In this dystopian, senseless, no-future wasteland, the end is both eagerly awaited and forever postponed, the apocalypse dreaded and longed for in equal measure while the actors on its stage engage in dull, repetitive, and pointless banter, assuring that things just go on as usual. The fantasy of the coming end as prevalent ideology announces the annulment of a fantasy articulated around making another world now. We are caught in a fantasy of the End Times that should not happen, but we are nonetheless fascinated and lured by its looming and tantalizing promises. In the meantime, postpoliticization, caught between these two ends—the end of politics and a dystopian end to come—rumbles on.

While many revel in the aestheticized, almost masochistic pleasures of a dystopian end foretold but conduct their business as usual, a real end may end things at any time. The imaginary of the end nurtures a repetitive and reactionary adaptation to the existing order, thereby deepening the very real mechanisms and dynamics that make a possible ending to the world as we know it more probable. Postpoliticization and its managed status quo are therefore stuck in the fantasy of the impossibility of an end to the end of history, on the one hand, and the incessant invocation of a potentially future ending of things, on the other. The one condition in all this that cannot possibly end is of course liberal capitalism and the enjoyment of its daily pleasures (and pains). There is indeed a great schism between the imaginary of a coming end that few believe will really come and the actually existing realities that are steaming forward to what may indeed be a life-threatening future. This is nicely captured in the Donald Trump event. While most liberals saw the first inauguration of Trump as president as truly catastrophic, Joe Biden's later installment at the helm was greeted with sighs of relief in the welcome return of old-style postpolitical technomanagerialism—a condition that insists that nothing can really change. Nonetheless, Joe's return to business as usual also reaffirmed the very mechanisms that may propel the world to a premature ending.

The phantasmagorical promise of the possibility of the end, Alenka Zupančič argues, assures that nothing is undertaken to stop things. The end foretold is this forever receding horizon that in its phantasmagoric promise permits not acting today to end those things that trigger the end. "I can end it any time," an addicted smoker or disgruntled partner in a relationship often exclaims but rarely does—and if they do, it invariably comes with a painful if not traumatic transgression of all manner of unacknowledged libidinal attachments to the very matrix that nurtures the desire to end it (the smoking or the relationship).[12] The fantasy of the end assures the repetition of the same and further cements the modalities, relations, and procedures that drive the processes, which nurtures the view of the necessity of the coming of the end to begin with. In other words, there is an enormous difference between the imaginary of an end to come, which is then used to interpret and guide our present condition (as in the case of environmental change or sustaining technomanagerial governance and capitalism), and the actually existing or coming socio-ecological and/or politicoeconomic catastrophes that become the reality of the situation. Paradoxically, the aesthetic of our routinized ways of making sense of the current order, sustained by the fantasy of the end to come, provides the foundation for repeating and solidifying in the present precisely the mechanisms that render the coming end increasingly plausible:

> To be sure, there is also a lot of catastrophism around, fascination with the apocalypse, with various disasters and prophesies of doom, with the spectacle of the End. Yet far from being the opposite of disavowal, this vivid catastrophism constitutes an important and integral part of it. The end of the world thus appears as a kind of general spectacular environment, a coulisse of the stage on which we go on with our business as usual. Images of apocalypse are precisely the fantasmatic screen obfuscating ("protecting" us from) the real apocalypse, which has already started creeping up on us, and is not looming, waiting for us somewhere in the future.[13]

The end does not stop being announced, and this is really catastrophic. With respect to climate change, Clive Hamilton ominously proclaims that "the greatest tragedy is the absence of a sense of tragedy,"[14] thereby echoing Walter Benjamin's insight that the fact "that things 'just go on' is the catastrophe."[15] The end is endlessly repeated as a never-ending end, and this eternal progress of the end is already part of the catastrophe itself. Of course, insisting on the end is illusionary, as Jean Baudrillard insists:

> When we speak of the "end of history," the "end of the political," the "end of the social," the "end of ideologies," none of this is true. The worst of it all is precisely that there will be no end to anything, and all these things will continue to unfold slowly, tediously, recurrently, in that hysteresis of everything which, like nails and hair, continues to grow after death.[16]

In sum, ensnared in between these two ends, politics seems no longer possible. The depoliticized contours of technomanagerial governance arrangements are all there is. The imaginaries of these ends solidify and deepen the deadlock of today's politics. Transgressing this deadlock requires recapturing the political from the debris of postpoliticizing stasis. This is predicated on recognizing that it is not only assumedly external events (like a comet or deadly virus) that may produce dystopian futures, but that changes from within the sociocultural and economic configuration, animated by internal class and other conflicts, harbor both potential cataclysmic outcomes as well as the enduring promise of emancipatory real change—a future that opens beyond the end. In other words, we have to welcome the return of the political as the recognition and expression of these conflicts and contradictions if another ending of the world is to be imagined, thought, and enacted.

Where Is the Political?

While there is now a wide-ranging debate on postpoliticization, and this book contributes in important ways to deepening our understanding of this process, relatively little attention has been paid to what precisely is evacuated from the political and public terrain through the installation of postpoliticizing practices, imaginaries, technologies, and modes of governing. Nonetheless, this is vital to appreciate fully the challenges that postpolitics poses to processes of social transformation in the End Times.

While there is no consensus, most interlocutors of the postpolitical debate insist that there is nothing truly foundational in politics; no ontological truth founds the nature of politics.[17] Our modes of organizing society are necessarily contingent and contradictory, even if they appear otherwise. Such postfoundational framing engages with what Paul Ricœur coins "the political paradox,"[18] insisting on the irreducible gap between politics as the ontic institutionalized form and ritualized practices of governing, on the one hand, and the political as signifier of the ontologically given heterogeneities, conflicts, antagonisms, and inconsistencies that cut through the social, on the other. The political therefore exposes the lie that views the people as a coherent, fully closed, and potentially harmonious political unity. The political asserts the radical heterogeneities that rupture any political form (that gives content to politics) through which the people are constituted and organized. The democratic political, then, is nothing else than the contingent proclamation of axiomatic equality of each and all in a context of constitutive conflicts and ruptures, and politicization becomes discernable in the process through which equality is staged and performed. What is seen as common sense becomes nonsensical, and a new common sense becomes seeable and actionable. The symptom of the political, therefore, always appears "at a distance from the state" but acts on and in the state of the situation.

The political is the (collective) act through which the given order is ruptured and inaugurates changing "the very parameters of what is considered possible in the existing constellation;"[19] it is the art and act of making the impossible possible. The key political question is whether today's postpolitical liberal capitalism can contain antagonisms powerful enough to prevent its indefinite reproduction[20]—a reproduction that operates through proliferating intersecting crises and potentially catastrophic endings. Interlocutors such as Slavoj Žižek, Jodi Dean, Todd McGowan, and Alain Badiou discern in the foreclosure of class antagonism the irremediable ensnaring of all within the postpoliticizing constellation. These interlocutors therefore insist on a return to the idea of communism. Such rebirth of history, the process through which a cut can be made in the fantasy of the double ending discussed above, resides in passing through the trauma of the disavowed class relations and becoming fully cognizant of the traumatic encounter with the real of class antagonism. The central metaphors that sustain the idea of communism are, of course, equality, solidarity, and democracy, held together by a fidelity to the conviction that these can be realized in the here and now.

In fact, class relations have never gone away. Nonetheless, this antagonism has been disavowed and displaced onto other terrains, such as race, identity, or ecology. These are infused not only by the spectrality of class relations but by its traumatic identification, which can be foreclosed because the former can be absorbed within the capitaloparliamentary order (Badiou's term for the postpolitical constellation) and rendered contentious within the existing order without fundamentally threatening its endurance.

Politicization therefore resolutely points toward traversing the deadlock of being between two ends. We either remain stuck in the fantasy that what exists can be perpetuated through adapting to or mitigating still existing problems and concerns (which nonetheless propel us to a catastrophic ending), or we begin seriously to think through and act on the reimagination of the utmost necessity of a real utopia in the present—one that simultaneously points to a beyond of the present dystopian future. Is it not precisely utopian to hold that the future remains a possibility under postpolitical consensus management that has us heading for a real catastrophe? Is it not therefore of the highest urgency to consider a different ending to the world?

Prolegomena for Another End to the World

In 1964, French intellectual and communist Maurice Blanchot wrote the incisive essay "The Apocalypse Is Disappointing."[21] In this contribution, he examined the thought of Karl Jaspers, a German philosopher who had written a then widely acclaimed book entitled *The Atom Bomb and the Future of Man*.[22] He argued that the capacity to annihilate the world humans had created demonstrated the urgency to transform thought and practice in order to (possibly) avoid the apocalypse. Blanchot, in his ruthless dissection of Jaspers's argument, claimed that it was precisely the absence in the world of a common humanity that made the nuclear apocalypse possible. If it were to happen, it would be the result of the contingent acts of a few powerful individuals in a particular context of intense conflict. In this sense, the apocalypse would be disappointing—a contingent nonevent that would nonetheless demonstrate the absence of a common humanity. The making of common humanity—as the only possible route to avoid catastrophe—is what Blanchot politically named communism. Only the making of humanity could retroactively inscribe the power of annihilation, symbolized by the bomb, into a collective process of making a different world. Alenka Zupančič turns to Blanchot (as does Giorgio Agamben)[23] in her essay "The Apocalypse Is (Still) Disappointing." While the reality of the bomb opens the perspective of the whole of humanity to be imagined as something that could be lost, it simultaneously affirms the absence of such totality in the reality of the present. As she puts it, "It only constitutes a whole in the perspective of being potentially lost. In other words, there is no (existing) totality, no 'whole of the world,' which could be eventually (actually) lost in an atomic apocalypse; it is, paradoxically, only the perspective of this very (potential) loss which constitutes it, or makes it appear, as such a totality or whole."[24] The fantasy of the potential annihilation of humankind inaugurates the imaginary of a global humanity, but this sense of coherence and unity is only emerging through the gaze of its potential destruction, not by a real sense of a global commons. In its potential destruction, humanity appears as a "negative virtual totality"—a totality that can only be conceived in its destruction to come. Yet it is the very absence of a humanity as a commons that unleashes the threat of annihilation (while all the same inaugurating its imaginary possibility).[25] In Blanchot's words, humanity is "something that cannot even be destroyed, because it does not exist."[26] There is no real humanity; it appears only as a fantasy emerging through the prism of potential destruction. Zupančič continues:

> When caught in the threat and fear of "losing it all" we are in fact held hostages of something that does not exist—yet. And is this kind of blackmail not in fact the very means of making sure that it never will exist? It makes us focus on preserving what is there, and what we have, but excludes any real alternative, any means of really thinking differently.[27]

Breaking through the deadlock of a declared end, and the reactionary repetition of the same that makes the end more likely to happen, ruptures the postpolitical order and its antinomies. While the nuclear threat is singular and abrupt if enacted, we are today ensnared in an intersectional knot of intensifying catastrophic entanglements that do not point to an instantaneous potential ending; rather, it unfolds like the slow death of a cancer patient whose treatment has run out. The promise of the end to come requires transgression; the aesthetic register is, as this book clearly demonstrates, pivotal in this.

Indeed, Blanchot's sentiment holds today more than ever. The realities of the climate condition, pandemics, geopolitical conflicts, and so on solidify the imaginary of a humanity that could be lost, while the modalities of managing these crises also demonstrate that humanity as such totality does not exist. It is the absence of a common humanity that structures the intersectional knotting of crises moments, but the actual making of humanity is what might rupture the highway to a dystopian future and open up the promise of a different ending of the world. The dominant fantasy that unfolds around insisting on the imminent danger of a catastrophic future not only assumes the presence of humanity but also insists that humanity requires or deserves salvation. However, as I have argued elsewhere, the realities of human actions and activities demonstrate the emptiness at the heart of humanity. The intersecting conflicts and struggles, the systematic violence and radical antagonisms that cut through the semblance of humanity, and the unequal power relations between humans radically exemplify this emptiness. Of course, there are occasional illustrations of the potential existence of a deep humanity in some forms of human action, demonstrating the potential to create a real humanity.[28]

Humanity does not exist (yet), and it may never do. The catastrophic dynamics that build to a potential end game are precisely an illustration of this. We are situated within a Manichean choice between continuing on a highway to an apocalyptic future, propelled forward precisely because of the dynamics unleashed by an absent humanity, on the one hand, or embarking on a political trajectory animated by the desire to construct an actual earthly humanity, on the other. Because the future of a really nonexisting humanity leads to catastrophe, the challenge is the creation of *a* humanity. This requires inaugurating a new temporality and spatiality articulated around a democratizing repolitization of the current socio-ecological state of affairs. As Lucas Pohl affirms, politicization is about demanding the impossible and rendering it geographically and historically real.[29] It is through this maneuver that we can cut through the trauma of not having a future at all.[30]

The ideological fantasy of a projected end game needs to be resolutely dismissed. The pull of a catastrophe to come reinforces our libidinal attachment to the present status quo, not only as a normalized condition but also one that needs to be cherished and sustained. Repetitive adaptation to unfolding crises conditions just normalizes the present post-political assemblage. The preservation of the present arrangements is considered not only as the horizon of the possible but also of the desirable.

Adapting to or mitigating existing problems and concerns is presented as a radical mechanism to sustain the present ordering of things and people. The incessant repetition of living in the End Times reinforces ever more our attachment to a reactionary desire to sustain the present.

However, as argued above, the lineaments of unfolding intersectional catastrophes are already there; it is too late already. It is within the contours of the current ecological catastrophe and other ruinations that social action and political intervention need to be situated.[31] The eschatological promise of the apocalyptic narrative as well as the redemptive, but illusionary, insistence on the importance of consensual and technomanagerial change has to be rejected. Confronted with recurrent fantasies, primarily fostered by the technomanagerial elite, that the catastrophe can still be averted if the right technomanagerial adaptive or mitigating actions are taken, the only reasonable response is to insist that ruination has already happened. It is too late; living in catastrophic times is already the actual, real condition for many planetary inhabitants. Achilles Mbembe captures this well in demonstrating the horrifying consequences of the necropolitics that animate the contemporary state of affairs.[32] Indeed, if the end is already here, no redemptive action is possible to save the existing configuration.

The hegemonic discourse of a threatened—albeit abstract and illusionary—humanity forecloses and disavows the reality of actually existing class and other contradictions that signal the nonexistence of *a* humanity. This fetishist disavowal or foreclosure of the antagonisms that form the matrix of the social assures that nothing will really change. Traversing the present fantasies of managing our troubles through postpolitical technomanagerial adjustments requires confronting the trauma of the nonexistence of humanity and the recognition that it is precisely this nonexistence—that is, the class and other conflicting axes that cut through humanity—that have already caused the catastrophe. Indeed, the only possible thing left to do is to engage in a process of constructing a real humanity—to produce a human world in the world. The end of history and the end of the world have to come to an End. Breaking through the deadlock of postpolitical repetition by making the impossible possible is our only hope for a livable common future.

Notes

I am grateful for the suggestions, comments, thoughts, and critical reflections offered by Juan Meneses, Joe Blakey, Lucas Pohl, Japhy Wilson, and Maria Kaika. I assume responsibility for any remaining errors of fact and inconsistencies of thought.

1. Japhy Wilson and Erik Swyngedouw, *The Post-political and Its Discontents: Spaces of Depoliticisation, Spectres of Radical Politics,* ed. Japhy Wilson and Erik Swyngedouw (Edinburgh: Edinburgh University Press, 2014).

2. Erik Swyngedouw and Henrik Ernstson, "Interrupting the Anthropo-obscene: Immuno-biopolitics and Depoliticising Ontologies in the Anthropocene," *Theory, Culture, and Society* 35, no. 6 (2018): 3–30.

3. Wilson and Swyngedouw, *Post-political and Its Discontents.*

4. Francis Fukuyama, *The End of History and the Last Man* (New York: Free Press, 1992).

5. Jacques Rancière, *Disagreement: Politics and Philosophy,* trans. Julie Rose (Minneapolis: University of Minnesota Press, 1999), 75.

6. Alenka Zupančič, "The End of Ideology, the Ideology of the End," *South Atlantic Quarterly* 4 (2020): 833–44; and Alenka Zupančič, "A Brief History of the End," *Alternator* 8 (February 22, 2021), www.alternator.science/en/long/a-brief-history-of-the-end.

7. Alex Callinicos, *The New Age of Catastrophe* (Cambridge: Polity, 2023).

8. Lauren Berlant, *Cruel Optimism* (Durham, N.C.: Duke University Press, 2011).

9. Bulletin of the Atomic Scientists, "2023 Doomsday Clock Announcement," January 24, 2023, thebulletin.org/doomsday-clock.

10. Lucas Pohl and Erik Swyngedouw, "Endgames: Enjoying Crises," in *Handbook of Environmental Political Theory in the Anthropocene,* ed. Marcel Wissenburg and Amanda Machin (Cheltenham, U.K.: Edward Elgar, forthcoming).

11. Zupančič, "End of Ideology."

12. Zupančič.

13. Alenka Zupančič, "Perverse Disavowal and the Rhetoric of the End," *Filosofski Vestnik* 43, no. 2 (2022): 94.

14. Clive Hamilton, *Defiant Earth: The Fate of Humans in the Anthropocene* (Sydney, Aust.: Allen & Unwin, 2017), ix.

15. Walter Benjamin, "Central Park," *New German Critique* 34 (1984): 50.

16. Jean Baudrillard, *The Illusion of the End,* trans. Chris Turner (Cambridge: Polity, 1994), 116.

17. Lucas Pohl and Erik Swyngedouw, "'What Does Not Work in the World': The Specter of Lacan in Critical Political Theory," *Distinktion: Journal of Social Theory* 24, no. 1 (2021): 1–19.

18. Paul Ricœur, "The Political Paradox," in *History and Truth* (Evanston, Ill.: Northwestern University Press, 1965), 247–70.

19. Slavoj Žižek, *The Ticklish Subject: The Absent Centre of Political Ontology* (London: Verso, 1999), 237.

20. Slavoj Žižek, *Living in the End Times* (London: Verso, 2011), 212.

21. Maurice Blanchot, "The Apocalypse Is Disappointing," in *Friendship* (1964; reprint, Stanford, Calif.: Stanford University Press, 1997): 101–8.

22. Karl Jaspers, *The Atom Bomb and the Future of Man,* trans. E. B. Ashton (1958; reprint, Chicago: University of Chicago Press, 1963).

23. Giorgio Agamben, "Atomic Warfare and the End of Humanity," *Medium,* October 12, 2022, lenabloch.medium.com/atomic-warfare-and-the-end-of-humanity-giorgio-agamben-d1335ca09e5c.

24. Alenka Zupančič, "The Apocalypse Is (Still) Disappointing," *S: Journal of the Circle for Lacanian Ideology Critique* 11 (2018): 18.

25. I thank Juan Meneses for suggesting this to me.

26. Blanchot, "Apocalypse Is Disappointing," 106.

27. Zupančič, "Apocalypse," 21–22.

28. Erik Swyngedouw, "'The Apocalypse Is Disappointing': Traversing the Ecological Fantasy," in *Haste: The Slow Politics of Climate Urgency,* ed. Håvard Haarstad, Jakob Grandin, Kristin Kjærås, and Eleanor Johnson (London: UCL Press, 2023), 17–26.

29. Lucas Pohl, "Geographies of the Impossible," *Dialogues in Human Geography* 14, no. 2 (2023), doi.org/10.1177/20438206231177069.

30. E. Ann Kaplan, *Climate Trauma: Foreseeing the Future in Dystopian Film and Fiction* (New Brunswick, N.J.: Rutgers University Press, 2016); Pohl, "Geographies of the Impossible."

31. Lucas Pohl, "Rem(a)inders of Loss: A Lacanian Approach to New Urban Ruins," in *The New Urban Ruins: Vacancy, Urban Politics, and International Experiments in the Post-crisis City,* ed. Cian O'Callaghan and Cesare Di Feliciantonio (Bristol, Eng.: Bristol University Press, 2021), 21–34.

32. Achille Mbembe, *Necropolitics,* trans. Steven Corcoran (Durham, N.C.: Duke University Press, 2019).

Contributors

JACQUELYN ARCY is associate professor of new media at the University of Wisconsin–Parkside.

CHRISTOPHER BREU is professor of English at Illinois State University. He is author of *In Defense of Sex: Nonbinary Embodiment and Desire, Insistence of the Material: Literature in the Age of Biopolitics* (Minnesota, 2014), and *Hard-Boiled Masculinities* (Minnesota, 2005), as well as coeditor of *Noir Affect.*

STEPHEN CHARBONNEAU is associate professor of film studies at Florida Atlantic University. He is author of *Projecting Race: Postwar America, Civil Rights, and Documentary Film* and coeditor of *InsUrgent Media from the Front: A Media Activism Reader.*

ERIC LEMMON is visiting assistant professor of music at Knox College.

ROBERT P. MARZEC is professor of English at Purdue University. He is author of *Militarizing the Environment: Climate Change and the Security State* (Minnesota, 2016) and *An Ecological and Postcolonial Study of Literature: From Daniel Defoe to Salman Rushdie* and editor of *Postcolonial Literary Studies: The First Thirty Years.*

JUAN MENESES is associate professor of English at the University of North Carolina, Charlotte. He is author of *Resisting Dialogue: Modern Fiction and the Future of Dissent* (Minnesota, 2019).

ALLISON PAGE is associate professor of media studies at Rutgers University, Camden. She is author of *Media and the Affective Life of Slavery* (Minnesota, 2022).

MATTHEW SCULLY is lecturer in English at the University of Lausanne. He is author of *Democratic Anarchy: Aesthetics and Political Resistance in U.S. Literature.*

ERIK SWYNGEDOUW is professor of geography at the University of Manchester and senior research associate at the University of Johannesburg Centre for Social Change. He is author of *Promises of the Political: Insurgent Cities in a Post-democratic Environment* and *Social Power and the Urbanization of Water: Flows of Power,* and coeditor of *The Post-political and Its Discontents: Spaces of Depoliticisation, Spectres of Radical Politics.*

SHERRYL VINT is professor of media and cultural studies and of English at the University of California, Riverside. She is author of *Biopolitical Futures in Twenty-First-Century Speculative Fiction* and coauthor of *Programming the Future: Politics, Resistance, and Utopia in Contemporary Speculative TV.*

Index